COLLECTED ECONOMIC PAPERS
VOLUME FIVE

COLLECTED ECONOMIC PAPERS

JOAN ROBINSON

VOLUME FIVE

The MIT Press
Cambridge, Massachusetts

First MIT Press edition, 1980
Published in Great Britain by Basil Blackwell, 1980

Library of Congress Cataloging in Publication Data

Robinson, Joan, 1903–
  Collected economic papers.

  Includes bibliographical references and index.
  1. Economics—Addresses, essays, lectures.
I. Title.
HB33.R6 1980   330   79–24584
ISBN 0–262–18093–6 (v. 1)
      0–262–18094–4 (v. 2)
      0–262–18095–2 (v. 3)
      0–262–18096–0 (v. 4)
      0–262–18097–9 (v. 5)
      0–262–18098–7 (Index)
      0–262–18099–5 (v. 1–5 & Index)

Printed in Great Britain

CONTENTS

PREFACE

The first of these papers was the response to a request for a survey of the state of contemporary economic theory as I saw it. The earlier papers in the first group are mainly elaborating various points covered by it. There is therefore some repetition. The theoretical papers operate on two planes, an attempt to get the logic clear in a tightly specified model and an attempt to loosen it up in the form of approximations to make it useful for discussion of actual problems. On the logical plane, I frequently had occasion to complain of the inability of neo-neoclassical writers to distinguish between a *difference* in the parameters of an equilibrium model and the effects of a *change* taking place at a moment of time. I suppose it is difficult for the reader to believe that such an error can be made by respected leaders of the profession especially by those distinguished for mathematical expertise. In this connection the interchange between Professor Samuelson and myself, following 'The unimportance of reswitching' is apposite. It is interesting that in my first publication, quoted in 'Thinking about thinking', I was already aware of the pitfalls of theoretical controversies.

The second group of papers consists of two surveys that I hope may be useful for teaching.

The third group returns to the subject of the Keynesian Revolution, and its disintegration in teaching in the 1970s.

The fourth group is mainly addressed to problems of the Third World, especially India.

The fifth contains a number of papers pleading for a non-dogmatic treatment of Marx.

Chapters 8, 11 and 24 are here published for the first time.

1

WHAT ARE THE QUESTIONS?

1

INTRODUCTION

THE 1930s have been described as the years of high theory, but all the great mass of work that has been done since and the proliferation of academic economic teaching has been very little illuminated by the ideas that emerged at that time, and there are no consistent and accepted answers to the questions that were then raised.

One reason for this lack of progress is connected with the origin of the new ideas themselves. George Shackle[1] treated 'high theory' as a purely intellectual movement, but in fact it arose out of the actual situation of the thirties – the breakdown of the world market economy in the great slump. Kalecki, Keynes, and Myrdal were trying to find an explanation for unemployment; the exploration of imperfect and monopolistic competition set afoot by the challenge from opposite directions, of Piero Sraffa[2] and Allyn Young[3] to the orthodox theory of value, though it proved to be a blind alley, arose from the observation that, in a general buyers' market, it could not be true that prices are equal to marginal costs. The movement of the thirties was an attempt to bring analysis to bear on actual problems. Discussion of an actual problem cannot avoid the question of what should be done about it; questions of policy involve politics (laisser-faire is just as much a policy as any other). Politics involve ideology; there is no such thing as a 'purely economic' problem that can be settled by purely economic logic; political interests and political prejudice are involved in every discussion of actual questions. The participants in every controversy

[1] *The Years of High Theory*, Cambridge, 1967.

[2] 'The Laws of Returns under Competitive Conditions', *Economic Journal*, December 1926, pp. 535–50.

[3] 'Increasing Returns and Economic Progress', *Economic Journal*, December 1928, pp. 527–42.

divide into schools – conservative or radical – and ideology is apt to seep into logic. In economics, arguments are largely devoted, as in theology, to supporting doctrines rather than testing hypotheses.

Here, the radicals have the easier case to make. They have only to point to the discrepancy between the operation of a modern economy and the ideals by which it is supposed to be judged, while the conservatives have the well-nigh impossible task of demonstrating that this is the best of all *possible* worlds. For the same reason, however, the conservatives are compensated by occupying positions of power, which they can use to keep criticism in check.

Benjamin Ward observes:

> The power inherent in this system of quality control within the economics profession is obviously very great. The discipline's censors occupy leading posts in economics departments at the major institutions. . . . The lion's share of appointment and dismissal power has been vested in the departments themselves at these institutions. Any economist with serious hopes of obtaining a tenured position in one of these departments will soon be made aware of the criteria by which he is to be judged . . . the entire academic program, beginning usually at the undergraduate level but certainly at the graduate, consists of indoctrination in the ideas and techniques of the science. . . .[4]
>
> These inside instruments of control are accompanied by outside instruments exercised by members of the larger society. Probably the most important of these is control of funds for research and, to a lesser ·extent, teaching. Consciences are not much troubled by such practices because economics has mixed its ideology into the subject so well that the ideologically unconventional usually appear to appointment committees to be scientifically incompetent.[5]

For this reason, the conservatives do not feel obliged to answer radical criticisms on their merits and the argument is never fairly joined.

Moreover, with the best will in the world, it is excessively difficult to find an agreed answer to any question concerned with reality. Economists cannot make use of controlled experiments to settle their differences; they have to appeal to historical evidence, and evidence can always be read both ways.

The laboratory sciences proceed by isolating a question and testing hypotheses about possible answers to it, one by one. In economics, questions

[4] *What's Wrong with Economics?* New York, Basic Books, 1972, pp. 29–30.
[5] Ibid., p. 250.

cannot be isolated because every aspect of human society interacts with every other; hypotheses can be put forward only in the form of a 'model' of the whole economy. Before a model can be confronted with empirical tests, it has to be examined for internal consistency and for the *a priori* plausibility of its assumptions. There is a whole branch of the subject – that which carries the highest prestige – which is concerned simply with criticizing and defending hypotheses. The 'high theory' of the thirties consisted of advancing alternative hypotheses to replace those, derived from the theory of supply and demand for labour, which had been too much discredited in the slump.

Even when it is possible to mark off some element in such a way that it can be confronted with evidence, the collection of evidence from available statistics is enormously laborious. To establish the simplest of statistical 'facts' requires years of patient toil. Since it is so laborious, there is a powerful temptation to take short cuts, to overloook awkward details and favour evidence that supports an attractive theory. No doubt natural scientists are also are subject to such temptations, but the experimental method provides a sieve to keep out error which has a much finer mesh than any that can be produced by an appeal to history.

There is a still more baffling difficulty in applying an economic model to statistical evidence. It may be possible to find evidence of the relationships within the model over a certain period of time and then to predict what they will be, say over the following years; but when it is found that the relationships turned out to be different, there is no way of telling whether it is because there was a mistake in specifying the model in the first place or because circumstances have changed meanwhile. And when they turn out the same, it is possibly by accident.[6]

> Difficult as it is to collect good physical data, it is far more difficult to collect long runs of economic or social data so that the whole of the run shall have a uniform significance. The data of the production of steel, for instance, change their significance not only with every invention that changes the technique of the steelmaker but with every social and economic change affecting business and industry at large, and in particular, with every technique changing the demand for steel or the supply and nature of the competing materials. For example, even the first skyscraper made of aluminium instead of steel will turn out to

[6] For instance, it has been found that a 'Cobb-Douglas production function' will fit any time-series of outputs, whatever the technology, provided that the share of wages in value added was fairly constant over the period.

affect the whole future demand for structural steel, as the first diesel ship did the unquestioned dominance of the steamship.

Thus the economic game is a game where the rules are subject to important revisions, say, every ten years, and bears an uncomfortable resemblance to the Queen's croquet game in *Alice in Wonderland*. . . . Under the circumstances, it is hopeless to give too precise a measurement to the quantities occurring in it. To assign what purports to be precise values to such essentially vague quantities is neither useful nor honest, and any pretense of applying precise formulae to these loosely defined quantities is a sham and a waste of time.[7]

Evading these difficulties, a great part of current teaching is conducted in terms of models that are evidently not intended to be taken seriously as hypotheses about reality but are used rather to inculcate an orthodox ideology. For a model to be taken seriously, the assumptions must be carefully specified, while a doctrine can appeal to a general body of received ideas. This distinction is illustrated below in terms of the contention that market prices provide an efficient mechanism for allocating scarce means between alternative uses, expressed in the proposition that 'a competitive equilibrium is a Pareto optimum'.

2

MARKET EQUILIBRIUM

In current teaching, a sharp distinction is usually made between micro- and macroeconomic problems, each being treated in terms of quite different concepts. It is necessary, of course, as the subject grows more complex, to focus upon particular questions one at a time, but a *general* theory cannot be split into these two parts. Micro questions – concerning the relative prices of commodities and the behaviour of individuals, firms, and households – cannot be discussed in the air without any reference to the structure of the economy in which they exist, and to the processes of cyclical and secular change. Equally, macro theories of accumulation and effective demand are generalizations about micro behaviour: the relation of income to expenditure for consumption, of investment to the pursuit of profit, of the management of placements in which financial wealth is held to rates of interest, and of wages to the level of prices result from the reactions of

[7] Norbert Wiener, *God and Golem, Inc.: A comment on certain points where cybernetics impinges on religion*, Cambridge, Mass., MIT Press; London, Chapman and Hall, 1964, pp. 90–1.

individuals and social groups to the situations in which they find themselves. Even the artificial conception of a stationary state has to be specified in terms of the behaviour of its inhabitants. Supposing all natural and technical conditions are constant, we still have to describe the individual and social behaviour which is conceived to make total consumption exactly equal to net output, neither more nor less, so that net saving and net investment are exactly zero. If there is no micro theory, there cannot be any macro theory either.

The analysis of markets is treated under the heading of micro theory, but it cannot be understood without some indication of the macro setting in which it operates. A prisoner-of-war camp, a village fair, and the shopping centre of a modern city cannot all be treated in exactly the same terms.

The macro setting of the analysis of 'scarce means with alternative uses' is very vaguely sketched. It appears to rely upon Say's Law, for the scarce means are always fully utilized.[8] The central concept is the production-possibility surface showing the combinations of quantities of a list of specified commodities that could be produced by various combinations of the given resources.

Nothing much is usually said about the inhabitants of the model. The ancestry of Adam Smith is often claimed for it, but his world was inhabited by workers, employers, and gentlemen. Here there are only 'transactors' or 'economic subjects.' To borrow Michio Morishima's trope, the people in this model are like the conventionally invisible property men of the Kabuki theatre, and only the commodities have speaking parts.

The 'scarce means' consist of 'labour', that is, workers who can be employed in various occupations, privately-owned land providing various kinds of natural resources, and the produced means of production (buildings and industrial equipment) that have already been accumulated. Thus, it purports to deal with a capitalist economy that has a future and a past, but the analysis applies rather to a once-over meeting of independent peasants at a rural market or to the prisoner-of-war camp where parcels were occasionally received from the Red Cross.

As Nikolay Bukharin observed when he was in exile in the West, there is almost no discussion of how scarce means are organized to yield outputs; the whole emphasis is on exchanges of ready-made goods.[9]

Robert Clower subsumes production under exchange:

[8] Strictly speaking, the rule is that any resource that is under-utilized has a zero price. When this applies to labour, presumably the workers must have died long ago.

[9] *Economic Theory of the Leisure Class*, English translation, London, Martin Lawrence, 1957. (In Russian, 1919.)

An ongoing exchange economy with specialist trader *is* a production economy since there is no bar to any merchant capitalist acquiring labour services and other resources as a 'buyer' and transforming them (repackaging, processing into new forms, etc.) into outputs that are unlike the original inputs and are 'sold' accordingly as are commodities that undergo no such transformation. In short, a production unit *is* a particular type of middleman or trading specialist.[10]

And he supports the view 'that "capitalists" are just individuals who have the wit and forethought to exploit profit opportunities by accumulating trade capital and engaging in the "production" of both trading services and new types of commodities.'

It is true, of course, that industrial capitalism developed out of commercial capitalism, but the process of exchange does not explain why there are so many (presumably dull-witted) individuals who are available to sell labour services.

There are various brands of micro theory; Clower has been critical of others, but all share the characteristic of stressing exchange and neglecting production.

Even the process of marketing commodities is not much discussed. Since the tastes of individuals are hard and fast, there is no scope for advertisement and salesmanship to affect them. Indeed there is no scope for competition at all. To quote Oskar Morgenstern:

> Competition means struggle, fight, maneuvering, bluff, hiding of information – and precisely *that* word is used to describe a situation in which no one has any influence on anything, where there is *ni gain, ni perte* where everyone faces *fixed conditions, given prices*, and has only to adapt himself to them so as to attain an individual maximum. . . .[11]

There is a large number of sellers of each kind of commodity, and though they are all assumed to be 'maximizing profits', none of them ever forms a group which could increase proceeds for each member above what they could get individually.[12] On the demand side, the market is made up of transactors each with a certain amount of purchasing power, in terms of some numeraire, which he spends on a selection from among the commodities offered, according to his tastes and their prices. Here the

[10] Private communication, quoted with permission, 1976.

[11] 'Thirteen Critical Points in Contemporary Economic Theory: An Interpretation', *Journal of Economic Literature*, December 1972, Vol. 10, No. 4, pp. 1163–89.

[12] It has been found by mathematical analysis that to ensure that combinations do not pay, the number of sellers must be indefinitely great.

argument does correspond to Adam Smith's treatment of the subject, for when he speaks of appealing to the self interest of the butcher, the brewer, and the baker to get us our dinner, he is evidently thinking of a gentleman with independent means spending money on the tradesmen, rather than of their competitive struggle to make a living.

At an equilibrium position on the production-possibility surface, the prices and flows of sales of the various commodities determine the earnings of various types of resources so that the income of each transactor depends upon the specific resources that he commands. An observing economist may make use of a single numeraire but, for each inhabitant of the model, the numeraire is a unit of whatever he has to sell.

The situation is described as an optimum when it is impossible to improve the position of one individual without doing harm to any other, but in Pareto's formulation individuals are not depicted in human terms. No aspect of economic life is considered but the individual's choice of how to spend given purchasing power, at a given moment, among a given assortment of goods. Pareto's optimum only repeats the definition of the production-possibility surface on which the output of one commodity cannot be increased without reducing the output of any other. (Only the commodities have speaking parts.)

The principle of measuring the cost of any benefit in terms of the alternative opportunities that must be foregone in order to get it can be applied in a general way to any decision-making unit, such as a family with limited income, a farm with limited space, a business with limited finance, or a planning commission with the limited investable resources of a particular socialist nation. But the choices that any such unit makes must depend upon the information at its disposal, both about technical conditions and market possibilities. In a perfectly static society, relevant knowledge might be handed down to everyone by tradition, but their behaviour also would be governed by tradition and no one would be conscious of ever making choices at all. In the world where we are living, choices have to be made in the light of more or less inadequate information. The full information required to make a correct choice can never be available because of the inescapable fact that:

> the basic data simply do not exist, and cannot exist, no matter what information is devised. There is no certain knowledge about the future, not even certain knowledge of probability distributions. There are expectations (or guesses) formulated with greater or less care; and unfortunately those formulated with the greatest care are by no means

always the most accurate. The New York State legislature has
deliberated on these difficulties, and enacted in Section 899 of the Code
of Criminal Procedure that persons 'Pretending to forecast the future'
shall be considered disorderly under subdivision 3, Section 901 of the
Code and liable to a fine of $250 and/or six months in prison.[13]

John Hicks, having repudiated the works of his former incarnation, J. R.
Hicks,[14] has observed that the very concept of equilibrium arose from a
misleading analogy with movements in space, which cannot be applied to
movements in time.[15] In space, it is possible to go to and fro, but time goes
only one way; there is no going back to correct a mistake; an equilibrium
cannot be reached by a process of trial and error. Since all individual
choices are based upon more or less independent and inaccurate judgments
about what outcomes will be, it is impossible that they should be consistent
with each other. The assumption of 'perfect foresight' carries the argument
out of this world into a system of mathematical abstraction, which,
although the symbols may be given economic names, has no point of
contact with empirical reality.

The question of scarce means with alternative uses becomes self
contradictory when it is set in historical time, where today is an ever-
moving break between the irrevocable past and the unknown future. At
any moment, certainly, resources are scarce, but they have hardly any range
of alternative uses. The workers available to be employed are not a supply
of 'labour', but a number of carpenters or coal miners. The uses of land
depend largely on transport; industrial equipment was created to assist the
output of particular products. To change the use of resources requires
investment and training, which alters the resources themselves. As for
choice among investment projects, this involves the whole analysis of the
nature of capitalism and of its evolution through time. Something like a
production-possibility surface might appear in the calculations made for
investment plans in a fully socialist economy, but in the world of private
enterprise it cannot exist.

A completely different approach to the analysis of markets was proposed

[13] B. J. Loasby, *Imperfections and adjustment*, University of Stirling Discussion Papers No.
50, 1977.

[14] 'Revival of Political Economy, the Old and the New', *Economic Record*, September
1975, Vol. 51, No. 4, pp. 365–7.

[15] John Hicks, 'Some Questions of Time in Economics', in *Evolution, welfare and time in
economics: Essays in honor of Nicholas Georgescu-Roegen*, edited by Anthony M. Tang, Fred M.
Westfield, and James S. Worley, Lexington, Mass., Heath, Lexington Books, 1976, pp.
135–57.

in *The Theory of Games and Economic Behaviour*.[16] This provides a powerful criticism of orthodox doctrine, but it is itself open to the objection that the type of games susceptible to mathematical analysis, such as noughts and crosses or go, are subject to set rules that all players accept and to the condition that each play has an agreed time limit. The scope of economic life, even that part of it which is concerned with markets, cannot be so narrowly confined.

The most basic objection to orthodox doctrine is raised by Kenneth Arrow, for he rejects the principle of individualism. The conduct of economic life requires the authority of institutions, such as corporations or national governments:

> There are many other organizations beside the government and the firm. But all of them, whether political party or revolutionary movement, university or church, share the common characteristics of the need for collective action and the allocation of resources through non-market methods. . . .

> There is still another set of institutions, if that is the right word, I want to call to your attention and make much of. These are invisible institutions: the principles of ethics and morality.[17]

The familiar story of the prisoners' dilemma illustrates this point. If each man acts selfishly, both will be worse off than if they follow the moral rule of refusing to betray a chum. But this rule cannot be introduced *ad hoc*. If it is followed at all it must be followed for its own sake, equally in circumstances where the individual will suffer for it.

With this objection, the whole structure of the model collapses.

3

THEORY OF THE FIRM

Keynes described the orthodox equilibrium theory as a pretty, polite technique 'which tries to deal with the present by abstracting from the fact that we know very little about the future.'[18] Alan Coddington observes:

> To stress the basis of all economic activity in more or less uncertain

---

[16] John von Neumann and Oskar Morgenstern, Princeton, 1944.

[17] *The Limits of Organization*, New York, Norton, 1974.

[18] 'The General Theory of Unemployment', *Quarterly Journal of Economics*, February 1937, Collected Writings of John Maynard Keynes (JMK) Vol XIV.

expectations is precisely to emphasize the openness and incompleteness of economic theorizing and explanation.[19]

Certainly it is true that a mechanical model cannot survive when it is set afloat in historical time. (It was recognizing the difference between the future and the past that caused Hicks to become disillusioned with the *IS/LM* model with which generations of students have been taught to misinterpret the *General Theory*.) But this does not mean that economic theory is useless. We cannot help trying to understand the world we are living in, and we need to construct some kind of picture of an economy from which to draw hypotheses about its mode of operation. We cannot hope ever to get neat and precise answers to the questions that hypotheses raise, but we can discriminate among the pictures of reality that are offered and choose the least implausible ones to elaborate and to confront with whatever evidence we can find. This is one function of economic models. The other is to satisfy the requirements of ideology.

Hypotheses are invented and die every day. The criteria by which some are chosen to survive and enter into the corpus of economic teaching are of two kinds. One is that a hypothesis seems life-like and offers some explanation that appears sufficiently promising to be worth exploring, and the other is that it fits into and supports received doctrine. Clearly the model of competitive equilibrium has a low score on the first criterion and owes its support to the second.

There is another approach to the analysis of competition in which the relations between observation and doctrine are more subtle, that is, the problem known as Marshall's dilemma.

Marshall's model was concerned not only with exchange but also stressed manufacture. The most basic micro-macro question for an industrial economy concerns the way production is organized in firms. Marshall had a picture, based on observation, of the family business in British manufacturing industry. He found it plausible to argue that as a firm's business expands, its costs of production fall because of 'internal and external economies of scale.' He observed, moreover, that in many cases the fortunes of a business are bound up with the life of a family. An individual sets it going and it prospers, but by the third generation its vigour is lost.

Now, on the plane of doctrine, Marshall held that in competitive conditions, prices are determined by costs, so that the benefit of economies of scale are passed on to the public. But how can competition be maintained if any firm that gets a start undersells its competitors, gains more economies,

[19] 'Keynesian Economics: The Search for First Principles', *Journal of Economic Literature*, December 1976, Vol. 14, No. 4, pp. 1258–73.

and therefore cuts prices further until it establishes a monopoly for itself? To get out of the difficulty, Marshall fell back on the observation, which was quite correct in many instances, that family firms lose competitive power as they grow. He made this into a general rule (allowing for monopoly as an occasional exception) and described industry as a forest in which each individual tree grows only to a certain height.

This raised the obvious difficulty that when the grandsons of its founder lose their grip on a business, it can go public and become immortal as a joint-stock company. Marshall recognized this possibility, but he did not allow it to spoil his doctrine. The joint-stock company loses 'its elasticity and progressive force', so that it is unlikely to be able to continue to grow in competition 'with younger and smaller rivals'.[20]

A. C. Pigou[21] was a loyal disciple of Marshall and quite innocent of any knowledge of industry. He therefore constructed a U-shaped average cost curve for a firm, showing economies of scale up to a certain size and rising costs beyond it. Pigou's firm, in a perfectly competitive market, is always selling the output that maximizes profits, that is, at which a small increase in production would cause marginal cost to exceed the price; when price exceeds average cost, the firm is making a super-normal profit, which will attract in new competition; when price is below average costs, some firms are dropping out. Equilibrium requires that both marginal and average costs are equal to price, that is, that the size of the firm is such that it is producing at minimum cost. In the ultimate equilibrium of a stationary state, the flow of profits obtained by each firm is just sufficient to cover interest at the ruling rate on the value of the capital that it operates, leaving nothing over as the 'reward of enterprise'.

In Marshall's world, however, profits accrue to 'business ability in command of capital'; successful firms retain part of their profits to invest in expanding their activities, and the more capital they own the easier it is to borrow outside finance. The conception is absurd that a firm when it is making more than normal profits sits around waiting for competition to invade its market and drive it back towards its optimum size. It would be the height of imprudence for a business to distribute the whole of its net profit to the family or to shareholders, and no business could borrow if prospective profits did not exceed its interest bill.

If Marshall's theory had been taken on its merits as a hypothesis, it would have soon appeared that the way out of his dilemma was the opposite of that proposed by Pigou. Successful firms accumulate finance and devour the

---

[20] *Principles of Economics*, Seventh edition, London, Macmillan, 1916.
[21] *Economics of Welfare*, Fourth edition, London, Macmillan, 1934, Appendix III.

unsuccessful ones. Most joint-stock companies continue to grow, and many competitive industries tend towards a condition of dominance by one or a few firms. But the great corporations do not behave monopolistically in the sense of restricting output in order to raise prices. They continue to compete with each other, invading new markets, introducing new products, and evolving new techniques, while at the same time throwing up opportunities for new small businesses to make a start.

Marshall's analysis was half in historical time and half in equilibrium doctrine. It is the first half that can pass the test of *a priori* plausibility and provide a starting point for a 'theory of the firm' appropriate to an economy of private enterprise.

Keynes developed his analysis in the setting of a short-period situation with given productive capacity and training of labour. This was appropriate to his problem: the influence of the level of effective demand on the utilization of resources already in existence. He had to concentrate upon forcing his readers to admit that there was such a problem. He was concerned with investment primarily as the source of instability and, apart from some quite conventional remarks, he did not have much to say about the process of accumulation either for firms or for nations.

Hicks[22] complains that Keynes' argument is not set wholly in historical time because the multiplier theory (and the theory of production that goes with it) is couched in terms of equilibrium. This is quite untrue. The original purpose of the multiplier was to work out what increase in income could be expected over the immediate future if the level of home investment were to be stepped up, beginning from a particular date. Admittedly the time-scheme was not very clearly worked out (Dennis Robertson complained a lot about this), but the main topic of the *General Theory* was the consequences of a *change* in the level of effective demand within a short-period situation with given plant and available labour.[23] The consequences of changing the stock of plant as investment matures hardly came into the story.

It is paradoxical that during the great Age of Growth – the twenty-five years that followed World War II – so-called macro theory was taught in 'Keynesian' terms, though Keynes himself had almost nothing to say about growth. Once he had thrown off the incubus of Say's Law, the whole field of the long-period theory of accumulation remained to be explored.

[22] Hicks, op. cit., 1976, p. 140.

[23] It must be admitted that there are many Marshallian remnants in the General Theory, which obscure exposition, but in the reply to Jacob Viner the point is made clearly (see J. M. Keynes, 'The General Theory of Employment'. JMK Vol XIV).

Side by side with the timeless equilibrium model, there have grown up a number of treatments of the behaviour of firms in a growing industrial economy, but no plausible simple general hypothesis has so far been found.[24]

The doctrine that firms 'maximize profits' collapses as soon as it is taken out of the equilibrium world and set in historical time. For a firm which is growing from year to year by investing retained profits, the maximum flow of profits will be reached when it commands an indefinitely large value of capital. Certainly, it is true that firms pursue profit, for without profits they would perish, but to 'maximize' profits over the long run is a meaningless phrase.

A less vapid statement would be that, in respect to each particular choice, say, of an investment programme, the firm will prefer the most profitable alternative. But, as Loasby has observed,[25] the firm does not know which would in fact be the most profitable alternative. The observing economist can only advance the hypothesis that the alternative actually chosen was that which was expected to be the most profitable.

Furthermore, any plan a firm makes is multidimensional – it involves the selection of products; the choice of technique, including the choice of workers to employ; it involves pricing policy and salesmanship; and it involves the availability of finance. In a small business, all these considerations revolve in the mind of the boss, who acts on business instinct and does not explain, even to himself, exactly what his motives are. In a large corporation, any decision involves the personnel of many departments in the technostructure – salesmen, accountants, engineers – each of which has its characteristic beliefs and interests, and which have to be coordinated by bureaucratic rules.

The stress that John Kenneth Galbraith[26] lays on the dependence of large corporations on their technostructures has been taken to suggest that they are not governed by the profit motive. This is a misunderstanding. The specialists who serve a particular corporation depend upon it for their incomes and careers and generally develop a kind of patriotism for it. They have just as much motive to promote its profitability as an old-fashioned capitalist. But the complexity of multidimensional choice in conditions of uncertainty means that maximizing profits, even in the limited sense of

[24] The question was opened by Edith Penrose (*The Theory of the Growth of the Firm*) in 1959. A recent contribution is *The Megacorp and Oligopoly*, Alfred S. Eichner, Cambridge University Press, 1976.

[25] See p. 8 above.

[26] *The New Industrial State*, London, Hamilton, 1967.

preferring more to less profitable policies, is by no means a simple matter.

An alternative hypothesis is that the motive of firms is to maximize their rate of growth. But this does not take us much further than the observation that firms that are not profitable do not survive, and those that are, grow.

Another approach is to start from the growth of the market for a range of products and suggest that each of a group of competing firms keeps its productive capacity growing so as to maintain its share. But fast-growing firms expand into diversified markets.

One view is that the growth of the productive capacity of an industrial firm is a function of its flow of profits – as fast as its cash flow comes in, it looks around for opportunities to invest. Another view is that when an investment opportunity offers, the firm adjusts the prices of its existing output in such a way as to get the profit that it needs to finance the investment.

All these hypotheses have turned up many interesting and plausible concepts, but it seems to me that the search for a single generalization is a hangover from the equilibrium model. There is no simple theory to cover the multifarious evolution of a private enterprise economy. The methods of ethology are more appropriate than mathematics to the study of industry, and, indeed, we do know a great deal about the natural history of business life from studies of the economics of industry, of finance, and of conditions of labour. But this knowledge cannot be well organized if it has to be squeezed into formulae that smooth over the distinction between the future and the past.

Galbraith sets out to substitute for Marshall a picture, based on general observation, of the New Industrial State. His account of the behaviour of giant firms appears plausible or, at the very least, worth discussing, but it has had no success as an ideological doctrine. As he points out, a very large proportion of the educated and professional class in industrial nations is employed directly or indirectly by great corporations, and the educational system is largely at their service. For this reason, the power that Ward refers to,[27] prevents critical views from penetrating into orthodoxy.

4

PRICES

Keynes complained of the theory in which he was brought up:

> So long as economists are concerned with what is called the theory of value, they have been accustomed to teach that prices are governed by

[27] See p. 2 above.

the conditions of supply and demand; and, in particular, changes in marginal cost and the elasticity of short-period supply have played a prominent part. But when they pass in volume II, or more often in a separate treatise, to the theory of money and prices, we hear no more of these homely but intelligible concepts and move into a world where prices are governed by the quantity of money, by its income-velocity, by the velocity of circulation relatively to the volume of transactions, by hoarding, by forced saving, by inflation and deflation *et hoc genus omne*; and little or no attempt is made to relate these vaguer phrases to our former notions of the elasticities of supply and demand.[28]

He proposed a micro-macro theory in which the prices of commodties are primarily governed by the cost of production, and he observed that the main element in the general level of costs (internal to one country) which can change in the short period, is the level of money wage rates. He was concerned to argue that cutting wage rates would lower prices. We now have to adapt the argument to the case where raising money-wage rates (relatively to the growth of productivity) causes prices to rise. Keynes's 'homely but intelligible' concepts now appear old-fashioned. A great deal of work remains to be done to establish a macro-micro analysis of prices appropriate to the modern world. Moreover, during the Age of Growth the industrial economies have gone through a mutation so that unemployment no longer prevents wage rates from rising.

Meanwhile the 'vague phrases' that Keynes complained of have come back into fashion. 'Monetarism' is now a powerful doctrine, but it is not easy to confront it with the post-Keynesian system, to discuss which is the more plausible, for the hypotheses on which the quantity theory is based have never been clearly stated.

The post-Keynesian system dwells in historical time; it is designed to analyse the consequences that may be expected to follow a change taking place at a particular date in particular circumstances. The system is set up like an artist's mobile. A flick on any point sets everything in motion, but it is possible to see which are the principle interactions and which way causation runs from one to another.

The old-fashioned formula, $MV = PT$, can be interpreted in terms of this mobile. Suppose that, since this time last year, there has been an all-round rise in money-wage rates and also some increase in employment. Both the flow of transactions (T) and the level of prices (P) are now higher. This has

[28] *General theory of employment, interest and money*, 1936, (JMK), Vol. VII, London, Macmillan, 1973, p. 174.

led to an increase in bank deposits, with a corresponding increase in currency in circulation because the value of working capital having gone up, many businesses have taken larger advances from banks or drawn upon overdraft facilities. At the same time, average velocity of circulation may have risen, as liquid reserves have been drawn upon so that a larger proportion of the total stock of money is now in accounts that are more frequently turned over. (It is in general more true to say that an increase in prices causes the quantity of money to increase than the other way round.)

However, if a spontaneous rise in M and V was not sufficient to provide for the higher PT, then interest rates must have risen, and a smaller proportion of the stock of money is now held by bearish owners who prefer cash to securities (in existing circumstances) as a placement for their wealth.

When the monetary authorities are endeavouring to prevent M from increasing, interest rates are raised all the more, and a credit squeeze checks the growth of activity or even precipitates a slump. But this, unfortunately, is not guaranteed to reduce prices.

The monetarist theory is not so easily described. The modern version of the quantity theory connects M, not to the flow of transactions, but to PQ, the value of gross output, so that V simply means GNP divided by some figure representing the quantity of money; all the interactions in the mobile are collapsed into one opaque relationship.

There seems to be a chronic confusion, in latter-day expositions of monetarism, between changes in the stock of money deliberately brought about by the authorities and the effects of changes in the flow of government expenditure. The story of currency notes dropped from helicopters is presumably intended to illustrate the case of a budget deficit financed by 'using the printing press'.[29] A shower of notes, picked up by passers-by, might be expected to produce a burst of expenditure that would peter out over a short time; a budget deficit continued from year to year tends to support a flow of expenditure as long as it continues. An *increase* in the deficit from one month to the next tends to increase expenditure over the following months in much the same way as a commensurate rise in investment or reduction in thriftiness. This is not a *monetary* phenomenon, though it is likely to be accompanied by an increase in MV. There is no way to distinguish between a rise in activity that is 'inflationary' in the monetarist sense from one that is not.

Monetary influences on the behaviour of the economy, in the proper sense, arise from changes in the stock of placements (including currency)

[29] M. Friedman, *The optimum quantity of money*, London, Macmillan; Chicago, Aldine, 1969.

available to the public relative to the demand for them. A shower of notes would leave behind (after the increase in expenditure with its multiplier effect was exhausted) an addition to wealth equal to the savings made out of the extra income generated by the expenditure and an equal addition to the stock of currency notes. Assuming that the demand for currency has been increased less than the supply, credit will be somewhat easier in the final position than it would otherwise have been. This is the only *monetary* element in the story of the helicopters.

A budget deficit may be financed by borrowing through the banking system and so increasing the quantity of money, but it need not be. A modern government has a large national debt to operate upon, not only what it borrowed last week. If it thinks right, it can sell long-term bonds and generate a credit squeeze whatever its budgetary balance may be. The trouble is that when money-wage rates and prices are rising, increasing values of working capital have to be financed and the authorities can prevent the quantity of money from increasing only by bankrupting business and bringing production to a halt.

Keynes, looking forward to a period of continuous high employment, expected money-wage rates to rise faster than productivity. He regarded this as an essentially political problem and did not suggest any remedy.[30] Michal Kalecki observed: 'If capitalism can adjust itself to full employment a fundamental reform will have been incorporated in it'.[31] The revival of monetary theory is a device for avoiding discussion of political problems. This makes it very attractive as a doctrine, but fails to provide any plausible hypotheses for interpreting experience.

Keynes intended to bring the theory of prices back from Volume II, Money to Volume I, the Principles of Economics, but Michal Kalecki [32] made a greater contribution than Keynes himself to carrying this programme forward.

Kalecki drew attention to the fact that there are two distinct systems of price formation in the modern world, one dominated by supply and demand and one by costs plus profits. This distinction has recently been rediscovered by Hicks.[33] The market for some commodities is created by specialist merchants who buy to sell again, and make their profits out of price differences. They carry stocks; when the outflow of sales exceeds the

[30] See Richard Kahn, *On re-reading Keynes*, London, British Academy, 1974.
[31] 'Political Aspects of Full Employment', *Political Quarterly*, Vol. 14, No. 4, 1943, pp. 322–31.
[32] *Essays in the theory of economic fluctuations*, London, Allen and Unwin, 1939.
[33] Op. cit., 1976, p. 149.

inflow of purchases so that stocks are falling, they raise prices, and conversely. A large part of the produce of agriculture and extractive industries is handled in this way. For manufactures, in modern times, the producers have taken over the merchanting function. They offer their commodities at an advertised price and produce for sale what the market will take. There are various intermediate forms and overlapping conditions, but the main distinction is between these two types.

Kalecki analysed industrial prices in terms of gross profit margins expressed as a mark-up on average prime cost. As his theory evolved, he rejected the view that Keynes had taken over from Marshall, that an increase in output requires a rise of prices because of rising marginal costs. On this, his opinion now generally prevails. In general, it seems that average prime costs fall rather than rise with rising utilization of plant. A sellers' market, in which the flow of output is limited by capacity, is rather rare because it quickly leads to investment to expand capacity for production of the commodities concerned; if it is expected to last, it will not. Even while it prevails, firms generally prefer to lengthen delivery dates rather than to choke back demand by raising prices.

Kalecki observed that prime costs are made up of two independent elements, the wage bill and the cost of materials and power. Here there is an interconnection between the two types of price formation, for costs of materials are strongly influenced by supply and demand. Bargaining for money-wage rates depends upon the balance of forces in the labour market. Assuming a stable pattern of gross profit margins, we can deduce the behaviour of prices to be expected in the short period. A rise in the overall level of activity entails an increase in demand for materials, which raises their prices. The rise in prime costs that this entails leads to a more or less proportional rise in prices. Now real wage rates have been reduced, while profits in money terms have risen. This sets the stage for a rise in money-wage rates. On the other tack, a decline in general industrial activity tends to lower material prices, but the resistance of organized labour is generally strong enough to prevent money-wage rates from being cut (though unemployment and short-time reduce earnings).

Kalecki's analysis reinforces Keynes' view that inflation is essentially a political problem by stressing the relationship between the formation of prices and the share of wages in the proceeds of industry, although the treatment of profit margins, which Kalecki derived from 'imperfect competition', was not thoroughly worked out.

Some evidence has been found to support the assumption that the ratio of gross margins to prime costs is fairly stable in respect to changes in the general level of demand.[34] But the hypothesis that the pattern of gross margins for various commodities can be explained solely by the 'degree of monopoly' was in the nature of a shot in the dark. A high degree of monopoly, in Kalecki's sense, means a weak state of price competition. It is true that the great oligopolistic corporations can set higher margins on their products than small competitive firms, but they may be using them partly to cover the expenses of nonprice competition among themselves. Moreover, the degree of monopoly is itself partly a function of the level of margins required to cover overhead costs of production. Risky investments requiring a heavy initial capital cost are made only by powerful corporations which have sufficient command over their markets to expect to be able to recover adequate gross profits.

Here we come to the border-line between long- and short-period theory of prices, which has been very inadequately explored.

5

LONG-RUN GROWTH

Hicks in the course of his 'long struggle to escape' from *Value and Capital*, came to the conclusion that models of steady growth are futile.[35] Certainly, if steady growth is proposed as a hypothesis, it sinks at the first step, but, as Hicks himself found, it is useful in what János Kornai describes as intellectual experiments, which are necessary to sort out the questions involved in analysing complicated processes.

Hicks describes his attempt to analyse disequilibrium growth in *Capital and Time*:

> I had to start very slowly. If I had started with a fine set of plausible assumptions, drawn from the real world, I am sure I should have got nowhere. I had to build up my model bit by bit. I began from a steady state (but that was simply because I had to have something firm, which I thought I understood, from which to start), but the point of the steady state . . . is that it is to be *disturbed*.[36]

I intended my golden age (which has often been mistaken for a hypothesis) to be used in this way, as I suggested in *Exercises in Economic Analysis*[37] in 1960:

[34] R. R. Nield, *Pricing and employment in the trade cycle: A study of British manufacturing industry, 1950–61*, Cambridge University Press, 1963. See also Wynne A. H. Godley and William D. Nordhaus, 'Pricing in the Trade Cycle', *Economic Journal*, Vol. 82, No. 327, September 1975, pp. 365–7.

[35] Op. cit., 1976, p. 143.

[36] Ibid., p. 145.

[37] Macmillan, pp. xviii–xx.

Most economic questions lead up to a discussion of what consequences may be expected to follow a certain event. We cannot isolate a particular causal element from its surrounding circumstances by a controlled experiment. . . . We have to proceed by breaking the question up into parts, and after discussing each separately, reassemble the pieces as best we may.

First, compare two economies which are alike in all relevant respects except the one which we wish to isolate. . . . Each has its own past and its own expectations about its own future. They need not be in stationary conditions provided that any change that has been taking place or is expected is smooth and regular so that we know where we are with it.

Next consider a single economy, following a regular predictable path, and consider how its subsequent course is altered by an event happening at a particular moment. . . .

Then consider an economy which is not following a smooth path, but is caught for examination, so to speak, at a particular moment in a more or less turbulent history. We have to try to work out what future development is inherent in the situation as it exists to-day. . . .

Finally, we have to try to see what effect upon this in any case turbulent path would be introduced by a particular event.[37]

This is what makes serious economics difficult.

A discussion of growth immediately raises the question of technical change. This was for a long time held up by the conception of a production function in labour and 'capital.' The concept of 'malleable machines'[38] was introduced precisely to abolish the difference between the future and the past so that a growing economy could be always in equilibrium. A pseudo-production function or 'book of blueprints' was a half-way house between history and a timeless production function. The pseudo-production function consists of the specification of a set of mutually non-inferior techniques, each requiring a particular stock of means of production per man employed. Each is eligible for at least one rate of profit, and none is superior to the rest at every rate of profit. When the techniques are listed in order of the flow per man employed of a homogeneous net output, it can be

[38] J. E. Meade, *A neo-classical theory of economic growth*, second edition, London, Allen and Unwin, 1967.

seen that a higher output is not necessarily associated with 'more capital,' that a technique that is eligible at a higher rate of profit may require a larger value of capital at the corresponding prices, and that the same technique may be eligible at widely different rates of profit. This killed off the doctrine of 'marginal productivity of capital' associated with the production function (though it has refused to get buried),[39] but it does not, by itself, provide the basis for an alternative analysis of accumulation. If techniques are invented, one after the other in historical time, there is no reason to expect them to be mutually non-superior. A new technique is normally adopted because, at existing prices and wage rates, it promises a higher return than the one in use, per unit of financial investment. It does not have to wait for a change in prices to make it eligible. But it will not remain exceptionally profitable for long. Copiers wipe out the initial competitive advantage of new commodities and rising real wage rates, of higher productivity. Meanwhile, new, more eligible techniques are being introduced. At each moment, the prospect of higher profits is inducing change, while, over a run of years, the *ex post* average realized rate of profit may be constant or falling.

To sort out the analysis of this turbulent scene involves the whole of economics and, as Hicks says, we must approach it bit by bit.

The first use to which the golden-age method was put was to examine the relation between accumulation and the rate of profit. Take Kalecki's assumptions that wages are currently consumed as they are received; gross investment is financed out of profits, which are also partly distributed to rentiers. On a steady growth path, g, the rate of growth per annum is equal to I/K, the ratio of net investment to the value of the stock of capital at the ruling rate of profit, and the rate of profit is equal to g/s_p where $(1 - s_p)$ is the proportion of profits consumed by rentiers' households. Thus, if two economies are alike in all respects except for the share of saving from profits, with equal growth rates and the same level of money wages, then prices are higher in the economy where rentiers are less thrifty.

This kind of argument is not confined to strictly steady growth. When each firm finances its own investment out of its own cash flow, and plans to invest its own retained profits, there is no problem of effective demand; the financial system, as Hyman Minsky[40] puts it, is robust, and investment has great inertia. When firms can raise outside finance direct from rentiers or

[39] See Martin Bronfenbrenner, 'Ten issues in distribution theory', in *Modern economic thought*, edited by Sidney Weintraub, Philadelphia, 1977, p. 419.
[40] *John Maynard Keynes*, London, Macmillan, 1976; New York, Columbia University Press, 1975.

through the banks, the system is liable to instability. The rate of investment is not tethered by a particular ratio to the value of the stock of capital. Any rise in investment above the former ratio increases the current flow of profits and encourages further investment and a rise in the proportion of borrowing to own finance. Soon schemes of investment are being planned that will be viable only if the overall rate of investment continues to rise. A fragile debt structure has been built up. When the acceleration in the rate of investment tapers off, some businesses find current receipts less than current obligations, and a financial collapse occurs. During the boom, equity holders have been experiencing capital gains and increasing the ratio of expenditure to income; when the boom breaks, thriftiness increases. Thus long-run average growth may occur in cycles.

There is no guarantee, because growth has been maintained on the average for a run of years, that it will continue. At any stage in the process of accumulation, a sufficiently drastic financial collapse may throw the investors into a state of self-fulfilling pessimism, which postpones recovery indefinitely.

The monetary characteristics of a growing economy would generate instability even if the 'real forces' developed smoothly, but (apart from wars and political upheavals) technology has never developed smoothly. As Joseph Schumpeter observed, great fundamental discoveries and inventions occur at random intervals and each is followed by a boom, or a series of booms, as investment is made in innovations embodying new techniques. When the appropriate changes have been made in the stock of industrial capital, investment tails off and recession supervenes.

Another problem also can be analysed by means of the golden-age method. We can distinguish the technical character of an innovation in terms of the cost of investment necessary to install the appropriate means of production. When the equipment involved in employing a man with the latest best-practice technique has required the same investment (at unchanged real-wage rates) as that which it replaced, the innovation has been neutral. When it has required a greater investment, the innovation has been capital-using, and when less, capital saving.

The 'stylized facts' − a run of years with a constant rate of profit, constant share of wages in proceeds, and a constant ratio of the value of capital to the flow of net output − are possible only if technical progress is neutral, though neutrality by itself does not guarantee a constant rate of profit.

To allow a constant rate of profit when a series of neutral innovations are being made, the real-wage rate must rise at the same rate as average net output per man employed. Then, if a steady rate of accumulation is being maintained, the value of the stock of capital is rising at the same rate as the flow of net output and the capital to output ratio is constant.

A round of capital-using innovations, with a constant rate of profit, requires real wages to rise in a smaller proportion than net output (to allow for the rise in the capital to labour ratio). Conversely with capital-saving innovations.

On an orthodox production function, there are no articulated techniques. 'Capital' is a kind of mush and, for some unexplained reason, a higher ratio of 'capital' to labour is eligible only at a lower rate of profit.

With neutral technical progress, it is possible to maintain both a constant rate of profit and a constant capital to output ratio. Neutrality is a necessary, not sufficient, condition. Steady growth requires not only that innovations are neutral, but also that the rate of accumulation is constant and that real wages rise at the appropriate rate. These are the characteristics of a golden age.

When real wages fail to rise in step with output, demand fails to expand as fast as supply (unless investment is expanding sufficiently to make up the difference). Underconsumption discourages investment, and the economy falls out of the golden-age into stagnation.

The analysis is quite complicated even on this high plane of abstraction, and this plane is very far removed from the turbulence of actual history. Here is a field where mathematical expertise combined with real-life observation has plenty of work to do. Meanwhile we may hazard some general remarks.

First consider the formation of prices. Innovating firms have to set prices *ex ante*. They may be supposed to aim at a price that will cover average total cost (including the interest bill) at some standard level of utilization of plant, plus an allowance for selling costs, plus an allowance for net profit. As well as the choice of technique, the choice of the standard of utilization, of selling costs, and of the ratio of net profit to price depend upon the policy of the individual firm. There is too great an element of luck in the game for an outside observer to tell which policies are proving the most successful in any particular circumstances.

The design of new commodities is a very important element in innovation. Here the large firms with an ample flow of finance have a great advantage. They can employ research staffs and try out a large number of innovations in the expectation that one will take off and become a winner.

Old commodities are constantly being dolled up with changes of design in the attempt to maintain demand.

The evolution of the general level of prices depends very much upon the strength of the labour movement. With constant prices and money-wage rates, a firm that has made an innovation which raises the value of output per man by more than the cost of investment per man is enjoying a higher rate of profit for the time being. Trade unions feel that it is a right and a duty to get a share of this profit for their members. They demand higher money-wage rates and the prosperous firms may concede this without a fight and without a fully-offsetting rise in selling prices. They may actually welcome a rise in real-wage rates because it helps them in competition with smaller and more backward firms, which cannot survive a rise in costs.

In a closed economy (without foreign trade), a general rise in average wage rates proportional to the average increase in productivity would keep the overall price level constant, but this cannot occur. Wages rise fastest in the most profitable industries. Less profitable industries have to raise the wages that they pay in response, and the firms in those industries have to raise their selling prices in order to survive. Thus, a general rise in real wages is accompanied by a change in the pattern of prices. As the cost of labour in terms of commodities rises, some lines of employment (say, domestic help) are squeezed out. Others (say, collecting garbage) have to be mechanized to maintain a necessary service, for in many cases machines have become cheaper than men. Here we find a grain of truth in the orthodox conception of substitution between capital and labour.

When accumulation has been going on vigorously while the population has ceased to grow, a condition arises of scarcity of labour in the sense that the flow of investable finance from retained profits has risen relative to the number of employable workers. This enhances the bargaining power of labour. (Marx failed to emphasize that growth of population is inimical to the interests of the proletariat.) It also stimulates inventions of all kinds. Even capital-using innovations save labour in the sense of raising output per man of the work force as a whole.

When there is a strong capital-using bias in technical progress, it requires a higher flow of gross investment to maintain a constant long-run level of employment. If sufficient gross investment is not forthcoming, a reserve army of long-period unemployment is created again.

Even when they are not capital-using, innovations may require a greatly increased minimum size of investment. This enhances the competitive advantage of large against small businesses.

A major side effect of technical change is on the nature of work. It is characteristic of modern industry to require highly trained personnel, while it has no use for the labour power of a great mass of unskilled workers.

Thus (as Ricardo admitted) technical development, which from the point of view of capitalism is progressive, may reduce the share of wages in the proceeds of industry and generate long-period unemployment. For a long time, this was hushed up in orthodox doctrine, but now it is becoming too painfully obvious to be ignored.

6

INTERNATIONAL TRADE

The most powerful and all-pervasive doctrine in pre-Keynesian orthodoxy was the case in favour of free trade. This was not invented by the neoclassicists, but derived via Marshall from David Ricardo.

Ricardo intended his model to exist in historical time; he claimed that *removing* protection would *increase* wealth, but in two important respects his argument runs in terms of timeless equilibrium. In the famous story which begins with England and Portugal both producing both cloth and wine,[41] resources can be moved instantaneously, when trade begins, from one industry to another in each country. Labour-value prices rule in each country. This means that there is a uniform rate of profit and a uniform capital to labour ratio in each. Output per man of each commodity determines their relative prices within each country. When it becomes profitable to expand one industry, resources are moved out of the other without trouble or loss and without changing the capital to labour ratio in the country concerned. (It is curious that wine, as well as cloth, is produced in conditions of 'constant returns'.)

Here is the first case of analysis couched in terms of a movement through time, which is really a comparison of equilibrium positions.

The second case is even more striking. Ricardo did not allow overseas investment (which he disapproved of) into his model. The value of the flow of imports and of exports had to be equal for each country. He relied upon gold flows and the quantity theory of money to establish equilibrium in the price levels of trading countries.

It is not legitimate to complain of Ricardo, who was hacking a pioneering path through unknown problems, but it is certainly permissible to reproach his successors for keeping the so-called theory of international trade on this narrow track ever since.

To broaden the discussion, the first question that we must ask is: What is

[41] *Works and correspondence*, edited by Piero Sraffa, Cambridge University Press, 1951. Volume 1, *On the principles of political economy and taxation*, Chapter VII.

a nation? In the equilibrium theory, from Marshall to Paul Samuelson,[42] and till today, a country is treated as a compact bundle of 'factors of production', at first in isolation, which remains physically unchanged as trade takes place. Samuelson prudently named his two factors 'land' and 'labour', but many of his followers postulate that each country is endowed with a particular 'quantity of capital'; though profit rates may differ, no financial flows take place.

Among modern industrial countries there is a great interpenetration of production of specialized components of traded commodities; rentiers in each country own placements in others; banking systems are interlocked; great corporations (sometimes operating under 'flags of convenience') install facilities in many countries and employ labour and technostructure personnel of many nationalities. They have become independent entities, each larger and more powerful than many nations, not burdened with patriotism for anything except their own command of capital. The native-born workers of a country regard themselves as a nation, but great capitalist businesses feel it their duty to 'maximize profits' by seeking cheap labour wherever they can find it.

There is one respect, however, in which a modern nation is a distinct economic entity: it has a current account of foreign payments and receipts and an exchange rate, which are of concern to its government and monetary authorities.

For monetary equilibrium, it is not necessary for the current account to be balanced. It is necessary that a surplus of foreign receipts is matched by equal net foreign lending or a deficit matched by borrowing. A surplus is correctly described as a *favourable* balance. It means that citizens of the home country are acquiring foreign assets and so improving its balance for the future. A deficit covered by borrowing may be welcomed if it is due to a high rate of investment at home, which is developing resources that will yield a surplus of exports in the future to repay the debt. But a deficit that is due merely to competitive weakness is highly unfavourable; moreover, the interest on the loans necessary to meet it imposes a growing burden on the balance of payments, which makes it progressively more unfavourable.

Ricardo, to make his case as dramatic as possible, gave Portugal a competitive advantage over England in the initial position. The output (say, per week) of Portuguese workers both of cloth and of wine was higher

[42] See Alfred Marshall, *Pure theory of foreign trade*, originally published in 1879, republished 1930 in Scarce Tracts in Economic Political Science, No. 1, London; Paul Samuelson, 'International Trade and the Equalisation of Factor Prices', *Economic Journal*, Vol. 58, June 1948, pp. 163–84.

than that of English workers. If money wage rates (in terms of gold) had been more or less the same when trade began, England would have been unable to export anything and would have had a drain of gold equal to the total value of her imports. Substituting a Keynes-Kalecki theory of prices for the quantity theory of money, we may say that equilibrium could not have been reached until relative money-wage rates were higher in Portugal in the same ratio as average productivity.

There is a certain tendency for wage differentials to adjust to trade balances. Where output per man is higher in one country than in others, if wages are *not* sufficiently higher there is a competitive advantage in trade leading to high exports and so to high employment and a high rate of profit. Both influences tend to cause money-wage rates to rise. Unemployment and low profits may not actually push down wage rates, but prevent them from rising, so there is tendency towards balance. But the mechanism of differential wage rates is weak and sluggish in its operations.

It was found in the 1930s that British and German costs were roughly equal, while productivity in comparable lines was double in the United States, and wage rates 50 per cent higher.[43] Then the high real-wage country was the cheap labour country.

In recent times, with both money-wage rates and productivity rising everywhere, there has been some tendency for a faster rise of wage rates to accompany a faster relative increase in productivity,[44] but this has been much too weak to maintain equilibrium. It has been supplemented by large deliberate appreciations and depreciations of exchange rates, but these have proved to be less efficacious than economists once expected. Unbalance between the major industrial countries still continues to cause great strain in the international financial system.[45] (The problems of trade with so-called developing nations and with the OPEC countries are not discussed here. Nor is the trade of the socialist world. There are more than enough questions to raise in one article about the problems of the advanced industrialized capitalist nations.)

The authorities of each nation desire to see a surplus on its current account balance of payments, though not all can succeed.

A surplus of exports is advantageous, first of all, in connection with the short-period problem of effective demand. A surplus of value of exports

[43] László Rostás, *Comparative productivity in British and American industry*, Cambridge, 1948.
[44] Richard Kahn, quoted in *Reflections on the theory of international trade*, below p. 141.
[45] Martin Fetherston et al., *Economic Policy Review*, Dept. of Applied Economics, Cambridge, March 1977, Chapter 6.

over value of imports represents 'foreign investment'. An increase in it has an employment and multiplier effect. Any increase in activity at home is liable to increase imports so that a boost to income and employment from an increase in the flow of home investment is partly offset by a reduction in foreign investment. A boost due to increasing exports or production of home substitutes for imports (when there is sufficient slack in the economy) does not reduce home investment, but creates conditions favourable to raising it. Thus, an export surplus is a more powerful stimulus to income than home investment.

In the beggar-my-neighbour scramble for trade during the great slump, every country was desperately trying to export its own unemployment. Every country had to join in, for any one that attempted to maintain employment without protecting its balance of trade (through tariffs, subsidies, depreciation, etc.) would have been beggared by the others.

From a long-run point of view, export-led growth is the basis of success. A country that has a competitive advantage in industrial production can maintain a high level of home investment, without fear of being checked by a balance-of-payments crisis. Capital accumulation and technical improvements then progressively enhance its competitive advantage. Employment is high and real-wage rates rising so that 'labour trouble' is kept at bay. Its financial position is strong. If it prefers an extra rise of home consumption to acquiring foreign assets, it can allow its exchange rate to appreciate and turn the terms of trade in its own favour. In all these respects, a country in a weak competitive position suffers the corresponding disadvantages.

When Ricardo set out the case against protection, he was supporting British economic interests. Free trade ruined Portuguese industry.[46] Free trade for *others* is in the interests of the strongest competitor in world markets, and a sufficiently strong competitor has no need for protection at home. Free trade doctrine, in practice, is a more subtle form of Mercantilism. When Britain was the workshop of the world, universal free trade suited her interests. When (with the aid of protection) rival industries developed in Germany and the United States, she was still able to preserve free trade for her own exports in the Empire.[47] The historical tradition of attachment to free trade doctrine is so strong in England that even now, in her weakness, the idea of protectionism is considered shocking.

[46] Sandro Sideri, *Trade and power: Informal colonialism in Anglo-Portuguese relations*, Rotterdam University Press, 1970.

[47] Eric J. Hobsbawm, *Industry and empire: An economic history of Britain since 1750*, London, Weidenfeld and Nicolson, 1968.

After 1945, the United States was far and away the strongest competitor and used her great influence to arrange free trade agreements, GATT, IMF, etc., but she has no objection to protection for her own industries when they are strongly pressed by Japan.

WHAT NOW?

The present situation raises new questions. The long boom of twenty-five years after 1945, interrupted only by shallow and local recessions, blew up into a violent inflation in 1973 and collapsed into a world-wide slump. The economists had sunk into complacency and now do not know what to say. Relatively high employment and continuous growth in the indicators of production and accumulation had been taken to show that an age of permanent prosperity had set in. It was natural scientists, not economists, who first pointed out that exponential growth in perpetuity is an impossibility for any physical entity. On the plane of doctrine, Keynes had been smothered in the neo-classical synthesis, and a new 'dynamic' version of Say's Law had come into operation.

Now that the Juggernaut car has come more or less to a halt, we must take stock of the problems that its passage leaves behind.

The consumption of resources, including air to breathe, has evidently impoverished the world; the long struggle over relative shares has implanted a chronic tendency to inflation in the industrial countries, which no resort to monetary stringency can master. The uneven development of trading nations has set insupportable strains on the international financial system. Growth of wealth has not after all removed poverty at home, and 'aid' has not reduced it abroad. Now unemployment exacerbates social problems and embitters politics.

In this situation, the cry is to get growth started again. The European countries in a weak competitive position plead with West Germany to spend money on something or other to improve the market for the rest so that they can permit employment to increase. Any up turn in the indicators in the United States is greeted as a sign that we shall once more be pulled up out of the slough.

Here we come upon the greatest of all economic questions, but one that in fact is never asked: what is growth for? Under the shadow of the arms race and its diffusion into the Third World, perhaps no merely economic questions are really of great importance; but even if it is a secondary question, we ought to consider it.

The obvious answer is that there is apparently no way to reduce unemployment except by increasing industrial investment. There is no question of choosing between alternative uses for given resources. Past development has dug deep grooves by physical investment, creation of financial property, and specialization of the labour force; existing resources cannot be redeployed; our only hope is to pour more resources down the old grooves.

The problem of the use of resources, and the institutional setting that controls it, cannot be confined within the bounds of theoretical economic analysis, but the economic aspect of the matter ought to be discussed. What is the object of production in a modern industrial nation, and if we could have more of it (through technical change and capital accumulation), what should we use it for?

For the classical economists, such a question did not arise. The wealth of a nation was its investable surplus; real wages were part of the cost of production, like fodder for cattle, and luxury consumption was deprecated; the neoclassicists conceived the object of production to be provision for consumption. But consumption by whom, of what?

The question was supposed to be settled by appeal to the individual's freedom of choice, but there are three very large objections to such a solution.

The first arises from inequality of the distribution of purchasing power between individuals. The nature of accumulation under private enterprise necessarily generates inequality and is therefore condemned to meeting the trivial wants of a few before the urgent needs of the many.

Do we want renewed growth in order to maintain and enhance disparities in consumption? Have we not become disillusioned with the doctrine that 'disease, squalor and ignorance' will soon be cleared away by the 'trickle down' from ever-growing conspicuous consumption?

Secondly, many kinds of consumption that are chosen by some individuals generate disutility for others. The leading case is the spread of private motor cars – the higher the level of consumption, the more uncomfortable life becomes; this fact is painfully obvious, but orthodox doctrine has not been able to accommodate it.

Thirdly, to keep the show going, it is necessary continually to introduce new commodities and create new wants. In a competitive society, a growth of consumption does not guarantee a growth of satisfaction.

Here is the problem. The task of deciding how resources should be allocated is not fulfilled by the market but by the great corporations who are in charge of the finance for development.

These questions involve the whole political and social system of the capitalist world; they cannot be decided by economic theory, but it would be decent, at least, if the economists admitted that they do not have an answer to them.

2

THE ABDICATION OF
NEO-CLASSICAL ECONOMICS

THE situation of orthodox economics today is not so much a crisis as an abdication.

In a recent article, 'The Irrelevance of Equilibrium Economics',[1] Nicholas Kaldor wrote:

> Taken at its purest and most abstract level, the pretensions of this equilibrium theory are modest enough. Although Debreu describes the subject-matter of his book as 'the explanation of the price of commodities resulting from the interaction of the agents of a private ownership economy', it is clear that the term 'explanation' is not used in the ordinary everyday sense of the term. It is intended in a purely logical and not in a 'scientific' sense; in the strict sense, as Debreu says, the theory is 'logically entirely disconnected from its interpretation.' It is not put forward as an explanation of how the actual prices of commodities are determined in particular economies or in the world economy as a whole. By the term 'explanation' Debreu means a set of theorems that are logically deducible from precisely formulated assumptions; and the purpose of the exercise is to find the minimum 'basic assumptions' necessary for establishing the existence of an 'equilibrium' set of prices (and output/input matrixes) that is (a) unique, (b) stable, (c) satisfies the conditions of Pareto optimality.

Kaldor was attacked by Professor Hahn,[2] who will die in the last ditch for equilibrium, for saying that Debreu claims to show the existence of a *unique* equilibrium. He only pretends to show that *at least one* equilibrium exists in his system. The equilibrium theory, Hahn proclaims, is even more empty than Kaldor supposed.

The irrelevance of orthodox economic theory to economic problems is

[1] *Economic Journal*, December 1972.
[2] *On the Notion of Equilibrium in Economics*, Cambridge, 1973.

From *Economic Theory and Planning: Essays in Honour of A. K. Das Gupta*, edited by Ashok Mitra, Oxford University Press, Calcutta, 1974.

sufficiently well known, particularly to students who are obliged to submit themselves to it. In this paper, I want to consider the logic of the theory to see how it has led to this 'lame and impotent conclusion'.

Ricardo maintained that 'The principal problem of Political Economy' was to determine the laws that regulate distribution.

> The produce of the earth – all that is derived from its surface by the united application of labour, machinery, and capital, is divided among three classes of the community; namely, the proprietor of the land, the owner of the stock or capital necessary for its cultivation, and the labourer by whose industry it is cultivated.

Ricardo was particularly concerned with distribution between profits and rent, but he also provided a theory of the relation of profits to wages. Capitalists are necessary to organize production. They are able to do so because there are men available to work who have no property and cannot live unless a capitalist is willing to advance them wages ahead of selling the product of their work.

Profit, in Ricardo's scheme, is the difference between the value of the product of a team of men, net of rent and of replacement of physical inputs, and the value of the wage that they receive.

Marx turned Ricardo's theory of profits into the theory of exploitation. Labour produces *value* and the capitalist takes a part of it.

The neo-classical theory that came into fashion after about 1870 was, consciously or unconsciously, a reaction against Marx.

It consisted mainly of dodging the question of distribution and concentrating on the analysis of the relative prices of commodities. In this sphere, the academics were able to score some points and I think that it was foolish of the Marxists to allow themselves to be drawn into an argument about this trivial question instead of taking the position that prices of particular commodities are not important – what matters is the over-all rate of exploitation in the economy as a whole.

Now that we have the benefit of Piero Sraffa's interpretation of Ricardo, we can state the whole analysis quite simply.

As a first approximation, assume both that there is a uniform rate of profit on capital throughout the economy and that the value of capital per man is the same in all lines of production. Then prices are proportional to the labour time required to produce the various commodities. We can read Volume I of Marx taking this approximation to have been made. (For Marx it may have had some deeper meaning, but there is no point at this time of day stopping to argue about it.)

The second approximation is a uniform rate of profit with different capital to labour ratios in different industries. 'Prices of production' then obtain. This is the point that Piero Sraffa has cleared up.

A third approximation would be to allow for a hierarchy of different rates of profit connected with the different levels of monopoly power amongst large and small firms. Even this, of course, is far too simple for the actual hurly-burly in which actual prices are formed, but it provides a starting point for the study of reality.

All this, however, is a development from Ricardo's theory of the prices of goods produced with the aid of produced means of production – equipment and stocks produced by labour with the aid of equipment and stocks.

The neo-classical theory had a completely different basis. It pretends to derive a system of prices from the relative scarcity of commodities in relation to the demand for them. I say *pretend* because this system cannot be applied to capitalist production.

The Walrasian conception of equilibrium arrived at by higgling and haggling in a market illuminates the account of prisoners of war swapping the contents of their Red Cross parcels.

It makes sense also, with some modifications, in an economy of artisans and small traders. This was the kind of world that Adam Smith evidently had in mind when he said that we do not depend on the benevolence of the butcher, the baker, and the brewer to get a dinner. (He did not mention this in connection with his pin factory.)

Two essential characteristics of industrial capitalism are absent in these economic systems – the distinction between income from work and income from property and the nature of investments made in the light of uncertain expectations about a long future.

Debreu's system (which Hahn defends in such a backhanded manner) attempts to get rid of time by supposing that all decisions about the whole future can be made today, but he fails to deal with the distinction between wages and profits. Everyone is to receive 'rentals' for the 'factors of production' with which they are endowed and 'factors', as for Walras, consist of such things as particular types of machines and labour trained in particular skills.

Now, an owner on day one of a machine, say for making buttons, can envisage himself retaining funds from its gross rental to invest in a machine for making sausages, if that is going to offer a higher yield. A capitalist is not interested in buttons or sausages *per se* but in the profit he can get from them. He is interested in the return he can get on the value of his investment; there must be a tendency to equalize the rate of profit on the value of means of production in different lines. The value of investment is influenced by the wages paid to workers operating machines for buttons or sausages. Thus the level of that rate of profit is related to the level of wages.

This is not discussed by Debreu, who operates only in terms of a rate of interest derived from subjective discount of the future in the minds of consumers.

Debreu's system (even if it could be made internally consistent) is just a *jeu d'esprit*, but in real life the principle of prices influenced by scarcity relatively to demand is of great importance, particularly for commodities of which supply depends mainly on natural resources. The neo-classicals had a right to point out that it was not given sufficient weight by Ricardo or Marx.

However, in their own system, the analysis is not at all well developed, because it leaves out the influence of expectations about the future.

Recently, in India when there was a drought, the price of grain began to rise in expectation of a bad harvest. The government, believing the text-book theory of supply and demand, began to release stocks hoping to lower the price. Dealers bought up the grain and sold it later at a handsome profit when the expected shortages occurred.

Marshall tried to combine neo-classical supply and demand theory for the short run with a classical theory of the rate of profit for the long run. There are many valuable ideas in Marshall but it must be admitted that they are in a terrible muddle. The modern text-book theory is mainly derived from Walras. It concentrates on the analysis of equilibrium and does not have any coherent theory of the distribution of the product of industry between wages and profits.

2

However, it is impossible to set up a theory that entirely neglects the question of distribution. The modern theory mixes two other strands of neo-classical thought with Walras.

One of these was concerned to provide an explanation of rentier income from interest and dividends. The rentier was said to provide the service of *abstinence* which provided capital to industry. (Income from property in land was put under a different heading.) Marshall though it more tactful to call owning property *waiting* rather than abstinence, but in the first account of the matter that he gave he was sufficiently candid to say that it means nothing more than owning wealth.

. . . That surplus benefit which a person gets in the long run by post-
poning enjoyment, and which is measured by the rate of interest
(subject as we have seen to certain conditions) is the reward of waiting.
He may have obtained the *de facto* possession of property by inheritance
or by any other means, moral or immoral, legal or illegal. But if,
having the power to consume that property in immediate gratifications, he chooses to put it in such a form as to afford him deferred
gratifications, then any superiority there may be in deferred gratifications over those immediate ones is the reward of his waiting. When
he lends out the wealth on a secure loan the net payment which he
receives for the use of the wealth may be regarded as affording a
numerical measure of that reward. . . .[3]

Later, Marshall evidently realized that he was giving too much
away. In later editions of the *Principles* a passage similar to the above is
linked to the justification of interest because 'few people would save
much without reward'.

Now, to treat interest as the reward of *saving* is a confusion. The
dimensions are wrong. The wealth on which a rentier receives interest
(if he chooses to lend it) is a stock in existence today; saving is a rate per
unit of time at which he is adding to the stock. Is he supposed to get
interest on the saving he is doing this week, or this year or this minute?

Obviously, the reward of saving is owning some more wealth. One
of the advantages, though by no means the only one, of owning wealth
is the possibility of getting interest on it.

But why is it possible to get interest? Because businesses make
profits and are willing to borrow.

The confusion between profits and interest ought to have been
cleared up once and for all when Keynes pointed out that profit is what
a businessman hopes to get on an investment and interest is what he has
to promise to pay for finance. But the confusion is still to be found in
the modern text-books.

Another strand of thought which is now being revived is the Austrian
theory which measures capital by the average period of production and
attributes interest to the superior productivity of more roundabout methods
of production. In this theory, also, the dimensions are wrong. It confuses
investment, that is, an addition to the stock of means of production, with the
stock already in existence and it confuses productivity from the point of
view of society as a whole with the share that goes to the capitalists as profit.

[3] *Principles of Economics*, first edition (1890), p. 614.

This point we must discuss further but first I will say something about the great capital-theory debate.

3

The modern text-book theory, as Professor Samuelson has confessed, was based on the vulgarized American version of neo-classical thought that was put out by J. B. Clark. On this view: 'What a social class gets is, under natural law, what it contributes to the general output of industry.' The class of owners of wealth provide a factor of production called 'capital' which is embodied in 'capital goods' – equipment and stocks. A single quantity of 'capital' can be extracted from one set of machines and embodied in another, receiving as its reward the profit determined by the 'marginal productivity' of 'capital' to the economy as a whole.

Thorstein Veblen, reviewing a book by J. B. Clark, immediately pointed out the fallacy:

. . . Here, as elsewhere in Mr. Clark's writings, much is made of the doctrine that the two facts of 'capital' and 'capital goods' are conceptually distinct, though substantially identical. The two terms cover virtually the same facts as would be covered by the terms 'pecuniary capital' and 'industrial equipment'. . . .

. . . This conception of capital, as a physically 'abiding entity' constituted by the succession of productive goods that make up the industrial equipment, breaks down in Mr. Clark's own use of it when he comes to speak of the mobility of capital; that is to say, so soon as he makes use of it. . . .

. . . The continuum in which the 'abiding entity' of capital resides is a continuity of ownership, not a physical fact. The continuity, in fact, is of an immaterial nature, a matter of legal rights, of contract, or purchase and sale. Just why this patent state of the case is overlooked, as it somewhat elaborately is, is not easily seen. But it is plain that, if the concept of capital were elaborated from observation of current business practice, it would be found that 'capital' is a pecuniary fact, not a mechanical one; that it is an outcome of a valuation, depending immediately on the state of mind of the valuers; and that the specific marks of capital, by which it is distinguishable from other facts, are of an immaterial character. . . . [4]

---

[4] 'Professor Clark's Economics', reprinted in *A Critique of Economic Theory*, pp. 180 and 181–2, *Penguin Modern Economics Readings*.

After the Keynesian revolution, Professor Samuelson (ignoring Veblen) took up J. B. Clark's interpretation of capital and this became the orthodox neo-neoclassical view.

In 1953 I tried to find out what it meant. I was reinforced by the publication of Piero Sraffa's *Production of Commodities by Means of Commodities* in 1960. Does a quantity of capital mean a number of dollars or a list of machine tools, railway lines and other hard objects? And which is it that has a 'marginal product'?[5]

The only answer we got was: Let us pretend that it doesn't make any difference.

Now, after twenty years, the state of play seems to be as follows. Profesor Swan has retired from the game. It was he whose 'Meccano sets' started off the idea of capital made of a physical substance which, like finance, can change its form in any way required.

Professor Samuelson has repudiated J. B. Clark but continues republishing his text-book just the same.

Professor von Weizsäcker, the most subtle of neo-neoclassics, points out that *if* there is no expenditure out of profits (as on von Neumann's growth path) so that net profit is identical with net investment, and *if* investment is at just the rate necessary to maintain full employment over the long run, then all profits are required to maintain employment. (If we had some eggs, we could have some ham and eggs, if we had some ham.)

Professor Solow has retreated into a one-commodity world where there is perfect substitutability between labour and inputs of the commodity and where there is no distinction between households and firms. (The propensity to save of the community controls the rate of gross investment.)[5]

Professor Hahn seems to maintain that there must be *some* meaning to a state of equilibrium but that no one can yet say what it is.[6]

However, the theory of profits based on the productivity of capital is still taught all over the world. It flourishes particularly in India. A great deal of talent and industry goes into the profession of economists in the sub-continent but very little of any relevance comes out.

4

What does 'the productivity of capital' mean? No one could deny that modern industry, for better or worse, causes output to grow as never

[5] See Joan Robinson, 'Solow Once More', *Collected Economic Papers*, Vol. IV; also 'Capital Theory Up-to-date' in the same volume.
[6] See above p. 32.

before. Capitalist accumulation, as Marx said, ripens the productive power of social labour as though in a hot house.

When accumulation has absorbed the reserve army of the unemployed, capitalists compete with each other in introducing labour-saving devices, raising output per man.

Until recently, orthodox Marxists stressed the 'growing misery of the workers' under capitalism, but the part of the Marxian argument that is relevant today is in Volume III of *Capital* where the rate of exploitation is expected to remain more or less constant while productivity increases. When the share of wages in the value of net output is constant while the total is increasing through time, wages in terms of commodities are continually rising. Rising real wages stimulate increasing productivity and increasing productivity provides for rising wages. (Marx predicted a rise in organic composition of capital that would cause the rate of profit to fall when exploitation does not rise fast enough to offset it. Organic composition was no doubt rising in his time but nowadays it seems to be on the whole fairly constant.)

Joseph Schumpeter took over his analysis from Marx and put it into a different ideological setting. Instead of explaining profits by exploitation, Schumpeter gives the credit to the heroic entrepreneur who takes the risks of investment in the 'gale of creative destruction' that competitive technical progress brings about. But entrepreneurs, that is, businessmen, do not make technical progress. They use what comes to them from the general development of science and engineering. They, in turn, foster development, so that investment generates knowledge and knowledge generates investment in an ever-widening spiral.

Thorstein Veblen, in his criticism of J. B. Clark, brings out the point.

J. B. Clark pictures an isolated primitive man, who 'makes by his own labour all the goods that he uses' and maintains that 'the inherent productive power of labour and capital is of vital concern to him'.

Veblen points out that the productive power of the primitive hunter does not reside in his bow and arrows.

> . . . The loss of these objects – tangible assets – would entail a transient inconvenience. But the accumulated, habitual knowledge of the ways and means involved in the production and use of these appliances is the outcome of long experience and experimentation, and given this body of commonplace technological information, the acquisition and employment of the suitable apparatus is easily arranged. . . .

As technology develops, the means of production which it requires grow more and more elaborate.

> .... Through 'difficulty of attainment' in adequate quantities, the apparatus and its ownership become a matter of consequence; increasingly so, until presently the equipment required for an effective pursuit of industry comes to be greater than the common man can hope to acquire in a lifetime. The commonplace knowledge of ways and means, the accumulated experience of mankind, is still transmitted in and by the body of the community at large; but, for practical purposes, the advanced 'state of the industrial arts' has enabled the owners of goods to corner the wisdom of the ancients and the accumulated experience of the race. . . .[7]

Capitalism fostered the application of science to technology and, so, by a spiral action, developed science and technology into the all-devouring system we know today.

Schumpeter remarked that in the great bureaucratic organization of a modern corporation, with its own laboratories, 'innovation itself has become a matter of routine'. There is no longer any need for the heroic entrepreneur. But still the corporations are cornering accumulated experience, as Veblen says, for their own ends.

They can still do so partly through 'ownership of goods', that is, the power to command great sums of finance that can be embodied in large units of productive equipment. But much more important is their power to command the educational system. The engineers, accountants, designers and salesmen – all the numerous highly specialized experts that man what Galbraith calls the technostructure of large-scale business, are provided for the corporations by the educational system. They are paid salaries above the level of operative workers; they are taught to feel themselves superior and they attach their loyalty to their employers rather than to their class fellows.

The educational system in a modern economy (even in the USSR) is devoted to providing the required numbers both of experts for the techno-structure and of operatives who are taught to think of themselves as too stupid to master technology, though they are allowed the necessary training required for productive work.

Today, the native workers in Europe are getting to feel superior in their turn, and 'guests' are called in from the underdeveloped world to do the low-class jobs.

Now we can return to the Austrian conception of the productivity of 'roundaboutness'. Whether we may evaluate a stock of capital in terms of

[7] T. Veblen, op. cit., pp. 174–5.

dollars discounted at a rate of interest corresponding to the over-all rate of profit or may use some rough physical measure, say, in terms of horse-power, in either case we find capital per man employed rising as modern industry develops. If we could measure capital as labour time embodied in the means of production in use, or, as the Austrians propose, as the length of the average period of production, equally we would find capital per man rising. But we would *not* find the 'marginal product' falling. Investment adds to productivity by embodying new technology in new types of means of production. It would not be possible to go on adding capital to labour for very long in a given state of knowledge.

The marginal productivity theory requires that the 'reward' of a 'factor of production' falls as its quantity increases, relatively to other factors. Do we expect to find a lower rate of profit on capital where, by any measure you like, capital per man is greatest? In the United States or in West Germany compared to India?

But if there were anything in the idea of substitution between capital and labour, we would find the rate of profit to be highest where capital per man is least, because low wages in terms of the product both make the rate of profit high and investment per man low.

5

The relations of 'waiting', saving, finance, investment, education and technology to rising productivity can be seen still more clearly when we transfer the argument from advanced capitalism to the setting of a would-be developing economy.

The technology pioneered, stage by stage, in capitalist industry is available to be copied in so-called backward countries. It does not have to be freshly invented. There are a variety of ways in which it may be transplanted.

The most striking example of development in modern times has taken place in North Korea. The Koreans, with a small amount of help from abroad, in the course of a decade, by a great drive for education, study and learning by doing, mastered the techniques of almost the whole range of modern industry, as well as mechanizing agriculture, and provided themselves with the equipment that it requires, in a country that had been blitzed to the ground. Their engineers read text-books or took machines to pieces to see how they were made. The workers were encouraged to put themselves through part-time schools, from primary to university level, side by side with regular education for the young generation.

By this means, with hard work and with the initial advantage of good mineral resources, they brought about the greatest 'economic miracle' that has ever been seen, in spite of feeling obliged to build up modern armaments as well.

They did not need a class of rentiers to perform the service of 'waiting', but 'abstinence' was provided by the whole country, in the sense that when a tolerable standard of life had been provided for all, they abstained from consuming luxuries so as to be able to devote a great share of resources to investment.

The economists in the Third World, on the other hand, under the influence of neo-classical orthodoxy, believe that what their countries need is 'capital' and that to get it, they need capitalists to take the risk of making investment. Capitalists have to be enticed by prospects of profit, and so they have to be allowed to consume a good part of the profits that they get. Moreover, they prefer to keep their workers ignorant, so that no one can put any dangerous thoughts into their heads.

Then there is 'foreign capital'. Foreign capital does not mean either equipment or technology, it means finance. Loans or 'aid' permit an economy to pay for a deficit in its balance of trade. When investment at home is going on, part of the finance may be used to import equipment, but a large part of the work must be done by labour at home and generate profits and saving at home. Then that part of the deficit that is not required to import ingredients for investment is used to import consumption goods (or means of production for them) which meet the demand for consumption out of profits.

Sometimes 'foreign capital' comes in the form of direct investment from multinational firms. This is more expensive than raising capitalists at home. The foreign firms pick the investment opportunities that yeld the highest returns and their profits are remitted abroad. This puts a greater burden on the balance of payments than the consumption of home-grown capitalists, which is not all of imports but largely of services at home.

Branches of foreign corporations are often welcomed because it is said that they bring know-how to the 'backward' country but they do not allow know-how to be digested in the Korean manner. They hold back enough to keep the local technostructure dependent and the local workers helpless.

But this is not fair, the orthodox economists reply. North Korea is a totalitarian communist regime and the others are part of the Free World. Yes, that is just my point. When orthodox theory cannot support itself by logic, it falls back on ideology.

Perhaps it is only natural that the orthodox economists prefer to blinker themselves with algebra rather than to take a look at the world.

3

MORALITY AND ECONOMICS

I WANT to speak about the philosophy of economics. It is an extremely important element in the view of life and the conceptions which prevail in this country. Freedom is the great ideal. Along with the concept of freedom goes freedom of the market, and the philosophy of orthodox economics is that the pursuit of self-interest will lead to the benefit of society. By this means the moral problem is abolished. The moral problem is concerned with the conflict between individual interest and the interest of society. And since this doctrine tells us that there is no conflict, we can all pursue our self-interest with a good conscience.

This doctrine is attributed to Adam Smith. Adam Smith was the founder of the economics of the modern world. He rejected regulation. He was against regulation and he was against government interference in trade and industry. He wanted to rely on the pursuit of individual self-interest to allow economic development. And, of course, he turned out to be quite right; in the modern world, there has been a fantastic degree of economic development with a level of productivity never attained in any other civilization.

Adam Smith says in *The Wealth of Nations*,

> In almost every other race of animals each individual, when it is grown up to maturity, is entirely independent, and in its natural state has occasion for the assistance of no other living creature. But man has almost constant occasion for the help of his brethren, and it is in vain for him to expect it from their benevolence only. He will be more likely to prevail if he can interest their self-love in his favour, and show them that it is for their own advantage to do for him what he requires of them. Whoever offers to another a bargain of any kind, proposes to do this. Give me that which I want, and you shall have this which you want, is the meaning of every such offer; and it is in this manner that we obtain from one another the far greater part of those good offices which we stand in need of. It is not from the benevolence of the butcher, the

---

Commencement Address (May 1977) at the University of Maine.

brewer, or the baker, that we expect our dinner, but from their regard to their own interest. We address ourselves, not to their humanity but to their self-love, and never talk to them of our own necessities but of their advantages.

In another passage, there is a famous phrase about the market leading individuals by an invisible hand to the benefit of all. He was talking in that particular context against protectionists. Adam Smith argued that there was no need to protect home industry because in fact every producer will prefer to sell in the home market if he can, rather than selling abroad. He intends only his own gain and his own security. In the pursuit of self-interest he is, 'as in many other cases, led by an invisible hand to promote an end which is no part of his intentions'.

The phrase 'invisible hand' – taken from this particular context, the case against protection, has been used as a central doctrine in the teaching of orthodox economics: the notion that individuals have no need to consider the collective results of their behaviour. Do not worry about social problems. Social problems will all be all right if everybody looks after his own self-interest.

This leads Professor Kenneth Arrow, himself a great exponent of the mathematics of the market economy, to say, 'The idealization of freedom through the market completely ignores the fact that this freedom can be, to a large number of people, very limited in scope'. (*The Limits of Organization*) I think that when Adam Smith was telling the story of getting his dinner from the butcher, the brewer, and the baker he was really thinking of a gentleman who has money to spend. He was not thinking of the struggles of those tradesmen to make a living. The price system can generate this kind of error. Kenneth Arrow writes:

> The price system can also be attacked on the ground that it harnesses motives which our ethical systems frequently condemn. It makes a virtue of selfishness. Some economists, much taken with this system, have argued that, for example, business corporations are committing a social wrong if they try to engage in socially desirable activities; their aims should be properly only to maximize their profits, and that this is indeed the socially most desirable activity that they can engage in.

This doctrine which, of course, is very widespread, favours those who have some base to start with. It follows the old rule: 'To him that hath shall be given; from him that hath not shall be taken away.'

There are many examples in the modern world showing how this doctrine of the free market – the pursuit of self-interest – has worked out to the disadvantage of society. You are well aware of the problems of environmental destruction which takes place with the development of high capitalist industry. The problem has come up now in Canada in a particularly horrible form with the spread of the minamata disease which was so devastating in Japan. This disease comes from emitting mercury into rivers. People who eat the fish from those rivers suffer from this incurable disease. If you are arguing in favour of maximizing profits, you must be in favour of allowing the industry to make cheap newsprint – so that you can have very thick newspapers at the expense of poisoning the rivers of Canada and allowing the Indian population to be killed (or worse, to remain half-alive).

There is another example which comes from the medical profession. Today there is some attempt to help poorer people who cannot afford the fees of doctors by giving them some medical aid. This is given to them in the form of payments which can be made to doctors. So the doctors fill out forms to say what services they have given. But as they are subject to the general doctrine of pursuing self-interest, they have to be checked. It becomes necessary to have a special bureaucracy to check these checks and to see whether the service has actually been given by the doctors who filled out the forms.

These are well-known examples – I think any of you can immediately think of innumerable examples – of what has happened as the result of upholding the doctrine that the pursuit of self-interest benefits society.

Now, I think it was a shame to associate Adam Smith with this doctrine. It is certainly true that he praised private enterprise and the market system as against state regulation. But he relied very much upon morality. He took it for granted that there is an ethical foundation for society, and it was against this background that he opened up his economic doctrine. In *The Theory of Moral Sentiments*, he wrote:

> It is thus that man, who can subsist only in society, was fitted by nature to that situation for which he was made. All the members of human society stand in need of each other's assistance, and are likewise exposed to mutual injuries. Where the necessary assistance is reciprocally afforded from love, from gratitude, from friendship, and esteem, the society flourishes and is happy. All the different members of it are bound together by the agreeable bands of love and affection, and are, as it were, drawn to one common centre of mutual good offices.
>
> But though the necessary assistance should not be afforded from

such generous and disinterested motives, though among the different members of the society there should be no mutual love and affection, the society, though less happy and agreeable, will not necessarily be dissolved. Society may subsist among different men, as among different merchants, from a sense of its utility, without any mutual love or affection; and though no man in it should owe any obligation, or be bound in gratitude to any other, it may be upheld by a mercenary exchange of good offices according to an agreed valuation.

Society, however, cannot subsist among those who are at all times ready to hurt and injure one another. The moment that injury begins, the moment that mutual resentment and animosity take place, all the bonds of it are broken asunder, and the different members of which it consisted, are, as it were, dissipated and scattered abroad by the violence and opposition of their discordant affections. If there is any society among robbers and murderers, they must at least, according to the trite observation, abstain from robbing and murdering one another.

Then he makes a comment on the sense of values which people have:

This disposition to admire, and almost to worship, the rich and the powerful, and to despise, or, at least, to neglect, persons of poor and mean condition, though necessary both to establish and to maintain the distinction of ranks and the order of society, is, at the same time, the great and most universal cause of the corruption of our moral sentiments. That wealth and greatness are often regarded with the respect and admiration which are due only to wisdom and virtue; and that the contempt, of which vice and folly are the only proper objects, is often most unjustly bestowed upon poverty and weakness, has been the complaint of moralists in all ages. . . .

The respect which we feel to wisdom and virtue is no doubt different from that which we conceive for wealth and greatness. It requires no very nice discernment to distinguish the difference. But notwithstanding these differences, those sentiments bear a considerable resemblance to one another. In some particular features, they are no doubt different, but in the general air of the countenance, they seem to be so very nearly the same that inattentive observers are very apt to mistake the one for the other.

Adam Smith believed in a natural order of morality. When man was formed for society he was endowed with the moral sentiments which would make society possible. But the second part of his doctrine, the 'Wealth of Nations', has succeeded in undermining those sentiments to a very considerable extent and putting in their place the doctrine that the pursuit of profit is a substitute for morality.

Now even Professor Kenneth Arrow, the great exponent of orthodoxy, has come to the conclusion that a society of individualists cannot succeed and prosper and that along with the necessary institutions of government and business we must have the invisible institution of the moral law.

I hope that the moral consciousness which has grown up in modern times in the youth of America, which has led them to protest against the unequal balance prevailing between morality and the market, will continue to prosper in this generation and that you will find that the doctrines of Adam Smith are not to be taken in the form in which your professors are explaining them to you.

4

HISTORY VERSUS EQUILIBRIUM

KEYNES regarded the triumph of Adam Smith over the Mercantilists and of Ricardo over Malthus as a victory of dogmatism over good sense, and he could not make head or tail of Marx; yet the conceptions of the *General Theory* have much more in common with the classical school of the first half of the nineteenth century than with the neoclassical doctrines in which Keynes himself was brought up.

The main preoccupation of the classical economists was with an historical process of accumulation in a capitalist economy and its relation to the distribution of the product of industry between the classes of society while the neo-classicals concentrated upon conditions of equilibirium in a stationary state.

When Keynes summed up what he felt to be the main difference between his theory and that from which he had had 'a long struggle to escape', he pointed to the admission into his argument of the very obvious fact that expectations about the future are necessarily uncertain. The uncertainty that surrounds expectations of the outcome of a plan of investment, of the course of technical progress, of the behaviour of future prices, not to mention the effects of natural and political cataclysms, cannot be reduced to a 'calculated risk' by applying the theorems of mathematical probability. Keynes described equilibrium theory as 'a pretty, polite technique' 'which tries to deal with the present by abstracting from the fact that we know very little about the future'.[1]

As soon as the uncertainty of the expectations that guide economic behaviour is admitted, equilibrium drops out of the argument and history takes its place. The post-Keynesian theory reaches back to clasp the hands of Ricardo and Marx, skipping over the sixty years of dominance of neoclassical doctrines from 1870 to the great slump. This accounts for the paradox that post-Keynesian analysis derives equally from two such apparently incompatible sources as Piero Sraffa's interpretation of Ricardo and Michał Kalecki's interpretation of the theory of employment.

[1] 'The general theory of employment', *Quarterly Journal of Economics*, February 1937 (JMK), Vol. XIV.

Thames Polytechnic, London, 'Thames Papers in Political Economy', 1974.

1

Equilibrium has been defined in these terms: 'Prices and input-output combinations are said to be equilibrium prices and input-output combinations if, when they rule, no economic agent has any inducement to change his method of production, and no input is in excess demand.'[2]

This entails that everyone knows exactly and in full detail what consequences would follow any action that he may take. (Indeed, the condition for reaching equilibrium is often stated to be 'perfect foresight'.) It rules out the holding of stock or money balances for contingencies, and it rules out any plans, say, for business investment or household saving, with consequences spread over future time in which circumstances are liable to change.

There is another curious feature of the concept. Equilibrium is described as 'the end of an economic process'; the story is usually told of a group of individuals each with an 'endowment' of ready-made goods or of productive capacity of some specific kind. By trading and retrading in a market, each ends up with a selection of goods that he prefers to those that he started with. If we intepret this as an historical process, it implies that, in the period of past time leading to 'today', equilibrium was not established. Why are the conditions that led to a non-equilibrium position 'today' not going to be present in the future?

Furthermore, the concept of 'stability', based on a mechanical analogy, is inappropriate in economic analysis. For mechanical movements in space, there is no distinction between approaching equilibrium from an arbitrary initial position and a perturbation due to displacement from an equilibrium that has long been established. In economic life, in which decisions are guided by expectations about the future, these two types of movement are totally different.

Some theorists, even among those who reject general equilibrium as useless, praise its logical elegance and completeness. A system of simultaneous equations need not specify any date nor does its solution involve history. But if any proposition drawn from it is applied to an economy inhabited by human beings, it immediately becomes self-contradictory. Human life does not exist outside history and no one has correct foresight of his own future behaviour, let alone of the behaviour of all the other individuals which will impinge upon his. I do not think that it is right to praise the logical elegance of a system which becomes self-

[2] F. H. Hahn, *The Share of Wages in the National Income*, Weidenfeld and Nicolson, London, 1972.

contradictory when it is applied to the question that it was designed to answer.

The specification of a self-reproducing or self-expanding system such as that of Sraffa or von Neumann exists in logical time, not in history. Any point on it entails its past just as completely as it entails its future. To confront it with a question such as: What would happen if demand changed? is nonsensical. A different composition of output requires a different set of equations. We could work out alternative von Neumann rays for different compositions of the real wage, comparing say, a diet of potatoes with wheat, postulating the same spectrum of technical knowledge, and see which path yields the higher rate of profit. But even this is a somewhat idle exercise, for the path an economy follows necessarily influences its technology. An economy that has developed the technology for growing potatoes does not have the same spectrum of technical knowledge as one which only grows wheat. In a Walrasian model, the stock of inputs in existence at any moment is quite arbitrary – perhaps it dropped from the sky, like Marshall's meteoric stones. But for Sraffa or von Neumann the inputs available today were produced by labour and inputs in the proportions required, with the technology in use, to produce tomorrow's output.

If we construct the equations for a single self-reproducing system and then confront it with an unforeseen change, an event taking place at a particular date, we cannot say anything at all before we have introduced a whole fresh system specifying how the economy behaves in short-period disequilibrium.

The most obvious application of post-Keynesian analysis (the behaviour of an economy in conditions of uncertainty) is to Keynes' own problems – investment decisions, the determination of the pattern and level of interest rates, and the evolution of the general price level – but it is equally necessary to apply it to so-called micro economics and the behaviour of markets.

2

In a Walrasian economy there are a number of individuals each with his endowment, his tastes and his technical expertise. Tastes, incomes and technical conditions determine the price and the volume of each output; from these are derived the hire prices or 'rentals' for the services of inputs; from the rental of his input and the quantity that he owns is derived the income of each individual. There must be sufficient substitutability between commodities and versatility of inputs to ensure that there is a position of equilibrium in which each individual has at least a subsistence income. (Anyone who did not, died long ago.)

The weakest link in the circle of simultaneous equations is that which connects prices to incomes. We do not seem to be able to say anything about it except in the form of a census. Mr. Jones owns x tons of input type 'A' so that at the equilibrium rental p_a (per ton per week) his weekly income is xp_a. Mr. Smith provides 40 hours of work type 'B' so that his weekly income is w_b, and so forth. The approach in terms of a census blurs the distinction between income from work and income from property and leaves no room for the classical problem of the 'distribution of the produce of the earth between the classes of the community'.

Nevertheless, supporters of the Walrasian system often maintain that it provides a link between demand and distribution that is missing from Sraffa's model.

To deploy this argument, Professor Harry Johnson provides a highly reduced form of general equilibrium.[3] The economy produces only two commodities; resources consist of a number of perfectly similar versatile workers and a particular lump of 'putty-capital' that is, a homogeneous physical input that can be squeezed (without cost) into any form required by technology; there is a well-behaved production function in putty and labour time for each commodity. In the context of accumulation, 'putty' is a way of getting rid of differences between the future and the past; putty investment, once made, can be undone and squeezed into another form while still representing the same 'quantity of capital'. But in the context of a static model, it might be defended as a way of representing the indefinite substitutability between physical inputs which is characteristic of the general equilibrium system.

Professor Johnson's assumptions provide the essential characteristics of the Walrasian system, while making it more perspicuous.

First, it brings out clearly the conditions for so-called instability in general equilibrium. For instance, where putty owners have a strong preference for the more putty-intensive commodity, a higher price of that commodity in terms of the other, which yields a larger income to putty owners, must be associated with a higher demand for the commodity, and so a higher demand for putty, whereas the rule of substitution requires that a higher price of putty is associated with a lower demand for it.

In such a case, as Professor Johnson shows, there may be several widely

[3] H. G. Johnson, *The Two Sector Model of General Equilibrium*, Allen and Unwin, London, 1971.

separated price ratios yielding potential positions of equilibrium. (This is analogous to 'reswitching' on a pseudo-production function.) In a 'well-behaved case' there is one equilibrium position corresponding to one set of equations.

Secondly, it is clear that the relation of prices to demand does not depend only on 'consumers' tastes' but also on the census of ownership of inputs, and on technical conditions which govern the interaction between the prices of the commodities and the rentals of inputs. (This seems to vindicate Marshall's one-at-a-time method of treating supply and demand. The world demand for, say, peanuts can be treated as independent of their conditions of production, but, in general equilibrium, supply and demand cannot be treated as independent of each other.)

With the aid of Professor Johnson's simplified model, we can examine the relations of tastes, rentals and technical conditions with prices and the composition of output, in alternative positions of equilibrium. The argument must be conducted, however, strictly in terms of comparisons of specified positions. We cannot say anything about how any position was reached from some other starting point. Nor can we say what would happen if there was a change in tastes. It is not legitimate to introduce an event into a system of simultaneous equations.

On a two-dimensional diagram, time lies at right angles to the plane on which the diagram is drawn, with the past behind it and the future in front. Suppose that Professor Johnson's economy has been living through history on a path passing through one equilibrium point and that, at some date, a change in tastes occurs. Then the position is no longer one of equilibrium. A change in the pattern of production must involve investment and disinvestment, at least in work-in-progress, and windfall losses and gains on stocks that have become inappropriate. To say how long it will take, or by what path, to find a new equilibrium (if there is one) we have to fill in a whole story about the behaviour of the economy when it is out of equilibrium, including the effect of disappointed expectations on decisions being taken by its inhabitants. The Walrasian system is no more capable of dealing with changes in demand than the system of Sraffa or von Neumann.

The theory of markets was in need of a Keynesian revolution just as much as the theory of employment. Keynes himself threw out some hints and anyone who is acquainted with the conduct, say, of trade in primary commodities, knows that it is dominated by *speculation*, that is by guesses about the future behaviour of demand and of supply. Such markets are made by intermediaries (often on several layers) between original producers and final buyers. Uncertainty tends to make markets unstable, since a rise of price is often a signal for buying in stocks and a fall for selling out.

The prices of manufactures are less volatile. The large powerful firms deal directly with retailers and set prices according to a more or less long range policy. Even they, however, cannot know the future; they work on estimates. The system of so called 'full-cost pricing' means calculating expenses, including amortization allowances, per unit of output on the basis of an assumed average level of utilization and length of earning life of plant and then adding a margin for the level of net profit that it seems prudent to go for. When actual utilization over the life of plant exceeds the standard, net profit exceeds the calculated level, and conversely.

There is a range of small businesses which operate in markets of an intermediate type. Such producers are subject to a large extent to the vagaries of supply and demand but not to the perpetual oscillations of commodity prices. They are an important part of an economy such as that of India, but in the West they are falling more and more under the control of oligopsonists (large retail chains) which administer prices for them. All this is ruled out from equilibrium theory 'which tries to deal with the present by abstracting from the fact that we know very little about the future'.

3

Another major characteristic that Keynes had in common with the classics was that they, like him, were concerned with actual contemporary problems and put their arguments in terms of the structure and behaviour of the economy in which they were living, while the neoclassics enunciated what purported to be universal laws, based on human nature – greed, impatience and so forth. The latter rarely say anything at all about the kind of economy to which an argument is to be applied. The suggestion is that the same laws which govern the supposed behaviour of Robinson Crusoe are equally valid for the conduct of Gosplan, or rather for what its conduct *ought* to be, and for analysing the vagaries of Wall Street.

Marshall retained something of the classical tradition. His world is inhabited by businessmen, housewives, workers, trade union leaders, bankers and traders. His moralizing tone – 'There are many fine natures among domestic servants . . .' sounds comical to modern ears, and he was not above twisting observation to suit his theory – Joint Stock Companies stagnate – but he was studying a recognizable economy in a particular phase of its historical development, in which recognizable classes of the community interact with each other in a particular framework of law and accepted conventions.

Pigou emptied history out of Marshall and reduced the analysis to a two-dimensional scheme. Marshall's argument had created a notorious dilemma. He believed in economies of scale for the individual firm; as a firm grows it acquires experience, invests in new techniques and lowers cost of production per unit of output. But in every market (with a few well known exceptions) there are enough firms competing with each other to keep prices in line with costs. Why does not one firm, that happens to get a start, undersell others, grow, reduce costs further, and finally establish a monopoly? Marshall's argument was that the life of a firm is bound up with that of a family; by the third generation, the vigour of the founder has been lost and the firm ceases to grow. This is certainly true of many actual case histories but as a universal law it had to be backed up by the remarkably untrue dictum that joint-stock companies stagnate.

Pigou set out to rescue Marshall from his dilemma by introducing the equilibrium size of firm. Every week, a firm is maximizing profits by selling such an output as to make the marginal cost of its product equal to the ruling price; over the long run, competition forces it to operate at the minimum point of a U-shaped curve, where marginal and average cost are both equal to price. There is a rate of interest (somehow connected with the discount of the future of owners of wealth) at which every firm can borrow as much or as little as it likes; when it is in equilibrium, its net profit per annum is just sufficient to cover interest, at the ruling rate on the value of its capital.

This rigmarole was the only legacy from Marshall that has been incorporated into modern orthodoxy.

Side by side with the Pigovian system, the heritage of Walras has been very much elaborated; in this sphere the specification of the character of the economy is not so much unreal as non-existent. Sometimes it seems that there are no people in the market at all – only prices and quantities of commodities are mentioned. Sometimes every individual has his own endowment both of labour power and of physical inputs, so that society consists of a number of Robinson Crusoes, living side by side and exchanging their products. Sometimes we seem to be in Adam Smith's world where a man (evidently of independent means) appeals to the self-interest of the baker and the brewer to get him his dinner.

But then again, society is represented as a pure co-operative, without distinction of classes or occupations. Society saves, as in Frank Ramsey's famous theorem, and society enjoys the benefit of the increased income that accumulation provides.

The leap from Walras to Pigou is made by means of a pun. For Walras, a 'factor of production' is something like a carpenter, a load of bricks, or a meadow. In the system, relayed by Pigou, that Marshall derived from Ricardo, the factors of production are labour, capital and land. Taking the word 'factor' in both senses at once, the argument about the prices of items in the available stock of inputs, established by higgling and haggling in a market, is applied to the determination of wages, interest and rent in long run equilibrium.

This pun, presented in mathematical notation, is the basis of so-called micro-economics offered in the fashionable text books.

4

Keynes pointed out the distinction between interest, which a business has to pay on borrowed finance, and profit, which it hopes to get on an investment. For his strictly short period problem, he did not need a realized rate of profit on capital, only a forward looking, uncertain expectation of profits. This could be formally expressed as the rate of discount that reduces the expected series of future quasi-rents to equality with the capital sum to be invested today; but uncertainty and prospective changes in the value of money make the calculation vague.

Marshall's normal profits and Wicksell's natural rate of interest were supposed to apply to a capitalist economy but their level was never explained. Adam Smith had quite a different story for the pin factory from that of the baker and the brewer; there, the share of profit was higher the lower the wage could be set, but a clear explanation of the determination of the rate of profit eluded him. Only Ricardo laid the basis for a theory of the rate of profit on capital and this was forgotten in the neoclassical era until it was disinterred by Sraffa. The neo-neoclassicals try to substitute the concept of 'the rate of return' for a theory of profits.

For Irving Fisher, the rate of return was the increment of income that a man could get from adding an increment to his wealth. Thus, in a modern economy with a gilt-edged rate of interest of 10 per cent, £10 per annum in perpetuity is the rate of return on a saving of £100. In an artisan economy, the return on saving is an addition to the flow of output, say of horse-shoes, produced with a given amount of work by a blacksmith who puts part of his energy into improving his forge. On Frank Ramsey's growth path, the rate of return in terms of utility to society as a whole on further saving varies as wealth accumulates. But the rate of return is connected with the rate of profit in a capitalist economy only by a methodological confusion.

Let us return to the picture of an economy in a static state of Walrasian equilibrium. Now compare it with another economy, with the same tastes and technology, in equilibrium with the same labour force and a larger amount of physical inputs (more of some and no less of any). There is then a larger output of some or all of the commodities being produced.

Professor Johnson could say that the second economy has a larger lump of putty, so that the hire price of putty per unit, taken as a whole, is lower than in the first economy, while the income of a representative worker is higher than in the first economy. The income of a representative putty owner may be less or greater according to the elasticity of substitution between putty and labour. (This follows from the assumptions of general equilibrium; it does not correspond to anything in real life.)

For such a comparison putty may be thought to be an adequate concept. But it does not enable us to say *how much* greater the second set of inputs is as a simple quantity (putty is a parable, not to be taken literally) still less, how the additional output in the second position is related to the additional inputs as a simple ratio.

The two lists of inputs and outputs are made up of items in different proportions and there may be some item in the second list that did not appear in the first. All relative prices are different in the two positions. A comparison of wage rates or of the value of stocks of inputs in the two positions would depend entirely on the numeraire chosen, and no one numeraire has more relevance than any other.

The question has been much discussed under the title of the 'measurement of capital'. But, properly speaking, there is no 'capital' in a Walrasian market. There are no capitalists who have invested finance in productive capacity with a view to employing labour and making profits. There is only a list of quantities of various kinds of available inputs.

In a Pigovian stationary state, there is a stock of capital, of which the value, say in terms of wage units, depends upon technical conditions and the rate of interest. Instead of an arbitrary list of objects, there is a flow of gross investment going on which is just sufficient to keep the balanced stock of equipment intact as it wears out and to renew supplies of raw materials used up in production. The flow of net output constitutes the income of the economy, which is all being consumed.

The Austrian theory, developed by Wicksell, attempted to 'measure capital' in such a case by the 'average period of production'. As Wicksell found, this is not exact; but even if it were, it would be no help in detecting the 'rate of return'.

We may imagine that we make a comparison between two equilibrium positions, with an identical labour force, one with a higher net output than the other. But it does not follow that the second has 'more capital' or a longer average period of production than the first. If we compare them at a common rate of interest, there is no guarantee that the one with the higher output has the higher value of capital. They are simply two equilibrium positions using different techniques, each with the stock of means of production appropriate to its own technique, and each with its own past history, that led to its present position.

The long wrangle about 'measuring capital' has been a great deal of fuss over a secondary question. The real source of trouble is the confusion between comparisons of equilibrium positions and the history of a process of accumulation.

We might suppose that we can take a number of still photographs of economies each in stationary equilibrium; let us suppose that the 'measurement' problem can be solved by calculating all values in terms of labour time, and that it happens that the economies can be arranged in a series in which a larger value of capital per man employed is associated with a higher net output per man of a homogeneous consumption good, as on Professor Samuelson's 'surrogate production function'. This is an allowable thought experiment. But it is not allowable to flip the stills through a projector to obtain a moving picture of a process of accumulation.

Before we can discuss accumulation, we must go back to the beginning and deal with the questions which Walras and Pigou left unanswered. In what kind of economy is accumulation taking place? Is it Frank Ramsey's classless co-operative, a collection of peasants and artisans, or a modern capitalist nation? Is it a property-owning democracy in which the rate of saving depends on the decisions of households? If so, by what means is saving converted into additions to the stock of inputs? Or if investment depends on the decisions of industrial firms, how do they get command of finance, and what expectations of profits are guiding their plans? Is there a mechanism in the system to ensure growth with continuous full employment? And if an increasing value of capital per man leads to a prospective fall in the rate of profit, do the firms go meekly crawling down a pre-existing production function, or do they introduce new techniques that raise output per unit of investment as well as output per man?

The data for periods of continuous growth in the industrial capitalist countries generally seem to conform pretty well to Kaldor's stylized facts – a fairly constant ratio both of the value of capital and of the wage bill to the value of output. This entails that the overall ex-post rate of profit on capital was fairly constant. With rising real wages and a constant rate of profit, it follows that each point of observation must have been drawn from a different technology. Even as a thought-experiment, it is meaningless to postulate the existence in a growing economy of a surrogate production function or a pseudo-production function, well or ill-behaved, on which a number of equilibrium positions, with different techniques, co-exist at a moment of time.

Certainly, for a developing country, the choice of technique is an important problem. The choice is not concerned with the ratio of 'capital' to labour or to output. It is concerned with the allocation of investible resources. The increment of future productivity of labour due to creating an addition to the stock of inputs might be called the return to investment (though it is not easy to express it as a rate) but it has nothing whatever to do with the rate of profit or the rate of interest on the pre-existing total stock of capital, or of wealth inherited from the past.

The problem of the 'measurement of capital' is a minor element in the criticism of the neo-classical doctrines. The major point is that what they pretend to offer as an alternative or rival to the post-Keynesian theory of accumulation is nothing but an error in methodology – a confusion between comparisons of imagined equilibrium positions and a process of accumulation going on through history.

5

The lack of a comprehensible treatment of historical time, and failure to specify the rules of the game in the type of economy under discussion, make the theoretical apparatus offered in neo-neoclassical text-books useless for the analysis of contemporary problems, both in the micro and macro spheres.

5

THE MEANING OF CAPITAL

THE controversies over so-called capital theory arose out of the search for a model appropriate to a modern western economy, which would allow for an analysis of accumulation and of the distribution of the net product of industry between wages and profits.

1

The old orthodoxy, which relied heavily on Say's Law and a natural tendency to the establishment of equilibrium with full employment, had been discredited in the depression of the 1930s. Keynes had cleared the way for a new approach. He broke down the old dichotomy between *Principles* and *Money*, treating the financial system as part of the general functioning of the economy. He observed that, because prediction of the future is necessarily uncertain, behaviour affecting economic life (or private life, for that matter) cannot be governed by strictly rational calculations of the outcome. He pointed out that accumulation depends upon decisions about investment taken by business firms and governments, not by decisions about saving taken by households, and he drew a clear distinction (which was confused in the old orthodoxy) between interest, as the price that a businessman pays for the use of finance to be committed to an investment, and profit, which is the return that he hopes to get on it. He pointed out that wage rates are settled in terms of money and the level of real wages depends upon the operation of the economy as a whole. All this cleared the ground for a model appropriate to modern capitalism, but Keynes' own construction was confined to dealing with short-period analysis.

In a short-period situation, here and now, the organization of industry, stocks of equipment, the training of the labour force and the habits of consumers are already settled. These elements in the situation are changing very slowly and for practical purposes may be taken as constant. The model is designed to deal with the causes and consequences of the changes in

---

Draft of the article which appeared in French in *Revue d'Economie Politique*, March 1977.

employment of labour and utilization of given physical resources which occur with swings of effective demand.

The stock of means of production ('capital goods') in existence at a moment of time can be represented by a who's who of particular items. The value of the stock is not a very precise concept. Businesses reckon book value in terms of the accounting conventions that they choose to follow. The stock exchange value of a corporation depends upon the market's estimate of future profits and on the level of interest rates. Market expectations are notoriously unstable and interest rates are influenced by monetary policy or, in any one financial centre, by events in others.

Since the value of capital is not a precise concept, the *rate* of profit is not precise. This did not matter for Keynes. He needed to consider only the flow of actual gross profits today and the expected return in the future on finance invested today. Finance to be invested is a definite sum of money, with whatever purchasing power it has today over labour time and physical inputs, but the expected return is far from definite; it is based upon extrapolation of past experience, guesswork or convention, coloured by the subjective mood, 'animal spirits', in which investment plans are being drawn up.

This was sufficient for short-period analysis, but once Keynes' theory was accepted, long-run accumulation became the centre of interest; it was therefore necessary to come to grips with the concepts of the quantity of capital and the rate of profit in the economy as a whole.

2

The 'mainstream teaching' being developed, particularly in the United States, seemed to be based upon three distinct types of model, often mixed up together.

In the first, the economy is represented by a grand co-operative without private property. Society saves, and society enjoys the benefit of the increased income which accumulation provides. To make sense of Frank Ramsey's elegant formula for the optimum rate of saving, it is necessary to suppose that output consists of some kind of homogeneous substance that can be consumed or used as means of production. Saving, that is, the excess of output over consumption, is added to stock and increases future production. The growth of output with the growth of stock is subject to diminishing returns, and so is the growth of utility for society as a whole with the growth of consumption.

The second type of model is based on the general equilibrium of Walras.

Here there is a stock of specific means of production, often called 'machines'. To overcome the problem of amortisation, machines are sometimes assumed to be indefinitely durable or, alternatively, subject to 'radio-active decay' so that their value at any moment is independent of their age. From one point of view this is similar to the short-period concept of a stock of equipment in existence at a moment of time, but from another point of view it is quite different. There is no utilization function, showing how output varies with employment. Labour and machines are fully utilized in equilibrium and the machines can be used, in different combinations, to make a great variety of alternative outputs, exhibited on a 'production-possibility surface'. The main emphasis of the analysis is on exchange. Production consists of hiring various inputs and combining them in various proportions. When the market is in equilibrium, the rentals of the various inputs required for each output absorb its value and there is no profit. This concept of equilibrium requires an exact definition of the number of workers in the economy (natives and immigrants?) and the hours of work per week and per year corresponding to 'full employment'.

The third type of model was derived from Marshall, vulgarized by J. B. Clark.[1] Here 'capital' is a factor of production, along with land and labour. The returns to factors are governed by their marginal productivities. 'Capital' is embodied in 'machines'; the marginal productivity of 'machines' governs the interest received by rentiers. There is a separate item for profits, which is the return to 'enterprise' or the 'co-ordinating function', that is, the management of business.

The concept of 'capital' as something distinct from physical means of production is connected with business experience. A new business sets out with a sum of money, whether owned by the proprietors or borrowed at interest. The money is invested in means of production and work in progress. So long as the business is successful, the value of the original investment is kept intact. It may be augmented by further investment financed out of profits or by further borrowing. A part of gross profit is treated as an amortisation fund. With the passage of time, the original form of the investment may cease to be the most profitable and the first stock of means of production is replaced by another, embodying a different technique or aimed at a different market. Thus the initial finance (so long as the business is successful) continues to exist as a sum of value being continuously embodied in different forms of productive capacity. But finance arises out of relationships within an economy. How can finance be treated as a factor of production?

[1] See *The Distribution of Wealth. A Theory of Wages, Interest and Profits*, 1899.

J. B. Clark blithely treated 'capital' as a quantity of something which could be embodied in various kinds of 'capital goods' and changed from one embodiment to another, but he did not try to explain what this quantity consisted of. Marshall at one moment pronounced that the factors of production should be regarded as land, labour and waiting.[2] Waiting means owning a stock of wealth. Thus the stock of capital is represented by the sum of the value of all assets owned by the individuals and institutions that the economy comprises. But Marshall was well aware that the value of assets is influenced by the level of the rate of interest and he admitted that it is impossible to derive the rate of interest from the value of capital without arguing in a circle. Wicksell was troubled by the same problem. Just before the eruption of the Keynesian revolution, Dennis Robertson posed the question of the meaning of a quantity of capital in terms of his story of ten men with nine spades.[3]

Apparently unaware that this problem had never been solved, the mainstream economists were drawing production functions of the form $0 = f(L, K)$, the quantity of output is a function of the quantity of inputs of labour and 'capital'. Moreover, they were using this formula to interpret statistics of the performance of industry, and treating the actual levels of wages and profits as the marginal products of labour and capital. In an article published in 1953, I revived the old question and asked whether K, the quantity of capital, was supposed to be a sum of money or a list of 'machines'.

One answer was that a production function can be drawn up in terms of specified inputs, and that the value of 'capital' is an unnecessary concept. But these inputs, seemingly, were not produced by profit-seeking investment. They may have fallen from heaven, like Marshall's meteoric stones; there is no means of discussing how further accumulation will take place.

The more usual answer was to set up a model in which physical products are as like as possible to money. Ouput consists of a single homogeneous, divisible commodity, say, butter, which is both consumable and can be turned into a stock of means of production. The stock is 'malleable'; a stock of butter which has been used for one type of production can be withdrawn and moulded into another form without cost and without change in quantity. (This model is not quite the same as Frank Ramsey's co-operative, because the income of 'society' is divided between wages and profits.)

---

[2] *Principles*, first edition (1890), p. 614 n. 1. In later editions the same concept is overlaid with various complications.

[3] 'Wage grumbles', *Economic Fragments*.

The butter model made it possible to revive all the propositions of pre-Keynesian orthodoxy. Say's Law prevails; saving governs accumulations; uncertainty disappears, for one investment can be turned instantaneously into another when circumstances change. Interest paid to rentiers is identified with profits accruing to firms. There is a well-behaved production function in labour and the stock of butter; when the ratio of the stock to the labour force is rising as accumulation goes on, the butter wage rises and the rate of butter profit on butter capital falls. Most remarkable of all, technical progress raises the productivity of the stock of butter without cost and without changing its quantity. (At first there was a mistake in the argument here that was put right by Professor Rymes.)[4]

This model was described as a parable. A parable, in the usual sense, is a story drawn from everyday life intended to explain a mystery; in this case it is the mystery which is expected to explain everyday life.

In order to interpret a time-series of statistics, the stock of butter in the model was identified with the book value of physical assets of firms comprised by US industry. As the relative shares of wages and profits in value added were fairly constant in the period studied, it was possible to go through the motions of fitting a Cobb-Douglas production function to the figures. But it was found that the ratio of the value of capital to value of output was fairly constant through time, thus (with a constant share of profit) the *ex-post* overall rate of profit on capital must have been constant over the period, while the average real-wage rate rose in step with the rise of output per head. On a production function representing the 'state of technical knowledge', rising real wages entail a falling rate of profit. Evidently, the statistics at each point of observation were drawn from a different state of technology. The figures might be interpreted to show that technical progress over a period had been roughly neutral; they could not exhibit a production function, or marginal productivities, 'in a given state of technical knowledge', as the mainstream theory required.

There was some argument about the problem of 'measuring capital' but there was no answer to the old problem that, if the total stock of capital is a sum of value, it already presupposes the overall rate of profit, whereas if it is a list of 'machines' there is no unit in which it can be reckoned as a quantity.

For some purposes, for instance a comparison between the industries in various countries, a very rough measure of the physical capital to labour ratio could be used, say horse power per man employed. But then it will not generally be found that where this ratio is highest, the rate of profit on capital is lowest.

[4] See *On the Concept of Capital and Technical Change*, Cambridge University Press, 1971.

The famous Leontief paradox was a result of this confusion. Because physical capital per man (by any measure) was highest in the United States, it was supposed that 'capital' there should be the cheapest factor of production and that therefore US exports should be more 'capital intensive' than imports. Leontief's calculation showed that the value of capital per man was on the average less in the export industries. This seems to indicate that, while US industry (at that time) was generally superior to its rivals in productivity, the superiority was most marked in the industries producing productive equipment. Why should this be considered a paradox?

The lack of an acceptable definition of a 'quantity of capital' was masked by the manner in which main-line teaching was (and still is) divided into two mutually exclusive departments. Micro theory was based on a mixture of the Walrasian model, in which there is an endowment of ready-made inputs (meteoric stones) with zero profits in equilibrium, and the Pigovian model in which each firm can borrow as much finance as it chooses at a given rate of interest and 'equilibrium firms' have earnings such that net profits exactly cover the interest bill. Macro theory was concerned with Keynes and the slump. Thus there was no place in the syllabus for a discussion of the mode of operation of a modern capitalist economy considered as a whole. 'Capital theory' was regarded as an esoteric doctrine which had no application to any question of general interest.

3

The discussion which I had tried to revive in 1953 took a new turn with the publication of Piero Sraffa's *Production of Commodities by Means of Commodities* in 1960.

In Sraffa's model, the treatment of physical capital, though highly simplified, is less fanciful than either meteoric stones or a stock of butter. We are presented with, so to speak, a snapshot of a process of production going on in a particular industrial economy. A particular labour force is producing a particular flow of output by means of a particular technique, specified in a system of equations. The technique dictates what physical inputs, in what proportions, are required for labour to produce the output, over what period of time. Stocks of inputs are continuously reproduced as they are used up (long-lived equipment is treated in a separate model which can be fitted into the same argument). The net output of any period is the excess of the product over stocks of inputs existing at the beginning of the period. Thus output consists of a list of quantities of particular commodities, independent of prices. Now, everything in physical terms remaining the same, the share of wages in net output is run through every value from unity to zero. Corresponding to each value of the share of wages is a set of prices (in any numeraire) for all outputs and inputs, and a uniform rate of profit on the value of the stocks of inputs at these prices.

These calculations must be regarded purely as an intellectual experiment. In reality neither the real-wage rate nor the rate of profit could be zero, and it is unnatural to suppose that the composition of output would be the same with widely different levels of real wages. In an actual economy of which a snapshot is taken, some particular pattern of prices is ruling. The 'changes' of the share of wages in the argument are not actual historical events, only calculations by the observing economist.

Sraffa was not trying to construct a model for positive analysis, though the concept of a technique of production as an input-output table in physical terms is certainly very useful. His own purpose was purely negative – to provide a prelude to the critique of economic theory.

The theory that Sraffa was preparing to criticize was the Marshallian orthodoxy that prevailed when he began to work on these ideas in the 1920s; but objections to his argument have been drawn mainly from the general equilibrium doctrines prevalent today. One objection is that he 'leaves out demand'. This objection does not stand. If we people his model with firms and households then, when a particular rate of profit obtains, firms are carrying out gross investment in order to earn profits from sales and households are purchasing goods at prices that yield the ruling rate of profit. The pattern of demand is evidently appropriate to the flow of production along with the distribution of income, and the flow of production is appropriate to the pattern of demand.

Another objection is that a Sraffa system is only a special case of general equilibrium with 'fixed coefficients', that is, with only one possible combination of inputs. This betrays a basic difference between two conceptions of the process of production. In the general equilibrium model, the story begins with an arbitrary stock of ready-made inputs which can be combined in various ways to produce a variety of different outputs. In Sraffa's model, the stock of inputs in existence today was the result of investments made in the past in order to produce today's output with the technique which is in use today. Which concept is the less inappropriate to an industrial economy?

Sraffa did in fact introduce a variety of techniques into his model. Where several techniques are known, it is assumed that, given the prevailing share of wages in net output, the technique has been chosen which maximizes profits when prices are such as to make the rate of profit

uniform throughout the economy. Making quite orthodox assumptions
about the character of technology, Sraffa showed that the same technique
may be eligible at widely different rates of profit. It was this which alerted
the mainstream economists to the fact that their orthodoxy was being
questioned.

4

The furore about 'reswitching' raged around the conception of a pseudo-
production function. There is supposed to be a book of blueprints
specifying all possible techniques for producing a flow of net output of a
given composition with a given labour force. Each technique is a Sraffa
system of equations requiring a specific stock of inputs, which are
continually reproduced as they are used up, and involving a particular time-
pattern in the process of production. The techniques are listed in order of
net output per unit of labour. Corresponding to each share of wages in net
output is a profit-maximizing technique. Inferior techniques are eliminated,
so that each technique in the book is eligible at at least one rate of profit.
Each point represents an economy on a steady-state growth path. The stock
of means of production in existence at that point has been produced in the
light of expectations of profit which are turning out to be correct 'today'
and are therefore renewed for the future. Since expectations are held with
perfect confidence, we may suppose that the ruling rate of interest is equal
to the rate of profit, but it is the rate of profit, determined by technical
conditions and the share of wages in net output, that governs the rate of
interest, not vice versa. (But here Piero Sraffa himself does not agree with
my interpretation of his model.) In an uncertain world, of course, positive
(or even zero) net investment will not take place unless interest rates are
appreciably lower than expected profits.

Between each pair of techniques is a switch point at which the ratio of
the two values of capital is equal to the ratio of the flows of profit per
annum, so that the rate of profit is the same for both.

Contrasting this construction with the well-behaved production
function in the butter economy, we see, first of all, that the production
function is continuously differentiable, for the smallest difference in the stock
of butter per man employed entails a difference in output per man, while
the pseudo-production function may have wide gaps between switch
points, over which the same output per head is associated with a falling rate
of profit and rising share of wages. Moreover, however dense the pages of
the book of blueprints, there must always be a discontinuity in engineering

terms between one technique and the next. On both constructions a higher share of wages is associated with a lower rate of profit, the most fundamental rule of the production function is that a larger stock of butter per man is associated with higher output, whereas on the pseudo-production function there is no presumption that a technique giving higher output per man requires a higher value of capital at the rate of profit at which it is eligible. And even when two techniques are compared at the same rate of profit, it is not necessarily the case, on the pseudo-production function, that a lower rate of profit is associated with a higher value of capital per man and a higher output per head. In short, a more labour-intensive technique may be eligible at a lower rate of profit than another which provides a higher output per man.

This was the point that caused all the trouble. A pseudo-production function may contain backward switch points at which a technique with a higher output per head than the next is eligible at a higher rate of profit. This may be associated with 'reswitching', since at the lowest rate of profit the eligible technique must be one with a high output per head.

The reason for these differences between the two constructions is obvious. The well-behaved production function conflates the concept of the value of capital with a stock of physical means of production while the pseudo-production function distinguishes between the physical means of production required for a particular technique and its value at various rates of profit.

After some hesitation, Professor Samuelson accepted the logic of the pseudo-production function. In the *Summing Up* of the debate ten years ago,[5] he even referred to 'a general blueprint technology model of Joan Robinson and MIT type' but his interpretation of it was (and still is) very different from mine. He recognized that each point on a pseudo function is supposed to represent an economy in a steady state, in which inputs are being reproduced in unchanged physical form, and yet he supposed that saving could raise an economy from one point to the position at another. He envisages a process of accumulation creeping up the pseudo-production function from lower to higher shares of wages, and higher to lower rates of profit. But an increase in gross investment above the rate required to maintain a steady state would entail an enlargement of investment industries (which would have to shrink again when a new steady state was reached). The former pattern of prices would be upset. Inputs appropriate to one technique would have to be scrapped and replaced by those appropriate to another. And how are we to imagine that the prospect

[5] 'Paradoxes in capital theory', *Quarterly Journal of Economics*, November 1966, p. 578.

of a lower rate of profit in the future induces these changes to be made?

A steady state implies that everyone concerned holds perfectly confident expectations that the future will continue to reproduce the past. If those expectations fail to be fulfilled, the economy is thrown into short-period disequilibrium and analysis has to be conducted in Keynesian terms.

This is nothing to do with 'reswitching'. Professor Samuelson's first reaction to Sraffa had been to construct a special case of a pseudo-production function (the 'surrogate production function')[6] in which, at each point, labour-value prices rule, so that the cost of the stock of means of production, for each economy, is independent of the rate of profit. A higher value of capital is then always associated with a higher net output per head. On such a pseudo-production function, backward switch points cannot occur. But, like the general case, it can be used only for comparisons of supposed steady-state economies, not for analysing a process of accumulation changing the value of capital per man.

A similar difficulty arises in arguing from Walrasian general equilibrium. At a point on the production-possibility surface at which supply and demand are in equilibrium for each commodity, buyers and sellers evidently expect the same prices which obtain today to be ruling next week. A change in demand ruptures the equilibrium, disappoints expectations – some for the better and some for the worse – and requires investment in one kind of stock and disinvestment in others. Here also, further developments can be analysed only in Keynesian terms.

The notion that conditions of demand allocate scarce means between alternative uses might apply to the case of an independent peasant deciding what crops to grow to feed his family, but in modern industry the greater part of resources, at any moment, are committed, in fixed equipment, to a narrow range of uses. The question of allocation concerns new investment, but both the level and form of investment are decided, for the most part, from political motives (armaments, hospitals) and from judgments of their own interests by the great corporations. This can hardly be identified with the beneficent operations of a hidden hand in a perfectly competitive market.

The exposition both of general equilibrium and of long-run accumulation seems generally to be conducted by drawing a two-dimensional diagram on a blackboard and then introducing historical events into it. A change cannot be depicted on the plane surface of the blackboard. Changes occur in time, and as soon as a point moves off the

6 'Parable and realism in capital theory: the surrogate production function', *Review of Economic Studies*, 1962, **XXIX**, 193–206.

blackboard into the third dimension of time, it is no longer bound by the relationships shown in the diagram.

It seems as though, all this while, mainstream teaching has been inculcating defective methodology.

5

Since the mainstream flows awry, we must return to the source. The classical economists did not treat society as a co-operative and they did not treat capital as a quantity of homogeneous stuff. For them, finance was the means of organizing labour and physical inputs to produce outputs, and gross profit was derived from the excess of physical output over the physical wage bill. Keynes condemned Ricardo for his neglect of short-period instability but, as Luigi Pasinetti says: 'Keynes' theory of effective demand, which has remained so impervious to reconciliation with marginal economic theory, raises almost no problem when directly inserted into the earlier discussions of the Classical economists.'[7]

This is still more true of Michał Kalecki's version of the theory of employment, which grew out of the Marxian schema of expanded reproduction and which related imperfect competition to the Marxian concept of exploitation.

Pasinetti continues:

> Similarly . . . the post-Keynesian theories of economic growth and income distribution, which have required so many artificial assumptions in the efforts to reconcile them with marginal productivity theory, encounter almost no difficulty when directly grafted on to Classical economic dynamics.[8]

The pseudo-production function was a very useful piece of scaffolding but it is not to be incorporated in the construction of a dynamic theory. Obviously, two stocks of inputs appropriate to two different techniques cannot co-exist in time and space. There is no book of ready-drawn blueprints appropriate to different rates of interest. As accumulation goes on, technology evolves, and no technique is blueprinted before it is about to be used. Moreover, no stock of means of production in real life is ever perfectly adjusted to the expectations of profit being entertained when it is in use. The pseudo-production function was not a model for the analysis of

[7] *Growth and Income Distribution*, Cambridge University Press (1974), p. ix.
[8] Ibid.

capitalism but a device to smoke out the contradictions in mainstream teaching.

The controversy has been a great waste of mental energy, for

> He who is convinced against his will
> Is of the same opinion still.

It is high time to abandon the mainstream and take to the turbulent waters of truly dynamic analysis.

GROWTH AND THE THEORY OF DISTRIBUTION

WHEN England was a 'developing country' Ricardo set out to find a theory of the distribution of the produce of the earth between 'the proprietor of the land, the owner of the stock or capital necessary for its cultivation and the labourers by whose industry it is cultivated'.

He set up a model of a society of three classes. Landlords, who lived in a feudal style, consumed rent which absorbed the surplus product of intra-marginal land. The output of a worker on marginal land was a certain quantity of corn, determined by technical conditions. His wage was also determined by technical conditions – the corn required for subsistence. The capital required to employ him was a year's wage bill in corn. The surplus per man and the surplus per unit of capital – the rate of profit – were thus technically determined.

From his share of the product each individual capitalist was free to decide how much to consume and how much to invest in an enlarged stock of corn-capital to increase the amount of employment he could offer.

Many elaborations and complications (in some of which Ricardo lost his way) were built on this basis but the essence of the theory was this simple and penetrating analysis of distribution.

In modern times what is basically the same model has been presented in mathematical form by von Neumann. On the one hand he elaborates the model by allowing the wage good to consist of a variety of commodities. On the other hand he simplifies by allowing no consumption out of surplus. The essence of his world is the same as Ricardo's. There is an indefinitely large supply of labour available at a physically determined wage rate, and the growth of the system depends on investment of the surplus. The rate of profit on capital is then identically equal to the rate of growth of the system.

Marx interpreted Ricardo to show capitalist exploitation as a cruel but necessary process by which accumulation, economies of scale and mechanization of industry raise productivity. He depicts the system wracked by internal contradictions, destined to bring itself to an end.

Reprinted from *Annals of Public and Cooperative Economy*, January–March 1967.

This interpretation of Ricardo was displeasing to those who were benefiting from the system. A new school of economics came into fashion which threw a veil over the theories of Ricardo and Marx. The great problems of distribution and accumulation dropped out of sight. The neo-classicals for the most part confined themselves to elaborating a theory of relative prices. Here they could triumph over Marx, for this part of his analysis is not satisfactory, and they could teach their pupils that his theory was erroneous and unimportant.

They did not however succeed in producing a theory of distribution.

There are two branches of the neo-classical system, one stemming from Walras and the other from Marshall. The Walrasian school operates mainly in terms of a stationary state, when accumulation has come to an end. There is a given quantity of 'capital' in existence, but it is no longer a homogeneous stock of 'corn'. It is capable of taking on various physical forms. Bohm Bawerk tried to find a measure of capital in the length of the period of production, but Wicksell very candidly pointed out that this does not provide a measure of capital independently of the rate of interest.

Marshall operates, not with a quantity of capital but with a normal rate of profit. What determines the normal rate, however, is left very vague. The whole argument (and it is very valuable in its own sphere) is about the effect of unforeseen changes in demand or in supply which cause profits in particular industries to deviate from the normal level.

The neo-classicals thus did not offer a theory of profits, but their pupils somehow got the impression that they were maintaining that profit measures the 'marginal product of capital'.

Keynes' General Theory was concerned only with short-period situations with a given stock of means of production in existence. He did not need a theory of the *rate* of profit. He provided the basis for a theory of the *share* of profits in a short-period situation, determined by the degree of utilization of given equipment under the influence of effective demand, but he was much more concerned with the problem of total national income than with its distribution.

Kalecki (who discovered the General Theory independently) paid more attention to distribution. He proposed a very useful simplification. Net income is exhaustively divided into wages and profits, and industry into an investment sector and a consumption-good sector. The workers spend their money wages week by week as they receive them. The gross profit on the sale of goods to the public is then equal to the wage bill for the investment sector plus consumption out of profits. 'The workers spend what they get and the capitalists get what they spend.'

The neo-classical school which has flourished, particularly in USA, since the war failed to notice that the neo-classicals did not have a theory of profits. Many of the leading exponents of this school, such as Paul Samuelson, are good Keynesians when they treat actual problems and policies, but keep a separate compartment in their minds in which there is a model of a private enterprise economy in equilibrium with full employment. In this compartment the rate of profit is governed by the 'marginal product of capital'.

However, when they were asked in what units a quantity of 'capital' is measured they hastily invented a mysterious substance which would adopt various forms and undergo technical progress while retaining its physical being.

Samuelson undertook to show that even when we allow for different techniques embodied in different kinds of machines, there is still some kind of 'capital' which is *like* a lump of jelly, though it is not actually made of jelly.

This attempt to justify the neo-neoclassical system has now broken down in a spectacular manner. In the November 1966 number of the *Quarterly Journal of Economics* Samuelson confesses that his jelly will not do.

The crisis arose over the so-called problem of reswitching. Piero Sraffa, reviving the classical tradition, produced, in *The Production of Commodities by Means of Commodities*, a solution of the problem which had bothered Ricardo – a system of prices providing a uniform rate of profit on all capital. He showed decisively that a quantity of capital cannot be defined independently of the rate of profit. Incidentally, he showed that, when we consider the problem of the choice of the profit-maximizing technique of production, it is perfectly possible that the same technique may be eligible at several different rates of profit. (I had come across this same point in the course of my attempt to make a 'generalization of the General Theory'.)

The important point is concerned with the nature of capital, but this had passed the neo-neoclassicals by. They seized upon the picturesque proposition about 'reswitching' and endeavoured to prove that it could not occur. The realization that it is impossible to disprove it *ought* to show them that the whole neo-neoclassical system is founded upon sand, but they evidently are not yet ready to draw the full consequences from the argument.

Meanwhile, following the line of generalizing the General Theory, an alternative approach to the theory of profits is offered. The simplest way of stating it is in terms of Kalecki's model, where all wages are spent on consumption and a proportion of profits saved. Then in long-run steady growth, the rate of profit on capital is equal to the rate of growth divided by the proportion of profits saved. (We have already seen, with von Neumann, that when that proportion is unity, the rate of growth is equal to the rate of profit.)

When the rate of accumulation is g, and the rate of growth of the effective labour force, allowing for technical progress, is n, and the proportion of profits saved Sp, and the rate of profit on capital π then, provided that g is not greater than n, $\pi = g/Sp$.

This formulation can be elaborated to allow for saving out of earned income, the relation of g to n, biases in technical progress, short-period fluctuations in g, and so forth – in short the whole post-Keynesian analysis, which brings economic theory down from the cloud-cuckoo land of full-employment equilibrium to discuss actual questions. In the present context we are interested in it as the basis for a theory of distribution.

The new approach represents a change from the moralistic to the functional view of profits. The neoclassics were looking for a *justification* for profit as the 'reward of waiting' or as a benefit derived from the superior effectiveness of roundabout methods of production, and this carried over into the neo-neoclassical 'marginal product of capital'.

Ricardo took it for granted that the *function* of capital was to extract a surplus for accumulation. The capitalists' business was to save and reinvest profits. The expenditure of profits on 'unproductive labour' for the personal consumption of capitalists was on a par with expenditure of rent – a draft on the surplus retarding accumulation.

The new theory, enriched by many complexities learned during the detour through neoclassical and neo-neoclassical realms, returns to Ricardo's conception.

The simplest and most striking illustration of this approach is the analysis of the contrast between socialist and non-socialist countries of the Third World.

After a socialist revolution, the surplus going to the feudal class becomes available for investment, while in the ex-colonial and semi-colonial countries it is still being wasted on consumption, largely of imported luxuries, which makes it doubly wasteful.

This surplus is not sufficient for the needs of rapid development. The socialist authorities need to prevent too rapid a rise in real wages. An acceleration of accumulation takes place as output per head rises faster than consumption so that a growing surplus can be deflected to investment.

This is made more tolerable, partly because there is no middle class to incite envy and partly because collective consumption of education and public shows can more easily be organized. At the same time investment can be planned with a view to national development rather than to private profit, so that the surplus is put to better use.

In the other so-called developing countries, accumulation is not fast enough to provide employment for a growing population, yet the capitalists as well as the feudal class are consuming a considerable part of the surplus. Moreover concessions have to be made to the industrial workers, so that they too begin to consume at the expense of investment. In short the capitalist method of development is less effective in extracting a surplus than the socialist method.

The neoclassics like to present this problem as a choice between the present and the future, but it is not so. It is a conflict of interest between the employed and the unemployed, or between the industrial workers and the landless labourers in agriculture.

Problems such as these, as well as the problems of latter-day capitalism, can be seen in a clear (and often painful) light when the mists of neo-neoclassical sophistry begin to lift.

7

THE UNIMPORTANCE OF RESWITCHING

1

INTRODUCTION

THE story of what is known as the debate over the reswitching of techniques is a sad example of how controversies arise between contestants who confront the conclusions of their arguments without first examining their respective assumptions.

How is it possible to have a controversy over a purely logical point? When various theorists each set out their assumptions clearly, after eliminating errors, they can agree about what conclusions follow from what assumptions. They have then prepared the ground for a discussion, not a controversy, about the relevance of various models to an explanation of whatever situation it is that they are trying to explain.

The reswitching debate arose from confronting the conclusions of an attempt to develop a post-Keynesian analysis of long-run accumulation with arguments drawn from pre-Keynesian assumptions.

In the pre-Keynesian model the rate of investment is governed by decisions about saving and the capital to labour ratio at full employment is governed by the level of real wages. In a Keynesian model saving in a given short-period situation is governed by decisions about investment and the level of employment is governed by investment and the share of saving in net income.

For our present purpose the exposition with both kinds of models may be simplified by setting them up in a pure capitalist economy, in which workers are all alike; there is no limitation on land or the supply of particular natural resources, and no government sector or foreign trade. At the first stage of the argument, we also rule out inventions and discoveries that change technical knowledge.

Quarterly Journal of Economics, February 1975. Professor Samuelson has kindly allowed me to quote from his reply.

2

A Post-Keynesian Model

Under the influence of Harrod's *Towards a Dynamic Economics*, I set out to make a generalization of the General Theory, that is, a Keynesian analysis of accumulation over the long run. (I am taking my own case because it is the one that I understand best.)

The first step was to set up a model for a single technique of production in which men with physical inputs, say machines of particular engineering specifications, reproduce these machines and a basket of consumption goods. There are no fixed technical coefficients in the short-period sense; there is a utilization function showing how output from a stock of machines varies with employment. This function may be perfectly well behaved, with output rising at a diminishing rate as employment increases, or it may not. In the long-run sense there is no flexibility. The production function consists of a single ratio of labour to machines, operating at normal capacity, for each composition of output.

Harrod assumed what has come to be called Harrod saving, that is, that a given proportion of net income is saved, independently of its distribution between households and firms, and he had no theory of a rate of profit on capital, though he discussed the influence of the rate of interest on household saving.

I adopted Kalecki's assumption – the workers spend what they get, and the capitalists get what they spend. Suppose that in the one-technique model accumulation is going on at a certain rate (there is always at least enough labour available to man the stock of machines as it grows). Then, when the composition of the stock of machines in existence at any moment is in harmony with the rate of investment, the output of consumption goods is determined. Then consumption out of profits determines the level of real wages and the rate of profit on capital compatible with the technique and the rate of accumulation.

Now compare a situation where everything else in the model is the same except that consumption out of profits is somewhat higher. There is now a higher rate of profit (with the same rate of growth). Unless labour embodied in machines per man employed is the same for machines as for consumption goods, and the time pattern of production is the same for both, the price of machines in terms of consumption goods is now either higher or lower, according as the time pattern of production is such as to require more machines per man in making machines or in making consumption goods.

The value of the stock of capital varies with the rate of profit in the general case, although it is identically the same in engineering terms.

Next, Nicholas Kaldor persuaded me that I ought to bring in the conception (which he has since repudiated) of deepening the stock of capital in a given state of technical knowledge.[1] To prepare for this (which I also have repudiated), I interpreted a given state of knowledge as a 'book of blueprints' giving the engineering specification of every technique that would be eligible (that is, that would yield the maximum rate of profit) at at least one level of real wages.

With each technique, an identical labour force is conceived to be replacing all the means of production required by that technique and producing a net output. The rate of growth is the same for each; when it is put at zero, net output consists of consumption goods, which may be specified in baskets of identical composition.

The techniques are set out in a pseudo production function in descending order of net output per man.

Each technique consists of the specification of the input-output table for producing the machines that it requires. These may be completely different for each. The machines for technique Alpha have to be made, say, of copper; for Beta, of iron; and for Gamma, of wood.

Running an eye down the pseudo production function, we observe the real wage rate falling and the rate of profit rising. Between each pair of techniques there is a switch point, at a level of real wages at which the rate of profit is the same, say, for Alpha and Beta or for Beta and Gamma. At the prices ruling at a switch point, the values of capital required for the respective techniques are in the same ratio to each other as net profit per man employed. (At a point where this is not so, only one technique gives the highest rate of profit at the real wage corresponding to that point, and it is not a switch point.)

Switch points may be either forward or backward. A forward switch occurs where, at a real-wage rate slightly less than that ruling at the switch point, the more labour-intensive technique (with a lower net output per man) offers a higher rate of profit. A backward switch means that the less labour-intensive technique (with higher output per head) offers the higher rate of profit at a lower real-wage rate. When the difference in the cost of machines required for two techniques is mainly or entirely due to differences in the labour time embodied in them, switching between them can only be forward. A backward switch involves a difference in time patterns, which makes the relative values of the respective machines markedly sensitive to differences in the rate of profit.

[1] See my *Accumulation of Capital* (London, Macmillan, 1956), p. vii.

The existence of a backward switch is a necessary but not a sufficient condition for the same technique to be eligible at two different rates of profit, that is, to show 'a reswitching of techniques'. The real scandal for the neoclassics was the possibility (within the accepted assumptions) of backward switching rather than reswitching, but the problem has come to be known under the latter name.

My treatment of this subject was clumsy and contained some errors. Piero Sraffa arrived at the same argument, in a more rigorous manner, starting from a different question – the classical theory of value.[2] The whole analysis has now been set out elegantly and perspicuously by Don Harris.[3]

3

THE PRE-KEYNESIAN ARGUMENT

The pre-Keynesian argument was developed in various forms.

The first was the contention that, in a Walrasian model, there is an initial endowment of an arbitrary assortment of machines of particular specification that can be combined in various ways with labour to produce output, so that accumulation can be described in terms of machines without mentioning a 'quantity of capital' at all. This was just a bluff. Obviously, a profit-maximizing scheme of investment is worked out by comparing the costs in dollars of various machines with the excess of dollar receipts over expenses that each may be expected to yield in the future. It cannot be planned in engineering terms alone, without taking account of values.

Another line was to set up a model comprising two sectors producing, respectively, say, steel and shirts.[4] In each sector there is a well-behaved production function in labour and steel with indefinite substitution between them (the isoquant for each commodity never cuts the axes, steel and labour, in which it is drawn). To exhibit a process of growth by accumulation of steel, the model has to be confined to the case where an output of steel requires less steel per unit of labour than an output of shirts, otherwise it could never get started.

Moreover, this model has to include some kind of monetary mechanism to ensure the equality of savings and investment, so as to reconcile the allocation of output between the commodities warranted, in Harrod's

[2] See *Production of Commodities by Means of Commodities* (Cambridge, Cambridge University Press, 1960), Part III.

[3] 'Capital, Distribution, and the Aggregate Production Function', *American Economic Review*, LXIII (March 1973), 100–13. 'Production funtion' is, of course, a misnomer.

[4] See H. Uzawa, 'On a Two-Sector Model of Economic Growth', *Review of Economic Studies*, XXIX (Oct. 1961), 40–7; and J. E. Meade, *A Neoclassical Theory of Growth* (London, Allen and Unwin, 1968), Appendix II.

sense, by the propensity to consume with the allocation required to maintain full employment over the long run.[5] For this reason it should be classed with bastard-Keynesian, rather than pre-Keynesian models.

In the pre-Keynesian model all machines and consumption goods are made of the same physically homogenous stuff. This is usually called a 'one-commodity world', but the stuff represents the inputs required for an indefinite range of techniques, or stuff-labour ratios, so that it is not like any single commodity in the everyday sense.

The well-behaved production function in labour and stuff was invented, I think, to answer the question: What is a quantity of capital? But the real point of it is to abolish the distinction between a short-period utilization function and a long-period isoquant. Saving consists of withdrawing part of the current net output of stuff and dumping it onto the stock. At whatever rate the stock is growing relative to available labour, there is always a point on the isoquant that provides full employment. A well-behaved production function with inputs and outputs made of the same stuff is necessary for the pre-Keynesian system in which accumulation is governed by society's propensity to save.

4

SWITCHING THE MODELS

Next, the professors at MIT took over my book of blueprints and tried to embed it in pre-Keynesian theory.

Professor Solow provided a mathematical proof that the definition of a switch point does define a switch point, that is, it shows a rate of profit such that two different sets of physical means of production (which we are calling 'machines') have capital values, per man employed, proportional to profit per man.[6] For Solow, the ratio of the additional output per man of the higher technique to the additional value of its capital is the 'rate of return'. At each switch point, forward or backward, this rate of return is identical with the rate of profit ruling at that switch point. If he regards a falling rate of profit as a process going on through time, due to accumulation *raising* the marginal product of labour, how is he to interpret a backward switch point, where an indefinitely small reduction in the rate of profit is associated with a sudden *fall* in output per man?

[5] Meade (op. cit. p. 3) keeps money prices constant and allows the level of money wages to regulate employment.

[6] This was published in 1967. See 'The Interest Rate and Transition Between Technique', in *Socialism, Capitalism and Economic Growth*, Essays presented to Maurice Dobb, C. H. Feinstein, ed. (Cambridge, Cambridge University Press, 1967).

Professor Samuelson[7] found out how to draw a pseudo production function in which the value of capital does not vary with the rate of profit. The machines required for different techniques on his 'surrogate production function' are different with respect to engineering specifications, but, with each technique, the ratio of labour to machines required to produce its machines is the same as that required to produce the homogeneous consumption good. That is to say, the cost of capital is determined solely by labour embodied in the machines required for each technique and the time pattern of all techniques is the same.

This may be interpreted, in a formal sense, as a one-commodity case;[8] from the point of view of cost of production, each type of machine is equivalent to a particular amount of the consumption good. But it lacks the essential characteristic of a pre-Keynesian model, that homogeneous stuff can be withheld from consumption and added to the stock of means of production.

For several years, everyone (except Piero Garegnani) was somewhat baffled by the surrogate production function. Then in 1965, a fortunate accident occurred. A disciple of Professor Samuelson claimed to have proved that reswitching can never occur, even in the general case where techniques differ with respect to their time patterns.[9]

It was fortunate because, after his argument had been challenged by a counterexample presented by Luigi Pasinetti at the Rome Congress of the Econometric Society in September 1965, the mathematical error in the supposed proof was a bait that attracted several others to the field, which they explored from various points of view.

At the end of it all, Professor Samuelson still thought that he could use a pseudo production function in describing a process of accumulation going on through time.[10] Many of his followers, even today, maintain that so long as they confine their arguments to cases in which technology is represented by a book of blueprints that does not give rise to any backward switch points, they ought to be free to talk about the marginal product of capital in the manner of J. B. Clark.

---

[7] 'Parable and Realism in Capital Theory: The Surrogate Production Function', *Review of Economic Studies*, XXIX (June 1962), 193–206.

[8] See Piero Garegnani, 'Heterogeneous Capital, the Production Function and the Theory of Distribution', *Review of Economic Studies*, XXXVII (July 1970), 407–36.

[9] D. Levhari, 'A Nonsubstitution Theorem and Switching of Techniques', *Quarterly Journal of Economics*, LXXIX (Feb. 1965), 98–105.

[10] See 'A Summing Up', this ibid., LXXX (Nov. 1966), 444–8.

5

A Nonexistence Theorem

Nothing could be more idle than to get up an argument about whether reswitching is 'likely' to be found in reality. Even if there was such a thing as a pseudo production function, there could be no movement along it to pass over switch points, and furthermore, in reality, there is no such thing as a pseudo production function.

Professor Solow seems to have forgotten that it was he who first called it by that name and explained it by saying that each point represents an economy on an island that has no intercourse with any other.[11]

On each island a particular rate of profit obtains, and each has the stock of machines appropriate to its own rate of profit. There is no way of moving across a switch point from one island to another, and no one takes any interest in blueprints for techniques that they are not using themselves.

What, then, is the meaning of postulating that they all have in common the same state of technical knowledge?

Two different economies are separated either in space or in time. No two economies separated in space have exactly the same technology, for many accidents of geography and history enter into the choice of technique, as well as the design of 'machines'. The same economy at different dates has a different state of technical knowledge.[12] Not only is every island at a different point, but every point is on a different production function.

When investment is being planned, whether for a single plant or for a socialist economy, the choice of technique is made by groping amongst incomplete information. There are no ready-blueprinted techniques to choose from. When the technique to be installed is designed to give a higher output per man than that formerly in use, it must be a recent innovation or an adaptation from one already known in the broad, though not in detail. The blueprints are drawn when the technique has been chosen, and it will rarely turn out, after the event, that exactly the best possible choice was made.

There is no such phenomenon in real life as accumulation taking place in a given state of technical knowledge. The idea was introduced into

[11] See 'Heterogeneous Capital and Smooth Production Functions: An Experimental Study', *Econometrica*, **XXXI** (Oct. 1963), 623–45.

[12] Technical progress can be represented in a vintage model, but this can be used for pre-Keynesian theory only by abolishing the distinction between firms and households so as to make the propensity to save determine the rate of gross investment.

economic theory only to give a meaning to the concept of the marginal productivity of capital, just as the pseudo production function was constructed in order to show that it has no meaning.

STEADY-STATE AND TRANSIENT RELATIONS: A REPLY ON SWITCHING

PAUL A. SAMUELSON

[The first three pages, after some flattering remarks, specify the 'factor-price frontier' for a single technique in a manner which does not conflict with the foregoing argument.]

SUBSTANTIVE VINDICATION?

Where then does the possibility of misinterpretation arise? It arises from the ambiguity of English speech and grammar. Thus, in my first paragraph, I speak of 'switching back at a low interest rate . . .' and of '. . . as the interest rate falls in consequence of abstention from present consumption. . . .' Suppose that here, and in a score of other innocent passages, I had rewritten these as '. . . a switch back had *permanently* occurred at a *permanent* low interest rate to the techniques *permanently* viable at a *permanent* high interest rate *subsequent* to successful saving-investment abstaining in the past from then-current consumption [as envisaged by the neoclassical writers being quoted].' If I had done this, even a hostile critic could not have managed to fall into a misunderstanding; and a critic of neoclassical views, sensitized to past propensities of some writers to err on related matters, would have had no reason to quarrel with my revised text.

So, to narrow down misunderstanding, I authorize any reader to make such purely verbal alterations at a score of places.

This done, how much of my substantive argument evaporates, or is vitiated, or needs amendment and elucidation? None that I can see. No diagram needs redrawing. No substantive contention need be withdrawn or qualified.

Since it is only too easy to be blind to one's own shortcomings, I have gone to some pains to check this complacent conclusion by reference to a detailed criticism on the same point by Professor Geoffrey Harcourt.[13] The conclusion stands.

[13] Harcourt, *Some Cambridge Controversies in the Theory of Capital* (C.U.P. 1972) pp. 122–3, compliments my 1966 discussion for 'handsomely admit[ting] the logic of the neo-Keynesian criticisms', but quotes a passage, as a sample of still others, that is

supposed (as an aside) to violate 'Joan Robinson's strictures that it is most important not to apply theorems obtained from the analysis of differences to situations of change (or, at least, to be aware of the act of faith in doing this). . . .' Because of length I do not reproduce the supposedly offending quotation, which consists of the complete sentences of the first paragraph on p. 577 of my 1966 paper. What it plainly says is correct, and I would write it again, namely the following: if above 100 per cent interest rate and below 50, technique A is viable over technique B, society can go from 101 per cent equilibrium to 49 per cent equilibrium without any physical movements at all. And so it can, as in my Table I between, say, time 7 and time 23 with all the intermediate times shown there skipped; or, as between time 4 and 5 (!) with the only changes between the equilibrium being the change in price tags that are *not* shown in the table. The point of the passage quoted was *not* to claim that the described move in time does go along the steady-state curve of my Figure Vb but to point out that it does not. Let me, however, not stick to the quoted passage but try rather to be responsive to the spirit rather than the letter of Professor Harcourt's unease. Suppose he had found a passage to quote that went like this: 'In going from the 51 per cent profit point on the curve to the 49 per cent profit point, the system goes through old-fashioned abstinence of present consumption for higher future consumption; but in going from the 101 per cent point to the 99 per cent point, it reverses the neoclassical parable and is splashed with current consumption and does negative abstinence.' If my pen had written that, would I be caught out in mortal or venial sin? Not at all. Not only does such a passage not say that the movement takes place *along* the steady-state locus, but to anyone who understands it and my Table I, it clearly indicates the contrary! The slopes between the $1 \cdot 01$ and $0 \cdot 99$ points and the $0 \cdot 51$ and $0 \cdot 49$ points in the relevant steady-state diagrams are the *reverse* of the described transient algebraic abstinences and splashings, and no 'act of faith' would permit of other than this even in the simplest neoclassical model. I believe that Professor Harcourt and I do not remain in any essential disagreement on substantive matters, but he does have the right to ask of me why a system might move along the warranted paths I so skilfully built into my discussion. Here we leave the realm of logic, but, too briefly, I would reply: Consider that a war breaks out between time 4 and 5 in my Table I (not amended as in this footnote). Perspicacious planners, or avaricious speculators in forward markets, act to produce the expansion of final output needed in the temporary war years. Etc., etc.

Countless other less dramatic scenarios could be written: change in optimal-control planners' Ramseyan time preference, a slow trend towards later retirements, tolerably well discerned by market participants, etc., etc. The warranted paths of my Table I are simply two of an infinity of alternatives. They were selected as the *fastest* transient paths, not for realism but to illuminate the nice Solow theorem on transition states of the 1967 Dobbs *Festschrift*, a theorem that Professor Robinson dismisses by the characterization that it merely says '. . . the definition of a switch point does define a switch point'. (The one point where my 1966 exposition does seem ungenerous is in my terming this theorem as 'merely' a 'book-keeping' or 'general accounting relationship, as applied to a constant-returns-to-technology'. An adversary in a debate would not merit the sneering 'merely' much less an admired colleague.) To conclude the reply to Professor Harcourt's query, the vast literature on the 'Hahn problem' should be consulted to form a reasoned opinion on how tolerably inefficient or efficient are market and planned systems in the real world in transient and steady-state analysis; I am not aware that my own part in this discussion contains *invalid* 'habits of thought so ingrained as for him [me] to be unconscious of their presence', but I shall be happy to recant if such logical errors can be found.

Deeper Issue of Non-Steady State Analysis

I do not think that the real stumbling block has been the failure of a literary writer to understand that when a mathematician says, 'y rises as x falls', he is implying nothing about temporal sequences or anything different from 'when x is low, y is high'. More important, I think there may well remain differences of opinion between some in Cambridge, England, and some in Cambridge, Massachusetts, over *whether non-steady state analysis can be meaningfully formulated and handled*. Thus, my 1966 Table I, p. 581, presents a warranted dynamic path, in which a system goes from one steady state to another. No reader who contemplates my exposition has reason to think that the technological relations of the transition are falsely derived there from relations valid only for the steady state. They clearly are not. But, what is a different and not a 'logical' point, a skeptic may legitimately doubt that (i) a planned economy would have the wit to follow such an 'intertemporally-efficient' warrantable path; or, withdrawing doubt about planned systems, a skeptic might legitimately doubt that (ii) a competitive market system will have the 'foresight' or the perfect-futures markets to *approximate* in real life such warranted paths that have the property that, if everyone knew in advance they would occur, each will be motivated to do just that which gives rise to them.

Another deeper issue has to do with hard-to-prove differences in empirical presumption. Thus, Sir John Hicks, in his 1972 Nobel Lecture,[14] comes full circle to his 1932 view that a successful raising of real wage rates (perhaps by real-wage sliding-scale contracts) is likely in the short and long

[14] J. R. Hicks, 'The Mainstream of Economic Growth', Nobel Prize Lecture, 27 April, 1973, Stockholm, in *Les Prix Nobel en 1972*, The Nobel Foundation, Stockholm, 1972, 235–46, particularly pp. 244ff. Professor Hicks is well aware of reswitching and other possibilities and therefore punctuates his text with the word '*usually*'. A perfectionist might want him to insert that qualification at a few other places, but I think that on a sensible interpretation of his text this can be taken as understood. No doubt too, except for the limitation of space, he would have spelled out in greater detail the time sequence of incidence of the postulated increase in real wages, but enough is given to register his empirical judgment about the importance of reswitching and related phenomena. For purposes of an anthology of readings, I had not been able to identify in Professor Robinson's voluminous writings a clear statement of exactly what, outside steady states, her theory of income distribution is. (In this respect Professor Kaldor is different, and one is splashed almost with an embarrassment of riches.) But it is clear that her theory is not neoclassical. And, from an aside (thrown off in her lecture before the 1970 World Econometric Congress in Cambridge) concerning the putative ability of Philippine workers to affect the distribution of income by militancy, I would infer that her empirical insights would not coincide with this of Sir John.

run to result in a reduction of employment. By contrast, one who believes technology to be more like my 1966 reswitching example than like its orthodox contrast, will have a more sanguine view about how successful militant power by organized labour can be in causing egalitarian shifts in the distribution of income away from property even in the long run. Indeed under such a reswitching technology, anyone who believes in the tautologies of the exponential paths of textbook-land might vote Social Credit to promote an easy euthanasia of the capitalist class merely by having the state (perhaps out of across-the-board taxation) finance larger shares of capital formation: when it relieves the profit savers of half the task, the tautological profit rate will halve, etc., according to the tautology,

$$r = (\text{growth rate/fraction-of-profits-saved}) \times (1 - f),$$

where f is the fraction of capital formation done by the government's fiscal system.

So even after logical issues have been put in their proper uncontroversial place, the arguments can go on as to whether the distribution of income does or does not depend significantly in real life on the *relative supplies of labour and of diverse capital goods*.[15]

In concluding this conciliatory note dealing solely with the logical points raised about my own works, I should say that failure to deal with other aspects of Professor Robinson's account does not mean that I would consider hers an optimal formulation of the issues agreed upon or in controversy.[16] It is valuable as *her* account: from *Rashomon*, we know how

[15] One who believes that class power can wrest great gains in absolute and relative income shares within a market system need not necessarily reject neoclassical constructs involving smooth marginal productivities and simple capital aggregates. For, as pointed out in P. Samuelson and F. Modigliani, 'The Pasinetti Paradox in Neoclassical and More General Models', *Review of Economic Studies*, **XXXIII** (Oct. 1966), 269–301, particularly around p. 213 and Figure 4, a one-sector model with $dK/dt + C = [(aL)^{-100} + (bK)^{-100}]^{-.01}$ and almost-zero elasticity of substitution would act much like a Pasinetto-Kaldor model with a fixed capital-output coefficient; on the other hand, a finite-activities model can be found, which at the same time that it lacks marginal productivities that 'determine' real wages and interest rates, has comparative-static and dynamic-path properties that come as near as we like to Cobb-Douglas Clarkian models.

[16] We all owe Professor Robinson so much that there is not the usual sting in such words as '. . . just a bluff', or 'The professors at M.I.T. took over my book of blueprints and tried to. . . .' Any reader of my three volumes of collected papers can verify that, whatever Walras did or did not do, I have on several occasions developed *logically correct*, nonsimple models of not-necessarily-steady-state economic development that eschewed use of *any* capital aggregate, and the same is true of many other writers. But it has been my sad experience that when a challenge in the realm of logic has been successfully met, that tends to

different the single reality will appear to different actors in the same drama. There may even be a viewpoint from which Professor Robinson's final Nonexistence Theorem belongs in the realm of deductive logic – like the Nonsubstitution or the Pythagorean Theorems, or the Impossibility Theorems of Frisch and of Arrow – but on this matter I must still reserve judgment.

REPLY

JOAN ROBINSON

The pseudo production function belongs to the class of theory that Janos Kornai calls a thought experiment. Anyone is free to draw it, just as he pleases, with or without backward switches and with appreciable or indefinitely small intervals between the rates of profit corresponding to different techniques, but no one is free to violate the logic of the assumptions on which the construction has been made.

Each point, or 'island', represents the input-output table of a particular technique. Each has its own past history, when investments were made in expectation of the prices and wage rates ruling 'today', and its own future in which inputs will be reproduced in the expectation that the same conditions will continue to rule.

Within the accepted simplifications (specified in Section I p. 76), it is possible to compare techniques in terms of *net* output per head of the whole labour force at a given rate of growth; but it is not possible, with this construction, to describe an actual process of moving from one equilibrium point to another. To 'change' the technique in use at an equilibrium point on the pseudo production function, it would be necessary either to go back into the past and rewrite the history of the investment that led to that point or to go into the future after changing both the rate and form of investment, thus throwing the starting point out of equilibrium. The 'neoclassical case' belongs to a quite different thought experiment – a one-commodity economy, malleable capital, and investment governed by saving, dwelling

move the objection into the realm of realism and relevance. Only into the logical realm does the present note enter. Also, politeness should not be confused with imitation: the activity analysis of von Neumann and programming theory was used by scholars all over the world before Professor Robinson used the terminology of blueprints, and yet it was appropriate that those who conducted discussions with the author of the *Accumulation of Capital* should have paid her the compliment of using her terminology. It is understandable that strong convictions should lead to strong language, as any reader of the 'capital controversies' can document in quantitative detail, author by author.

in a timeless world without any distinction between the future and the past. The attempt to incorporate a book of blueprints into this construction can only cause confusion.

Professor Samuelson claims that his 'parable' (1962 and 1966) was a construction of the first kind, with the amendment, now, that transitional paths are not necessarily 'efficient'. Two different rates of profit, on either side of a switch point, represent two different techniques, each requiring a different bundle of specific physical inputs, or, in the case of 'reswitching', the same technique occurs at different rates of profit with correspondingly different sets of relative prices.

Professor Samuelson reminds us that a plane diagram can show relations between only two variables. He observes that a writer of prose may slip into saying: As real wages rise, the rate of profit falls, but a mathematician knows that a functional relationship is timeless and makes no reference to history or to the direction of change.

Exactly. There cannot be a movement between points on a plane diagram. A movement can take place only in the third dimension of time, either forward into the unknown future or backward into an investigation of past history.*

However, Professor Samuelson continues to use his construction to describe a *process* of accumulation that *raises* wages, *alters* technology, and *changes* a stock of inputs made, say, of wood into one made of iron and then into copper.

To Kornai, Harcourt, and myself, this methodology is unacceptable, but Professor Samuelson assures us that it is quite all right. The argument rests in a difference of opinion about a purely logical point.

The discussion has been involved, over the last twenty years, with the problem of 'measuring capital'. When we turn from thought experiments to reality, that is, to the interpretation of statistics, some rough-and-ready measure must serve – say, horsepower per man employed, labour embodied in the stock of inputs, or the book value of business capital.

In comparisons across countries, American industry is generally found to have the highest ratio of inputs per worker, by any such indicator, but I do not know that anyone has ever suggested that the rate of profit on capital is exceptionally low in the United States.

In a time series of the figures of industrial growth in a prosperous period, it is found that neither the share of wages in value added nor the ratio of value of capital to value of output varies very much. It follows that the overall ex-post rate of profit has been fairly constant. Rising real wages with

* Paragraph added.

a constant rate of profit entail that the observation at each date is drawn from a different technology. The thought experiment of accumulation *in a given state of technical knowledge* has not been a success.

A planning authority has to consider the choice of technique ex-ante, but it is concerned with allocating investable resources between alternative possible *increments* to be made in the stock of inputs. The relation of total profits to the value of the total existing stock has nothing to do with the case.

Professor Samuelson is kind enough to make me a number of compliments in his comment. I would be more gratified if he would answer my point.

8

THE DISINTEGRATION OF ECONOMICS

PROFESSIONAL economics grew and flourished on an unprecedented scale, especially in North America, after the end of World War II. At the same time, the Western industrial nations were enjoying a period of continuous growth and high employment, interrupted only by brief and shallow recessions and accompanied by only a mild rate of inflation in the price level. The central teaching of orthodox economic theory was the natural tendency to 'equilibrium' in the free market system, and this did not appear to be in obvious contradiction to the facts of experience.

Since 1974, the occurrence of a serious world-wide recession accompanied by increased inflation has left the economists gaping. Othodoxy has nothing to offer and all kinds of fanciful notions are floating around.

HOLLOW ORTHODOXY

However, it is not only the slump which has exposed the bankruptcy of academic economic teaching. The structure of thought which it expounds was long ago proved to be hollow. It consisted of a set of propositions which bore hardly any relation to the structure and evolution of the economy that they were supposed to depict. The reason for this intellectual aberration seems to have been that the very notion of an economic system, as a particular historical phenomenon, developing through time, was associated with the doctrines of Marx. The aim of teaching was to build up a screen to prevent students from glancing in that direction. This was reinforced during the McCarthy period by the fear of being suspected of dangerous thoughts. Thus the academics were anxious to present the economy in a pleasing light and did not care to examine it to see what it was actually like.

As a matter of fact, a very robust defence of capitalism can be derived from Marx's analysis. Exploitation, that is the payment as wages of less than the value of the net proceeds of industry, is necessary for the emergence of profits. Profits provide both the motive and the means for the accumulation of capital and the competitive struggle amongst capitalists to accumulate leads to technical innovation which 'ripens the productive power of social labour as though in a hot-house'.

The academics (except for Joseph Schumpeter) did not follow up this line. They pretend that the Marxian 'labour theory of value' means that workers have the right to the whole product of industry – the view of the Utopian socialists whom Marx despised – and protest that capital also produces value and has a right to its share.

Before the great slump of the 1930s, Alfred Marshall was the dominant influence on economics in the English-speaking world. He was a subtle thinker who allowed for exceptions to every rule that he propounded but the effect of his doctrines as they were generally interpreted was to support laisser-faire – government intervention in economic life, however well-intentioned, will do more harm than good; belief in a natural tendency to equilibrium in the free-market economy at a level of real wages consonant with full employment of the available labour force; the beneficial effects of free trade; the defence of the gold standard and of sound finance. Many arguments drawn from this complex of ideas are being trotted out again now, as they were in the 1930s; for instance, the view that there cannot be any 'involuntary' unemployment, because any individual could always get a job by offering to work at less than the going wage rate, or that government borrowing draws upon a given fund of savings (or is it of finance?) and so 'crowds out' private-sector investment. However, during the great debate that was broken off by the war in 1939, the arguments of Keynes were gradually prevailing over orthodoxy, and by the end of the war Keynes had become orthodox in his turn.

In the course of his endeavour to understand the causes of unemployment, Keynes had reintroduced the concept of capitalism as a particular economic system, evolving through history. He saw it as containing an essential flaw – its inherent instability and chronic failure to make full use of its potential resources – but he thought that his theory showed how this could be patched up and in any case, as an economic system, it 'was the best in sight'.

This was not good enough for the new orthodoxy burgeoning in the United States. The subject was split into two parts; Keynes was safely corralled in the section called 'macro economics' while the main stream of teaching returned to celebrating the establishment of equilibrium in a free market.

This section of theory was described as 'micro economics', that is, the study of prices of particular commodities and the behaviour of individual sellers and buyers; however, it is obviously impossible to discuss the behaviour of individuals in a vacuum without saying anything about the legal, political and economic setting in which they are to operate. The setting in which the equilibrium of supply and demand is analysed has no resemblance to modern capitalism. It is suited, rather, to the discussion of a rural fair where independent peasants and artisans meet to exchange products that are surplus to their own requirements.

A great point is made of the freedom of the consumer to choose what commodities to consume, according to his individual 'tastes', but obviously the main influence upon the pattern of demand for commodities is the distribution of purchasing power between families. Nothing is said about this except that each individual has an 'endowment' of some 'factor of production', such as the ability to work, or property in land or (though this is scarcely consistent with the rest of the story) property in various types of industrial equipment.

In the old Marshallian theory there had been a discussion of 'welfare' and it was admitted that a given flow of production of commodities would provide more 'satisfaction' to a given human population the more equally it was distributed amongst the consumers concerned. Marshall himself favoured a more equal distribution of national income provided it could be brought about without any revolutionary upheaval. This whole question, however, was eliminated from the analysis of the equilibrium model, first by passing very lightly over the question of the relative amounts of 'endowments' possessed by different individuals while concentrating on the determination of the relative price per unit of the various 'factors'; secondly, by concentrating upon the choices made by a single consumer under a 'budget constraint', that is, with a certain amount of purchasing power to spend. When it has been shown that his 'tastes' and the prices of the commodities determine what he buys, the suggestion is slipped in that the choices of consumers in the aggregate determine what is to be produced. In acclaiming the 'sovereignty of the consumer'. the problem of distribution of consuming power amongst the population somehow gets lost to view.

The great claim of equilibrium theory was that it showed how scarce means are allocated between alternative uses in accordance with consumers' tastes. The existence of scarce means (materials, energy, cultivable land) has recently come very much to the fore in public discussion, while consumers' tastes run to large cars, overheated rooms, and an excessive consumption of meat. The central doctrine of orthodox economics is the defence of the freedom of anyone who has money to spend, to spend it as he likes.

SMOTHERING KEYNES

In the other department, so-called macro economics, the discussion is all about instability and how slumps could be prevented by applying Keynes' conceptions of demand management. This complete break, like a geological fault, between the two departments of economic theory, makes it impossible for students to form a coherent view of what it is all about. If there is a natural tendency in the free market system to equilibrium with full employment, why do we need Keynes; and if Keynes was right, that the capitalist system is inherently unstable, why do we have to spend so much time working out the mathematics of an equilbrium system? Such doubts, however, were smothered by reducing 'Keynesian' theory to a kind of equilibrium in its turn and swallowing it up in the 'neo-neoclassical synthesis'.

Keynes himself, when he had worked out the argument of the *General Theory*, was startled by the indictment of the free-enterprise system that it seemed to represent and he wrote the last chapter in a very mollifying style which made it possible for orthodoxy to accept it and to pass very lightly over the awkward questions that earlier chapters had raised.

The synthesis was very soothing. A natural tendency to steady growth took the place of equilibrium. The subject split up into a number of compartments – business economics, labour economics, urban economics, and so forth which provided many fields of work for academics to burrow into without questioning the central structure of theory. The elaboration of mathematical theorems (though devoid of empirical content) kept many brilliant practitioners happily occupied. When some dissidents tried to attack the basis of orthodox doctrines from a Marxist point of view, they were absorbed into the profession; now 'radical economics' is one of the standard compartments of the subject along with the rest.

Under this cover a great deal of work has been done and a mass of information collected, much of which is of great interest, but it has been confused and distorted by the need to stuff it into the restricting frame of equilibrium analysis.

A case in point is the so-called theory of the firm. Marshall was a great moralizer. His aim was to justify the ways of Mammon to man. The labourer is worthy of his hire, and the capitalist is worthy of his return. The interest received by a rentier is the 'reward of waiting' that is, of keeping his wealth intact. For an entrepreneur it is the reward of 'business ability in command of capital'.

Marshall knew that the main source of finance for the growth of a business is reinvestment of its own profits, but he refused to accept the corollary that any business which gets a good start will go on growing indefinitely. He maintained that there is an upper limit to the size of firms so that every market will normally be served by a sufficient number of sellers to ensure competitive pricing.

His theory is one of the fossils of nineteenth century doctrine that has been carried down till today in mainstream teaching. The mutation in capitalism which has come about with the establishment of the great, and still growing, multinational corporations is largely ignored. Kenneth Galbraith has examined the characteristics of the *New Industrial State*, but as he writes in a bright, readable style, his views need not be taken seriously. Many realistic studies of actual business performance have been made but they are excluded from the mainstream textbooks which still depict competitive industries composed of a large number of firms each unable to grow beyond the equilibrium size.

ANOTHER VERSION

There was a serious weakness in the neo-neoclassical synthesis to which most of the profession seems to have been oblivious. The theory of market equilibrium, with given 'endowments' and given 'tastes' for a specified list of commodities is essentially static. It can accommodate accumulation and change only by making the assumption that buyers and sellers have 'correct foresight' of the future course of prices. A world of correct foresight is not the world in which human beings live. From this point, the argument takes off into an elaboration of mathematical structures which have no point of contact with empirical reality. But if steady growth had been substituted in the synthesis for static equilibrium, it was obviously necessary to discuss accumulation. This required an account of the the nature of capital and of the generation of profits.

There had been another version of the central theory derived from Marshall, often mixed up in the textbooks with market equilibrium. In this, the 'factors of production' are not individual endowments but the total amounts, available to the economy as a whole, of land, labour and capital. When all are fully employed, each receives a 'reward', rent, wages and interest, according to its contribution to the product of industry. This doctrine was propounded in the USA by Professor J. B. Clark, at the beginning of the present century. Thorstein Veblen immediately pointed out that the 'capital' which receives interest is rentier wealth that can be lent to business or to government, while the 'capital' that contributes to the product of industry is the technology embodied in equipment and stocks that permits labour to produce output. But no one from the orthodox camp deigned to answer him. Veblen (the most original economist born and bred in the USA) was a maverick whose views could be laughed off.

When the question was raised in Cambridge (England) twenty years ago, the orthodox answer was: let us pretend that 'capital' consists of a physical substance that is just like finance so that the problem does not arise. It is homogeneous, divisible, and measurable, and can be embodied in any variety of equipment, instantaneously, without cost and without change in the initial quantity. The distinction which Keynes had drawn between interest – the price of loans, and profit – the return on investment – was muddled up again and the rate of interest was taken to measure the productivity of this imaginary substance.

Orthodoxy seemed to be quite content with this concoction, until the publication by Piero Sraffa of a book with the eccentric title: *Production of Commodities by Means of Commodities*, roused a sharp controversy. Cambridge (Massachusetts) challenged Cambridge (England) and failed to win the point. Professor Samuelson very candidly admitted that his system did not hold water. This knocked the bottom out of the logical structure of orthodox theory, but mainstream teaching goes on just the same.

THE PRESENT AS HISTORY

Piero Sraffa's formal analysis re-established (though in a somewhat cryptic manner) the classical doctrine that the rate of profit on capital depends upon the technical structure of production and the share of wages in net output. The classical economists, such as Adam Smith and Ricardo, had naturally thought in terms of accumulation as a historical process. (The equilibrists are fond of claiming Adam Smith as the founder of their school, but he certainly did not intend to set up a static model of an exchange economy.)

Keynes abused Ricardo for neglecting the problem of effective demand, and he had no time for Marx, but he himself instinctively thought in the classical manner of the institutions of capitalism evolving through time. His own analysis was confined, for the most part, to strictly short-period problems but it fits into a classical, historical approach. (Modern attempts to force Keynes into the equilibrium mould are causing a great deal of unnecessary confusion.) By acknowledging that life is lived in time and that today is an ever moving break between the irrevocable past and the unknown future, he had shattered the basic conception of equilibrium, though he sometimes felt a nostalgic reluctance to give it up.

When we view our problems in historical terms, it is obvious that the twenty-five years of continuous growth after the end of the Second World War was a special epoch (indeed, every decade in the history of capitalism is a special epoch). It was characterized by the rise to dominance of the United States over the free-enterprise world economy, with the cold and hot wars that that entailed. Keynesian doctrines had very little to do with its success, except, first, that the monetary authorities had learned how to prevent a recession in industry from developing into a severe credit crisis, and second, that deficit finance had been made respectable; this was an important contribution to the development of the military-industrial complex, to which President Eisenhower vainly attempted to alert public opinion in America.

The high rate of consumption of natural materials entailed by the growth of industrial production gradually caused demand to overtake supply so that the terms of trade were turned against manufactures. The uneven development of the free-enterprise nations set intolerable strains on the world financial system, and the attempt by Nixon to devalue the dollar in 1971 was a further shock. Trying to counter an incipient recession due to rising costs by cheap money led to a wild inflation in 1973. Then OPEC threw a spanner into the works and the long boom finally collapsed.

Now there is a revulsion against Keynes, and the popular view seems to be that it was really all his fault.

INFLATION

The characteristic of the present slump which makes it markedly different from the slump that Keynes was trying to diagnose in the 1930s, is that it is accompanied everywhere by a greater or less degree of inflation, that is, by world-wide rising price levels. During the long run of high employment, as Keynes predicted, there was a tendency for money-wage rates to rise faster than the general productivity of industry, and so for prices to rise to cover rising costs. This experience led to the concept of a 'pay-off' between unemployment and inflation. Some rather slap-dash historical research produced a statistical 'law' showing an inverse relation between the level of unemployment and the rate of rise of the price level. The concept of a pay-off is typical of the way economists argue from statistics without thinking about human beings. Clearly, the cost of unemployment falls mainly upon workers, while the inconvenience of inflation is felt mainly by the middle class. The economists do not hesitate to tot them up and set one against the other. When the 'law' broke down in the late 1960s, with inflation and unemployment rising together, the economists proclaimed that the terms of the pay-off had shifted, and it was necessary to have more unemployment to keep inflation in check. This is how the matter rests at present.

During the long boom, while 'Keynesian' policies seemed to be working satisfactorily, a dispute developed between two schools of thought as to whether monetary policy, operating through the banking system, was to be preferred to fiscal policy operating through central and local budgets. The prevalence of inflation has given a great boost to the monetarists, who flourish particularly in Chicago, for traditionally inflation was always regarded as a 'monetary' problem. The strong point in their case is that a rise in the value of transactions, due to increased activity at rising prices, generally cannot take place without an increase in the stock of money. The weak point is that for the authorities to prevent the quantity of money from increasing requires a severe credit squeeze, which acts directly upon industry, causing bankruptcies and reducing employment, and only indirectly, if at all, on the level of prices.

The monetarist argument supports the idea of a 'pay-off'. If a high level of unemployment can be maintained for long enough (some say two years, some say five) the rate of inflation will gradually fall until stability is established (does this include the price of oil?). Meanwhile, the stock of industrial equipment would be degenerating for lack of investment and the labour force would be degenerating as juveniles fail to get jobs. But that does not matter. Inflation, to the monetarists, is the worst of all evils and there is no remedy for it but keeping production low.

Business opinion seems rather to favour fiscal policy and hopes for an injection of profits into industry through enlarged expenditure on armaments. In a wider context, it might be argued that this remedy is worse than the disease.

PERMANENT UNEMPLOYMENT

The immediate problem of unemployment is serious enough, but the long-period problem lying behind it is still more menacing. Industrial technology is continually developing and continually reducing the requirement for manual labour. From one point of view, of course, it is a benefit to humanity to reduce the burden of heavy toil, but for the individual, the purpose of work is to earn money and it is no benefit to him to reduce the burden of toil if it reduces the possibility of earning a living at the same time.

It is true that modern technology is very destructive of amenities, including fresh air, but the individual would prefer to earn money in the smog rather than not earn it at all.

No less an authority than Arthur Burns (in *Challenge*, January/February 1976) has pointed out that American industry, at its most flourishing, offers employment to a limited number of highly skilled workers. (He might have added that, when the great corporations do require unskilled labour, they often prefer to get it in South Korea and Taiwan, where wages are lower and trade unions not allowed.) Even if growth could be started up again at the old rate, there is no possibility of reaching full employment in the long-period sense, that the economy provides everyone with the opportunity to support himself without resorting to crime.

The most pertinent question to ask is:

What characteristic of the private enterprise system is it that condemns the wealthiest nation the world has ever seen to keeping an appreciable proportion of its population in perpetual ignorance and misery?

The professional economists keep up a smoke-screen of 'theorems' and 'laws' and 'pay-offs' that prevents questions such as that from being asked. This situation is, I think, inevitable. In every country, educational institutions in general, and universities in particular, are supported directly or indirectly by the established authorities and whether in Chicago or in Moscow, their first duty is to save their pupils from contact with dangerous thoughts.

9

VALUE BEFORE CAPITALISM

1

AT the present time, the most elementary propositions of economic theory are the most in dispute. This is true of Adam Smith's famous statement:

> If among a nation of hunters, for example, it usually costs twice the labour to kill a beaver than it does to kill a deer, the beaver should naturally exchange or be worth two deer. It is natural that what is usually the produce of two day's or two hour's labour, should be worth double of what is usually the produce of one day's or hour's labour. In this state of things, the whole produce of labour belongs to the labourer, and the quantity of labour commonly employed in acquiring or producing any commodity is the only circumstance which can regulate the quantity of labour which it ought commonly to purchase, command or exchange for.[1]

There are two aspects of this proposition. First, in general: 'In the original state of things, which precedes both the appropriation of land and the accumulation of stock, the whole produce of labour belongs to the labourer. He has neither landlord nor master to share with him.[2] Second, in particular, the view that exchange takes place at labour-value prices.

On the first point, we must observe that Adam Smith has chosen a case where the physical inputs required for production are provided by nature – wild game, which is evidently still in plentiful supply. (The labour required to produce arrows or traps is not mentioned.) Therefore, there was no stock of produced means of production and, it appears, no exclusive rights in the use of the terrain. In agriculture, however primitive, there must be some system of property (whether individual or collective) in the right to cultivate land and in the stock required at least to provide seed and subsistence from harvest to harvest. For artisan production, a stock of

[1] *Wealth of Nations* (Everyman Edition), Vol. 1, pp. 41–2.
[2] Ibid., p. 57.

implements is also necessary. There is no economy so simple that it does not require some rules of property, and whatever the accepted rules may be, they have an influence on the distribution of the product among producers.

The second aspect of Adam Smith's proposition concerns exchange. There is no explanation of why the hunters are exchanging their kill. Exchange implies specialization. If the forest is open to all and there is no difference in technique between one line of production and another, each hunter can catch what he wants for himself. The individual hunter might be aware of a subjective cost ratio — deer need less time to catch than beavers; they are cheaper in terms of effort — but there would be no occasion for exchanges to take place.

We might suppose that there are two tribes of hunters each with its own inherited lore, or one may have an accepted right to hunt in the hills and the other in the valley; then, if each consume both commodities, exchanges will take place.

What is the meaning of Adam Smith's contention that the quantity of labour 'is the only circumstance that can regulate' exchange value? Does he mean that this is an accepted rule in the society of hunters or does he mean that it is the only possible explanation for the observing economist?

The first interpretation is the more plausible. The idea of a pre-capitalist world in which 'natural' values ruled is very close to the idea of a 'just price' and, certainly, in any actual primitive society, prices are regulated by rules which reflect what that society considers proper.

But if Adam Smith meant that labour value is the only circumstance that could ever explain prices, he was not correct. When trade is taking place between specialized groups of producers, exchanges (if not regulated by the just price) are governed by the laws of supply and demand. The price ratio then depends upon the quantities produced of the two commodities relatively to the demand for them by the whole population, and it is liable to vary from time to time with changes in the relation of demand to supply.

A Marshallian might try to defend Adam Smith by arguing that, whenever say, the deer-price of a beaver was greater than two, some sons of deer hunters would penetrate into the valley and raise the supply of beavers till price came down to the 'normal' ratio. But Marshall was concerned with a normal rate of profit on capital; the whole point of Adam Smith's story is that there was no capital in the forest.

Marx accepted the doctrine that exchanges at labour values obtained in the pre-capitalist economy — simple commodity production — though he emphasized the various kinds of stock that different lines of production require. The problem of the transformation of labour values into 'prices of production' with a uniform rate of profit on capital is sometimes presented as an arithmetical puzzle, but sometimes the transformation is treated as an historical process. When labour-value prices rule, the potential rate of profit on an investment in a stock of inputs is highest where the value of inputs per man is lowest. When capitalists turned dispossessed artisans into workers – employed at a uniform wage rate – then, if prices of commodities initially remained the same, the rate of profit on the value of inputs in different lines would be highly unequal. A process of competition between capitalists is then supposed gradually to bring the rate of profit to a uniform level, thus transforming labour values into prices of production. This seems excessively fanciful. There is no reason to suppose that there was ever a moment when prices were all proportional to values, still less a time when capitalism had been generally established without any change in prices having occurred. This piece of history is even less plausible than Adam Smith's anthropology.

The concept of labour value prices arose under capitalism, where all kinds of work are reduced to a common measure by wages per man hour. In an artisan economy, each producer has his own skill and his own stock of tools; the 'labour commonly employed in acquiring or producing any commodity' has its own special character; it cannot be reduced to a simple quantity expressed as a number of hours of work.

2

There is an equally basic dispute about the neoclassical concept that the rate of interest is derived from a subjective rate of discount of the future.

Irving Fisher gave the most systematic formalization of this theory.[3] To make the argument simple, he confines it to the case of an expected life time of two periods. The less a man consumes of his income this year, the greater will be his wealth and his income next year. The rate of return on saving is the ratio of the increment of consumption next year to the saving out of potential consumption this year that makes it possible. The man disposes of his consumption between this year and next so as to make his rate of discount of the future (the preference for present consumption at the margin, given his existing stock of wealth) equal to this rate of return.

What are the rules of the game in the economy to which this analysis is to be applied? If we seek to apply it to a modern economy with a gilt-edged rate of interest of, say, ten per cent, expected to remain constant over the

[3] See *The Theory of Interest as Determined by Impatience to Spend Income and Opportunity to Invest*, New York, Macmillan 1930.

relevant period of future time, we might say that any one who is saving evidently discounts the future at less than ten per cent, and anyone who is dissaving, discounts it by more. However, this is a hypothesis which is in principle impossible of verification. It does not add anything at all to the observation that some individuals are saving and others dissaving. Moreover, the argument is derived from the fact that there is a gilt-edged rate of interest with which the supposed subjective discount rate can be compared. It cannot throw any light at all upon what the level of the rate of interest is, or why there is a rate of interest, or how it is related to the rate of return on investment in an industrial economy.

When we put the argument into the setting of an artisan economy, it is less vapid. We might suppose that a village blacksmith can choose to make fewer horseshoes for sale (thus reducing his current consumption) and put time and materials into improving his forge. The return on his saving is then greater productivity per unit of work in the future.

Each artisan is a small classless economy like Robinson Crusoe which, however, may be exchanging products with others.

The blacksmith's motive for saving may depend on whether or not he has more than one son. Let us take a case where the population in the artisan economy is stationary so that an addition to stock, in any family, is an addition to stock per head. Then each family may be supposed to go on accumulating until the increment of output per unit of work due to an addition to their stock does not seem worthwhile. When all families have reached this position, the economy has sunk into a stationary state.

But how much is while worth? There are two difficulties in reducing the return on an increment of stock to a rate of discount. First, the blacksmith does not necessarily have a predetermined income to be divided between consumption and saving. He might make his investment by extra work while keeping his output for sale unchanged. His flow of current income, when he is not investing, consists of two elements, consumption and leisure. How is the sacrifice involved in accumulation to be measured? Secondly, the benefit, in terms of consumption, to be expected from greater productivity with the improved forge, depends very much upon the future price of horseshoes in terms of other commodities, so that the return is a subjective estimate, not a simple rate of discount.

To meet these difficulties the one-commodity world was invented. There, there are no prices, no need for expectations, and saving and investment are physically identical. Moreover, in that story, there is a well-behaved production function which specifies the rate of return on an increment of stock at every ratio of stock to work.

To reduce the commonsense story of the blacksmith to terms of the theory all the common sense has to be refined out of it.

3

A parable offered by Professor Christian von Weizsäcker[4] is intended to illustrate both the principle of labour value prices in a pre-capitalist economy, and the concept of saving limited by impatience for present consumption.

There is a peasant economy (with free land) in which two commodities, wheat and wine, are produced and exchanged. The population is constant. Each wheat-growing family has inherited a stock sufficient for an annual harvest. Wine takes five years to produce: a wine growing family has inherited a stock of maturing wine produced by work put in over the past five years. The economy is in a stationary state; each family is keeping its stock intact, neither saving nor dissaving. Measured in terms of labour embodied, the stock of a wine grower is five times the stock of a wheat grower, but the investment that went into it occurred long ago. At the time that the story is being told, every producer is equally doing a unit of work every year and drawing off a year's net output, to consume or exchange for the other commodity.

Now, the author first postulates that the wheat-price of wine is such that every producer receives the same wheat value of income per year. He argues that this must be so because there is no special know-how required for either line of production and workers are free to move from one to the other. But, in his story, they are not free to move. Each is tethered by the stock that he has inherited. If wine yields a higher income than wheat for a year's work, there is nothing that the wheat-growers can do about it. The concept of stock as a sum of value that can be changed from one form to another by amortization and re-investment belongs to capitalism and has no place in such a model as this.

The economy has reached a stationary state with a particular amount of productive capacity being maintained; the wheat-price of wine must depend either on the community's notion of what is proper or on total demand for the two commodities relatively to the flows of output being produced. Labour value prices might rule, but if so, it would be only by a fluke.

Next, the author introduces 'impatience' into the model. Professor von Weizsäcker defends the Austrian view of capital, but his is not Austrian

[4] 'Morishima on Marx', *Economic Journal*, December 1973.

wine. If the wine were of the Austrian type, it would mature gradually and it would be drinkable after four years, though less agreeable than at five years old. In such a case, impatience might be supposed to lead to drinking four-year old wine, while the reward of patience would be the addition to agreeableness to be got by waiting for another year.

The Austrian fallacy, of course, is to try to derive the interest yielded by the stock of privately owned wealth in a capitalist economy from the *increment* of output due to an *increment* in the stock of means of production.

But this does not arise in Professor von Weizsäcker's story. His wine has to be matured for five years to be drinkable at all. Where then does impatience come in? There is a market in wine of all ages. An individual wine grower, impatient to consume this year more than this year's income, could offer to sell part of his stock of immature wine in exchange for mature wine. But he can do so only if there is a counter-party who is prepared to buy immature wine, so as to carry purchasing power into the future, for instance for old age. The premium on mature wine in terms of immature would be positive or negative according as impatience predominated over prudence or vice versa.

Irving Fisher believed that impatience must predominate because he supposed that the existence of a positive rate of interest is evidence that it does so, but in a modern economy the rate of interest is positive because a business which borrows money can invest in such a way as to make a profit. This does not provide any evidence as to what the rate of interest would be in an economy in which lending and borrowing was only for consumption.

In any case, even if impatience predominates, it could not effect the physical flow of output, which is determined by the stock that is being kept intact in the stationary state.

It seems that Professor von Weizsäcker has cut himself off from deploying the argument he wants to illustrate by putting his economy into a stationary state. He wants to argue that impatience must make the wheat-price of wine higher than it would be at the labour-value ratio. To illustrate this contention we should look at the period when stocks were still being accumulated.

Peasants have taken up residence in an unbounded, uniform fertile plane; each family is free to decide which commodity to produce. But this economy is not like Adam Smith's forest, where nature provides the inputs required for production. Each type of cultivation requires some stock, and wine requires five times as much as wheat. How can the first wine growers live for five years? We might suppose that there is a surplus of wheat available which wine growers can borrow at interest. Then the price of mature wine must exceed its labour value by at least enough to cover interest payments. But this is proto-capitalism, in which property without work is a source of income. Moreover, the cause of borrowing, here, is not impatience but the need to live.

A better case for Professor von Weizsäcker would be to suppose that each family had had to borrow to begin with and that, in the present stationary state, all loans have been paid off long ago out of the proceeds of production in early years. Then wheat growing, which needed a smaller loan and a shorter period of stinting consumption for repayment, would have been initially more eligible than wine.

The stationary state which has now been reached bears the mark of this past history. The stock of wine would have been kept down by it and the wheat-price of wine would be so much the higher. Then we might argue that the expectation of this higher price was what induced some of the peasants, in the first place, to undertake the stinting necessary to build up the stock required for the production of wine. This appears to fit the requirements of Professor von Weizsäcker's argument, but it seems rather artificial to call the excess of a wine grower's income over its labour value an implicit rate of interest on the consumption forgone by his ancestors long ago.

4

The moral of all this is that the labour theory of value does not mean that a man can produce anything with his bare hands. Stock is necessary for production and stock (even when provided by nature) necessarily involves property in some form or other. The rules of the game in respect to property in each type of economy largely determine its mode of operation. It is of no use to erect an argument based on 'human nature' without examining the setting in which it is to apply.

10

GUNNAR MYRDAL

THERE is no doubt that, of all economists alive today, Gunnar Myrdal has made the most important contributions to the subject, but it cannot be said that they have been the most influential, because of the entrenched resistance of the profession to ideas that challenge received orthodoxy. In this volume of collected essays and addresses he records and reflects upon the various phases of a long life's work.

In 1929 Myrdal published *The Political Element in the Development of Economic Theory* in Swedish (A German edition was published in 1932). The English translation, which did not appear until 1935, was reviewed by the *Economist* under the title 'Time Bomb for Welfare Economics'. In that book he showed how the orthodoxy of the day had been evolved in order to glorify the economic system of the day and how the doctrine of 'utility', which logically points to extreme egalitarianism, was twisted into a defence of laisser-faire. He found an explanation in 'the need of the economists to protect themselves from their own radical premises from the era of the Enlightenment'. Nowadays they defend themselves by expressing circular arguments in elaborate mathematics. Myrdal believes that this phase will pass and 'that much that is now hailed as most sophisticated theory will in hindsight be seen to have been a temporary aberration into superficiality and irrelevance'.

In 1931, Myrdal published *Monetary Equilibrium*, which drew out from the heritage of Wicksell the conceptions that became known as the Keynesian Revolution (though here Myrdal's patriotism claims too much). The victory of a theory that demanded Government intervention in a slump was assured by the convergence of all interests behind a policy to increase both employment and profits; but on the present problem of stagflation (a term which Myrdal put afloat) economists are divided and policy is confused because any possible solution involves sharp conflicts of interest.

Partly by good luck and partly by enlightened management, the great slump was quickly overcome in Sweden. Gunnar and his wife Alva devoted

---

A review of *Against the Stream*, by Gunnar Myrdal, Panther Books, 1973.

themselves to problems of social welfare and population. He is a patriot for the achievements of the welfare state in his own country; there is sometimes a hint in his comments on other peoples that if only they would be sensible like the Swedes their problems could easily be solved. In 1938 he began his great study of what was then called the Negro problem in the southern United States. As a citizen of a neutral country he was able to carry on during the war. *The American Dilemma* was published in 1942. It is not primarily a study of the poverty and disenfranchisement of the blacks, though it is a rich source of information on those subjects; it is concerned chiefly with the divided conscience of the whites – the gulf between their actual behaviour and the political tenets that they believe themselves to hold.

Still today: 'The whites continually live in moral confusion. They proclaim ideals that are bluntly disobeyed in their daily life. This is the dilemma'.

This inquiry brought Myrdal to see that the character of economic life depends very much upon what the profession regards as 'non-economic' factors. He tells us that when he first came to the USA in the twenties, it seemed that the 'wind of the future' was institutional economics, in the line of the great Americans, Veblen, Commons and Mitchell. He himself was passionately attached to the 'theoretical' school and played some part in founding the Econometric Society. But when it came to a study of poverty, he realized what was the flaw in traditional teaching – the separation of the problems of production from those of distribution. This

> distinction had been used by economists as a means to escape from the problems of distribution by concentrating on those of production, usually with only a general reservation in regard to distribution, and then thinking about distribution as a simple matter of money incomes. This reflected a bias in economic theory which is still with us, not least in research on underdeveloped countries, implying the view that egalitarian reforms are necessarily costly in terms of economic growth, and very definitely not productive.

To the study of underdevelopment, which has occupied Myrdal for the last twenty years, he brought an acute sense of the hypocrisy, which he politely describes as 'bias', in orthodox opinion.

In the colonial period, the problem of world poverty was simply ignored. Welfare theory and the ideals of egalitarianism applied only at home. The miserable conditions of the mass of the subject peoples was a perfectly acceptable consequence of their natural inferiority. Now there has

been a reversal in fashion; diplomatic language is always used and the
spokesmen of the capitalist world have a vested interest in optimism, for if
'development' is on its way, popular demand for radical reforms can be
held off.

Self-interested optimism is no more helpful than the old attitude of
complacent superiority. It would be better to recognize the great burden
that history and geography has laid on those countries – harsh climate,
overpopulation, a family tradition that favours corruption.

But what is to be done? Myrdal sees problems more clearly than
solutions. In spite of pious sentiments about aiding development, the
policies of the Western countries have been aimed at inhibiting it:

> It is understandable that business interests in the West would be more
> willing to invest in an underdeveloped country where the reins were
> tightly held by an oligarchic regime bent upon preserving the social,
> economic, and political status quo. It was also natural that they
> preferred to deal with the rich and powerful there. Indeed they had to.
> That this, in turn, strengthened these people in their own countries is
> equally self-evident. They are, however, exactly the groups who raise
> the resistance to domestic reforms or see to it that they became
> ineffective or even distorted. The governments in developed countries
> felt inclined to take into account the interests of their business firms
> operating in underdeveloped countries. In their aid policies the
> governments, like business firms, also had to deal with the groups in
> power.
>   . . . Financial and unilateral aid was, and still is, very firmly awarded
> to utterly reactionary regimes.

When he turns to American problems he is no less blunt. After Vietnam,
the American nation needs to go through 'a catharsis in order to be at
peace with itself. . . . To have an "honourable end" to a thoroughly
dishonourable war, implying continued backing of an American puppet
government in Saigon, is not acceptable'.

A genuine 'war on poverty' would be costly and 'the healing process
will take at least a generation even if begun with courage and determination
and pursued persistently' and though it would be a good investment in the
long run, many vested interests are working to prevent the necessary
reforms.

All the same Myrdal's optimism and belief in the power of
enlightenment shines through all his argument. In an address to the youth of
America, after listing the unprecedented dangers facing every country in

'spaceship earth', he concludes with a warning against defeatism. His faith is in our inherited ideals of justice, liberty, equality and brotherhood. His life's work has been to show where they have failed, in the hope of showing how they might succeed.

11

THINKING ABOUT THINKING

My first publication, in 1932, was devoted to the methodology of economics. It was a small pamphlet called *Economics is a Serious Subject*. This was during what Professor Shackle has called the years of high theory[1] when it seemed that 'imperfect competition' was going to revolutionize the analysis of prices and when the discussions that brought Keynes from the *Treatise on Money* to the *General Theory* had already begun.[2]

It seemed, at the time, that economics was emerging from the long sleep of laisser-faire doctrines, 'marginal products' and equilibrium under Say's Law and that it was an important subject, dealing with urgent problems. The title of my essay, however, turned on a pun. It opens as follows:

> The student's heart sinks when he is presented with a book on the Scope and Method of his subject. Let me make a start, he begs, and I will find out the scope and method as I go along. And the student is perfectly right. For a serious subject, in the academic sense, is neither more nor less than its own technique.

I never had the pamphlet reprinted because I soon ceased to believe in its main argument – that if economists could avoid certain bad habits and arrive at a consistent set of assumptions, however abstract, they could approach reality step by step merely by making more complicated models.

I soon realized that to avoid unacceptable methods of argument is a necessary but not a sufficient condition for establishing a genuine discipline. But some of the negative points in the essay still seem to be valid forty years after it was written. One of those points concerns controversy among economists.

> Economic controversies sometimes occur in which one of the contestants is right and the other is wrong. One has made a logical error, and the other has seen it. But this is the rarest kind of controversy. More often, like the two knights in the story, they are fighting about whether a shield is black or white, only to find, after it is

[1] G. L. S. Shackle, *The Years of High Theory*, C.U.P., Cambridge 1967.
[2] See (JMK), Vol. XIII.

all over, that one side was black and the other side white. Now, conducting an economic controversy is a delicate business. It is fatal to be too rude – an interchange of: It's black. No it's not, it's white – never leads to any results. On the other hand it is fatal to be too polite. When you are looking at a black shield, and the other man says it is white, it is of no use to say: Perhaps so, but I think on balance the evidence in favour of its being black is stronger; and then, when he politely replies: But I think it is white, to part from him saying: Of course there is a lot of difference of opinion nowadays, and we each have a right to our own. The proper technique of controversy is to say: That's interesting – what makes you say it is white?

Now when the argument is approached in this spirit the differences, other than logical, boil down to a difference of assumptions. One side of the shield is white, and the other is black, and there is no need to quarrel.

But when the two rival sets of assumptions are examined and compared, the argument can continue in an amicable manner.

Some people consider the style of argument prevalent in Cambridge, England, too rude, but it is aimed at getting points clear. I have suffered far more, especially in the USA, from politeness, being fobbed off with compliments just when I was hoping to clinch an argument.

The children's story of the knights illustrates an important point. When controversies arise through confronting contradictory conclusions, they can easily be resolved by examining the arguments that led to them. Each party should set out clearly the assumptions on which his argument is based; by mutual criticism they can arrive at agreement about what consequences follow from what assumptions and then they can join in an amicable discussion about what evidence must be found to show which set of assumptions (if either) is relevant to the problem in hand.

For this method to be successful, both parties must follow it. An attempt by one party to proceed in this way is frustrated if the other continues to reiterate his conclusions or insists that his own set of assumptions is the only one that can legitimately be made. Unfortunately, the greater part of economic controversies arise from confronting dogmas. The style of argument is that of theology, not of science. This has grown with the growth of a large and flourishing profession, in which jobs depend on supporting opinions acceptable to those in authority.

The concept of a change of paradigm, introduced by T. S. Kuhn,[3] has

---

[3] See *The Structure of Scientific Revolutions.*

become very fashionable among economists. The Keynesian revolution had many features in common with the scientific revolutions that Kuhn describes, but the subsequent development of the subject was not at all like that of any natural science when a shift of paradigm has occurred. In economics, new ideas are treated, in theological style, as heresies and as far as possible kept out of the schools by drilling students in the habit of repeating the old dogmas, so as to prevent established orthodoxy from being undermined.

On the plane of practical affairs, the importance of the Keynesian revolution was to break through the inhibitions of laisser faire and make governments accept, in principle at least, responsibility for maintaining a 'high and stable level of employment'.

On the plane of academic theory, the importance of the Keynesian revolution was to show that all the familiar dogmas are set in a world without time and cannot survive the simple observation that decisions, in economic life, are necessarily taken in the light of uncertain expectations about their future consequences.

Orthodox theory reacted to this challenge, in true theological style, by inventing fanciful worlds in which the difference between the past and the future does not arise and devising intricate mathematical theorems about how an economy would operate if everyone in it had correct foresight about how everybody else was going to behave.

Professor Hahn defends this manoeuvre; he maintains that it is an important achievement to have formulated the orthodox theory 'so sharply as to enable such an unambiguous verdict to be reached' as that it has no practical application.[4] But the labour that has gone into that achievement could have been saved by recognizing that, at any moment in real life when a decision is taken, the past is already irrevocable and the future is still to come.

The Economics of Imperfect Competition, on which I was working with R. F. Kahn in 1932, was pre-Keynesian and it is based on a fudge – confusing comparisons of possible alternative equilibrium positions with the analysis of a process taking place through time. I postulated that every manufacturing firm is faced by a demand curve for its own product, showing how much could be sold at various prices, and that the firm finds out its position and shape by trial and error. For this to be feasible the demand curve would have to remain rigidly fixed for long enough for the firm to discover it, and the experiments of raising and lowering the price to find out the response of sales would have to have negligible cost and no reaction upon the behaviour of the firm's customers.

---

[4] 'The Winter of our Discontent', a review of Janos Kornai, *Anti-Equilibrium, Economica*, August 1973, p. 324, Note the misprint in the last complete line of the page.

Keynes himself fudged his own argument. He defined aggregate supply price as 'the amount of the proceeds which the entrepreneurs expect to receive from the corresponding output' and appended this footnote:

> An entrepreneur, who has to reach a practical decision as to his scale of production, does not, of course, entertain a single undoubting expectation of what the sale-proceeds of a given output will be, but several hypothetical expectations held with varying degrees of probability and definiteness. By his expectation of proceeds I mean, therefore, that expectation of proceeds which, if it were held with certainty, would lead to the same behaviour as does the bundle of vague and more various possibilities which actually makes up his state of expectation when he reaches his decision.

Furthermore he treated long-term expectations in the same way; the 'marginal efficiency of capital' is derived from the profits expected from investment, allowing for risk; the level of investment at any moment is said to be such as to equate the marginal efficiency of capital to the rate of interest (the cost of finance). Interest charges represent an obligation to pay certain definite sums of money. What is said to be equated to the rate of interest is an uncertain expectation of profit. But this statement is vacuous, for it is impossible to separate out the expected rate of profit from the allowance for the degree of uncertainty with which expectations are held. Keynes later denounced the conception that uncertainty in economic affairs can be reduced to calculable risks as one of the 'pretty, polite techniques, made for a well-panelled board room and a nicely regulated market' which 'tries to deal with the present by abstracting from the fact that we know very little about the future.'[5]

This kind of fudging comes from a sort of instinctive self-defence mechanism. At a time of crisis (in Kuhn's sense) there is nothing solid and reliable in traditional theory – everything has to be thought out afresh. No question can properly be asked before every other question has been answered. In pursuing one line of argument, it is necessary to block off others, by fair means or foul, or else no question can ever be posed. I remember pointing out (when I was going through the proofs) that that footnote in the *General Theory* would not do, but Keynes left it unaltered – he could not afford to remove the block that was temporarily providing some space within which he could develop his system.

[5] 'The General Theory of Employment' *Quarterly Journal of Economics*, February 1937, reprinted in (JMK), Vol. XIV.

This, of course, is not a legitimate excuse for fudging; it is a fact about how original work gets done in our ill-disciplined discipline.

The basic fault in the method that I was pursuing in *Imperfect Competition*, and defending in my pamphlet, was to start the argument from a purely *a priori* set of assumptions – the assumptions that Pigou had distilled from Marshall – and then to introduce a minor improvement in them, instead of making a radical critique of the relationship between the traditional assumptions and the actual economy that they pretended to describe. All the same, the work was not wasted because, over the bridge of Kalecki's 'degree of monopoly' it led on to the modern theory of the determination of profit margins and so was linked up with the theory of employment.

My twin, Professor Chamberlin, spent many years protesting that his 'monopolistic competition' was quite different from my 'Imperfect Competition'. (It used to be said at Harvard at one time that any student could be sure of getting a good degree by abusing Mrs. Robinson). This was partly, I think, due to human weakness. We had to share reviews and footnotes that Chamberlin would rather have had to himself. (The fact that I was quite bored with the subject annoyed him all the more.) But there was a deeper reason. I was delighted to find that I had proved (within the accepted assumptions) that it is not true to say that wages equal the marginal productivity of labour, while Chamberlin wanted to maintain that advertisement, salesmanship and monopolistic product differentiation in no way impaired the principle of consumer's sovereignty and the beneficial effect of the free play of market forces.

The one-sided controversy of Chamberlin against Robinson was a bad case of confronting the conclusions of two arguments without examining their assumptions. Where he and I set up the same questions (errors and omissions excepted) we found the same answers and where the questions were different, the answers were too. In some respects Chamberlin's assumptions were more realistic than mine, though he did not want to draw realistic conclusions from them.

Nowadays we have both been swept aside in the revival of neoclassical orthodoxy which cannot admit any realism at all.

Keynes had to break out of the orthodoxy in which he had been brought up because he was considering a real problem – the causes of unemployment in an industrial economy – and he had to examine how the economy really works. Even in the well-disciplined natural sciences, it is recognized that an original idea comes in the first place by a flash of intuition. Keynes certainly was an intuitive thinker. In a serious subject, intuition must play over reality and draw hypotheses from it, to be worked over consciously and critically to see if reality does not reject them. Originality means discovery, not invention. It is not like designing an elegant façade for a new building but like exploring an old ruin and trying to make out what its ground-plan must have been.

Because Keynes was trying to understand how the economy works, he was unwittingly following the line of Ricardo and Marx, who were engaged in the same quest, each trying to understand the operation of capitalism in his own day. Keynes was clearing up a particular element in it (effective demand) that Ricardo had ignored and Marx imperfectly understood. This explains the apparent paradox that the post-Keynesians in Cambridge find an affinity with the classics.

Jevons declared: 'That able but wrong-headed man David Ricardo shunted the car of economic science onto the wrong track'. In fact Jevons himself shunted the train onto a loop line round which it still circulates, but Keynes and Kalecki managed to detach a few coaches and got them back on to the main track.

I had a very literary education and to this day I know only the mathematics that I was able to pick up in the course of trying to formalize economic arguments, but it seemed to me obvious that a quantity that is to be manipulated by the methods of applied mathematics must be specified as a number of some unit, and that the very definition of a unit implies its method of measurement.

I was quite naïve when I wrote my pamphlet. I thought that this fact had only to be mentioned to receive universal recognition.

I observed that, to make economics into a serious subject it was necessary to

> continue the labour of removing out of the tool-box of the analysts all tools which appear to involve conceptions that are not capable of measurement. If any reader of this essay practises any other serious subject, I must pause to explain why this is still necessary. Economists are subject to many vices, and one of them has been to talk about 'utility', which is a quantitative conception that there is no known way of measuring. Such a scandal must be frankly admitted. For confession and penitence must precede the recognition of economics as a serious subject.

Not all economic concepts can be reduced to strictly quantitative terms. To treat something that is in principle unmeasureable as though it were a quantity is a confusion of thought pretending to be scientifically precise.

Twenty years later when I made a similar point about the meaning of a 'quantity of capital', I was still naïve. I really thought that if I asked a reasonable question I ought to get a reasonable answer. I was quite surprised at the rage and indignation that my question aroused. 'Everyone except Joan Robinson knows perfectly well what capital means.' It became quite a joke in the profession. I once happened to hear a tape of a meeting at which a speaker was saying 'As Mrs. Robinson is not in the room, I suppose you do not object to my talking about capital.'

I only recently discovered that Thorstein Veblen had made my point, much better than I did, in 1908.

> Much is made of the doctrine that the two facts of 'capital' and 'capital goods' are conceptually distinct, though substantially identical. The two terms cover virtually the same facts as would be covered by the terms 'pecuniary capital' [finance] and 'instrumental equipment'.
>
> . . .
>
> The continuum in which the 'abiding entity' of capital resides is a continuity of ownership, not a physical fact. The continuity, in fact, is of an immaterial nature, a matter of legal rights, of contract, of purchase and sale. Just why this patent state of the case is overlooked, as it somewhat elaborately is, is not easily seen.[6]

In the natural sciences, controversies are settled in a few months, or at a time of crisis, in a year or two, but in the social so-called sciences, absurd misunderstanding can continue for sixty or a hundred years without being cleared up.

The cause of this difference, of course, lies in the difference of methods. My saying: 'A serious subject is neither more nor less than its own technique' was a half truth, but it is the important half. In the natural sciences, experiments can be repeated and observations checked so that a false hypothesis is quickly knocked out. I agree with Kuhn's view of science as a particular kind of social activity which is carried on for its own sake, with a particular set of accepted rules. That it enables us to understand an aspect of the universe is, so to speak, an accidental by-product of this activity. Economics is also a social activity but its rules are such that its by-products are much less impressive.

The modern style of so-called mathematical economics came into fashion after the period when my pamphlet was written. Mathematical

[6] 'Professor Clark's Economics', reprinted in *The Place of Science in Modern Civilization*, pp. 195–7.

logic is a powerful tool of thought, but its application in economic theory generally seems to consist merely of putting circular arguments into algebra. Mathematical theory of statistics, also, was developing fast. At first there were high hopes that observations of reality by the method of econometrics would produce truly scientific results.

Since I have confessed that I am no mathematician, my views on this subject might be thought to be those of the fox who had lost his tail, but that reproach could not be made to Norbert Wiener.[7]

> An econometrician will develop an elaborate and ingenious theory of demand and supply, inventories and unemployment, and the like, with a relative or total indifference to the methods by which these elusive quantities are observed or measured. Their quantitative theories are treated with the unquestioning respect with which the physicists of a less sophisticated age treated the concepts of the Newtonian physics. Very few econometricians are aware that if they are to imitate the procedure of modern physics and not its mere appearances, a mathematical economics must begin with a critical account of these quantitative notions and the means adopted for collecting and measuring them.

He continues: 'Difficult as it is to collect good physical data, it is far more difficult to collect long runs of economic or social data so that the whole of the run shall have a uniform significance.' This means that an attempt to test hypotheses by data in the form of time series is posing two questions at once – whether the forces at work were correctly diagnosed for one period and whether they have remained the same over subsequent periods. When there are elements in the forces involved such as the militancy of trade unions or the effect of advertising on household expenditure, this difficulty appears to be insuperable.

Keynes' review of Tinbergen[8] pouring cold water on the pretentions of econometrics caused a great deal of offence but it seems to have turned out in the main to have been correct. Ragnar Frisch, himself a great practitioner, has sadly remarked that most of the work done in this field has been playometrics not econometrics.[9] Only for a few narrow and tightly specified questions has the method turned out to be fruitful.

Yet there have been some notable cases where hypotheses drawn from

---

[7] See *God and Golem*, cf. p. 4 above, note.

[8] (JMK), Vol. XIV.

[9] 'Econometrics in the world today' in *Essays in honour of Sir Roy Harrod*, ed. Eltis, Oxford 1970.

economic analysis have been broadly vindicated. Keynes in 1925 predicted that the return to the gold standard at an overvalued sterling exchange rate would be followed by a period of pressure to reduce wages which would be bitterly resisted. (In 1926 there was a general strike.)

In 1931, he pointed out that falling prices were putting a great strain on the banks. (In March 1933 the banking system in the USA came to a standstill.) In 1936 (following Keynes) I observed that a period of continuous near-full employment would lead to continuous inflation; and (most remarkable of all) Kalecki predicted in 1944 that after the war we should be living under the regime of a political trade cycle (stop-go). These predictions were not at all exact; they were not derived from studying time series, but from a diagnosis of how the contemporary economic system operated. It seems as though what success economics has had depends more upon insight than upon precision and that its affinity must be with history as much as with mathematics.

History can never give a final knockdown answer to any question. Each generation rewrites its own past in accord with its current ideology. Certainly, economics can never escape from ideology. In every human activity or line of inquiry there is always a right and a left, orthodox and radical views, defence of the status quo and demand for change. This is true even of the natural sciences at a time of crisis. As long as I have known economics, it has always been in crisis.

At the present time [1970], it seems that the neo-neoclassical orthodoxy is quite discredited but I do not think that the swing of opinion against it owes so much to the exposure of its logical defects by Gunnar Myrdal, Maurice Dobb and Piero Sraffa as to the revolt of the young generation against an unjust society that began with the Civil Rights Campaign in the USA. Myrdal and Dobb have been available for thirty or forty years and no one would have understood Sraffa who was not in revolt already.

Then, the question may be raised: if the choice between one theory and another is always made by their ideological colour, not their logic, why is a reasonable theory any more use than a spurious one? Is there any point, after all, in trying to make economics into a serious subject?

At the present time, there are a great many radicals who seem to feel that any argument is justified by being anti-neoclassical no matter whether or not it is internally coherent or in accord with evidence.

I believe, however, that there is a lot of difference between good analysis and bad, apart from ideological tendencies. Logic is the same for everyone (though I could never get Professor Solow to admit it) and the reading of evidence, though always biassed to some extent, can be more or less fair. I do not think it was a waste of time to try to understand the great slump, post-war growth and the present crisis and, for understanding, an adequate system of analysis is indispensable. It was not a waste of time, either, to try to examine the neo-neoclassicals to find out why their logic is at fault, as well as their opinions.

It is often said that one theory can be driven out only by another; the neoclassicals have a complete theory (though I maintain that it is nothing but a circular argument) and we need a better theory to supplant them. I do not agree. I think any other 'complete theory' would be only another box of tricks. What we need is a different habit of mind – to eschew fudging, to respect facts and to admit ignorance of what we do not know.

Honesty and hard work are required of radicals, while the orthodox can doze over their dogmas. But I do not think that radicals need fear that they will have to sacrifice their convictions in order to make economics a serious subject. My old saying about technique was a half truth. The other half concerns the subject to which technique is to be applied. I believe that the proper subject matter of economics is an examination of the manner of operation of various economic systems, particularly our own, and as long as our economy system continues to survive, a clear-sighted examination of it is more likely to favour radical views than to support the defenders of the status quo.

12

THE AGE OF GROWTH

THE slump from which we are told the United States economy is now recovering has been an extremely important event. It was the first serious recession since World War II. It brought to an end the epoch in which continuous steady growth in the industrial economies was generally taken for granted. Certainly, there were quite sharp setbacks, particularly in 1958 and 1966, but the very fact that they were overcome maintained confidence that a real recession was a thing of the past.

It was believed that this was a new era in which government policy could be relied upon to control the levers of economic activity. The spokesmen for capitalism were saying, in effect: we have to admit that the unemployment that prevailed in the interwar years was a serious defect in the free-market system. Now we are going to give you capitalism with full employment, so what have you got to complain of?

Indeed, capitalism without a serious slump for 25 years was something new in history. In Western Europe and in Japan, statistical GNP per capita had been growing for a long run of years at never less than 4 per cent per annum. In North America growth was only at 2·5 per cent, but starting from a higher base, the great mass of consumption grew prodigiously, though poverty, which is largely relative was not much reduced.

High consumption struck a blow in the cold war. When tourists from the affluent countries began to pass through the ex-iron curtain, they naturally came from the affluent classes; the slum dwellers stayed at home. The display of the tourists' possessions was quite a shock in the socialist world, creating envy and discontent.

Experience of *almost* continuous prosperity built up a belief in perpetual growth as a normal state of affairs.

It is for this reason that the slump from which we are now assumed to be recovering was a unique event. It has been a very great shock, all the more because recession was accompanied by rising prices, so that all the old rules fail to hold – inflation no longer makes profits buoyant and rising unemployment no longer keeps inflation in check.

The Gildersleeve Lecture delivered at Barnard College, 2 March 1976.

BASTARD KEYNESIANISM

The doctrines of the new era have been attributed to Keynes, but the dominant economic theory of the time, in North America and spreading from there over the world, was what I have called the bastard Keynesian doctrine. I do not use this term just as abuse. It has a definite meaning. The old orthodoxy, against which the Keynesian revolution was raised, was based on Say's law – there cannot be a deficiency of demand. Spending creates demand for consumption goods, while saving creates demand for investment goods such as machinery and stocks. Keynes pointed out the obvious fact that investment is governed by the decisions of business corporations and public institutions, not by the desire of the community to save.

An increase in household saving means a reduction in consumption; it does not increase investment but reduces employment.

According to the bastard Keynesian doctrine, it is possible to calculate the rate of saving that households collectively desire to achieve, and then governments, by fiscal and monetary policy, can organize the investment of this amount of saving. Thus Say's law is artificially restored, and under its shelter all the old doctrines creep back again, even the doctrine that any given stock of capital will provide employment for any amount of labour at the appropriate equilibrium real-wage rate. Then unemployment occurs only because wages are being held above the equilibrium level.

Keynes, and Kalecki, who found out the same theory independently, were diagnosing an inherent defect in the laisser-faire system but the bastard Keynesians turned the argument back into being a defence of laisser-faire, provided that just one blemish was going to be removed.

The complacency of the age of growth covered what, in the legal phrase, can be called *inherent vice* in the free-market system. The present situation was quite unexpected. Economists lost track of their formulae and the politicians got their slogans mixed up.

First consider inflation. A major point in the theory of Keynes and Kalecki is that the general level of prices in an industrial economy depends mainly upon the level of money-wage rates. The Keynesian revolution began by refuting the then orthodox theory that cutting wages is the best way to increase employment. Keynes argued that a general cut in wages would reduce the price level more or less proportionally, so raise the burden of debt, discourage investment, and increase unemployment. Kalecki added that if prices do not fall, it is still worse, for then real wages are reduced and unemployment is increased directly by the fall in purchases of consumption goods.

Such arguments obviously cut both ways. If falling money wages reduce prices, rising money wages must increase them.

Keynes expected that a long run of high employment and high profits would lead to continuously rising prices though he did not suggest what to do about it. Any rise of prices leads to a demand for a compensating rise in wages and every rise in wages leads to rising prices again.

Professor Weintraub and his disciples drew this moral from Keynes' theory, but the bastard Keynesians somehow managed to sweep it under the carpet.

It is sometimes said that the trouble arises from monopoly. But according to the textbook theory competitive prices are governed by marginal costs. A rise in wage rates raises marginal costs for a whole group of competitors and prices go up proportionately.

But of course perfect competition never did exist except in the textbooks, and a growth of huge monopolistic corporations is a necessary consequence of competitive growth in a long run of prosperity.

THE CLASS WAR AND INFLATION

The trouble does not lie in monopoly but in the class war – workers must struggle to keep their share in the product of industry and corporations must struggle to prevent them from increasing it.

There is not only a class war between employers and workers as a whole. There is an internal struggle of each group to maintain its relative position. Looking back now, after experience of inflation at 20 per cent per annum, anything less than 5 per cent seems moderate and acceptable. But even 3 and 4 per cent, year after year, was a great nuisance.

Expectations of 3 per cent were quite enough to set going speculative booms in property of every kind, causing huge arbitrary redistributions of wealth and falsification of values. There was a joke after a sudden dip in the art market. One dealer was saying to another: Do you think we could get them to buy paintings because they *like* them?

The long run of what now seems mild inflation gave rise to the cynical doctrine that the private enterprise economy *needs* unemployment to preserve the value of money. The spokesmen of capitalism were saying: Sorry, chaps, we made a mistake. We are not offering full employment, but the natural level of unemployment.

Of course, they suggested that a *little* unemployment would be enough to keep prices stable, but now we know that even a lot will not do so.

Inflation at 3 or 4 per cent was quite enough to set going the struggle for relative shares and to break through the solid belief that a dollar is a dollar. Resistances and conventions were progressively undermined so that any chance shock would set the vicious spiral spinning in earnest.

The shock came from the other part of the price system. The price level in the market economy is in two parts – the cost-plus system in the industrial sector and the supply and demand system in the markets for primary commodities. A sharp rise in activity in the industrial sector raises the prices of raw materials, puts up the cost of manufactures relative to money-wage rates and so sets up a demand to raise wages in turn.

Even before OPEC threw a spanner into the works, a sharp rise in material prices had occurred. This was the spark that fell upon the inflationary tinder that had been accumulating over the years. It was bound to happen sooner or later. For my part, I was surprised that the era of mild inflation (which survived the Korean war boom) could last for so long, not that it finally gave way.

Now that this element of inherent vice in the free-market system has broken out in a virulent form, it is not easy to see any way to return to the era of continuous growth with an 'acceptable' level of inflation.

THE POLITICAL TRADE CYCLE

The next point to observe is that so-called Keynesian policy was not really applied in such a way as to maintain stability. It turned out to be very much like the political trade cycle predicted by Kalecki. A continuous high level of employment is not acceptable to the leaders of industry. It is true that it is accompanied by high profits, but it weakens their position in the class war. As Kalecki remarked, ' "discipline in the factories" and "political stability" are more appreciated by business leaders than profits,' though, of course they require profits as well.

Near-full employment can be established by means of a government deficit, but if it goes on too long the captains of industry fear that the workers will get out of hand and want to 'teach them a lesson'. Rentier interests grow tired of a boom that generates inflation, and, as Kalecki presciently observed, more than one economist will be found to say that the situation is manifestly unsound. Then government outlay is cut, dear money imposed, and unemployment emerges again. But after a year or two it is time for the next election. No government wants to go into an election with too much unemployment. The tap is turned on again and employment and profits revive.

A particular feature of the political trade cycle as it is played out in the

United States is that when a political boom is required, it is arms expenditures that expand; when a political recession is required, it is social services that are cut.

One of the contributing factors to the outbreak of inflation in 1973 is that both Mr. Heath in Great Britain and Mr. Nixon in the USA were playing up for a political boom in 1972 with exceptional vigour.

Another Keynesian diagnosis of instability has been developed by Professor Minsky. He maintains that a capitalist economy in general, and in the USA in particular, is inherently incapable of steady growth. When investment is increasing from year to year, the flow of profits is increasing and providing finance to maintain the growth of investment. Then good prospects of profit lead corporations to increase their investment plans beyond their capacity for self-finance, and raise their leverage. The more cautious hold back at first, but when they see that the daring ones are successful they are led to follow suit. Now the ratio of payments required to service debt is continually rising relative to the flow of actual cash receipts. Sooner or later some industrial businesses have to curtail their investment or financial business to sell out assets. With the indebtedness that has grown up, the system is vulnerable, and any check to expansion sets the dominoes of credit falling; the search for liquidity spreads from one business to another and a real slump grows out of the financial crisis.

The Minsky thesis and the Kalecki thesis are not mutually exclusive. Rather, the expansion and collapse of credit act as an amplifier of the political cycle, bringing an undesigned, exaggerated reaction to a political stop and preventing a political go from sustaining itself.

Minsky also has a more long-run diagnosis of recent history: when the war ended, both the industrial and the financial systems had a fat hump of liquidity, which was gradually eaten up in successive financial crises and is now pretty well exhausted. Moreover, the very fact that the authorities would never allow a financial crisis to go too far meant that a residue of debt was left each time so that a robust state of liquidity was never restored.

Nowadays, it seems that even the political trade cycle has come to an end, and the governments of all the capitalist nations are stuck in immobility, dithering between the fear of inflation and the fear of unemployment.

Where Do We Go From Here?

An American economist might very well reproach me: You call me a bastard, but what would *you* do? I could only answer with the quip about the motorist who asked the way to Oklahoma. The man by the roadside answered: If I wanted to go to Oklahoma I should never start here.

The problem has developed far beyond the point where it makes sense to discuss any simple remedies. Keynes himself did not propose *simple* remedies. It was the bastard Keynesians who concocted bromides from his acid treatment of orthodox nonsense. Now the old guard, who stood out against him in the thirties, are saying Keynes has failed. We must return to strict laisser-faire and sound finance. If you are uncomfortable in the frying pan you can jump into the fire.

In the famous last chapter of the *General Theory*, Keynes describes his political philosophy as 'moderately conservative'. This was offered as a paradox. All his life he had been treated by the establishment as an *enfant terrible*, so that to present himself as a conservative was partly ironical. Moreover, the preceding chapters of the book were a powerful polemic against received ideas. It was because Keynes was shocked by the force of his own indictment of capitalism that he wrote the last chapter in a mollifying tone.

On inflation, he agreed with my deduction from the *General Theory* that rising prices would prove to be the great unsolved problem of full-employment policy. When money-wage rates do not rise as fast as productivity, the market economy falls into stagnation through sluggish demand, but when the bargaining power of organized labour is sufficient to keep wages rising enough, it will generally raise them too much to maintain stable prices. Keynes regarded this as a political problem which, when he died, still lay in the future.

Kalecki took a more radical view:

> 'Full employment capitalism' will have, of course, to develop new social and political institutions which will reflect the increased power of the working class. If capitalism can adjust itself to full employment a fundamental reform will have been incorporated in it. If not, it will show itself an outmoded system which must be scrapped.

It is precisely because such changes in social and political institutions did not occur that the age of growth has been so uneasy and is now in danger of bringing itself to an end.

In Great Britain, the trade unions were in a strong position while employment was high but they did not want to ask for the kinds of changes that Kalecki recommended. They only asked for freedom in wage bargaining. However, inflation rising to a rate of 25 per cent per annum has been a great shock and the trade unionists found that they were alienating all the rest of the population, including their own wives. Now they are willing to discuss the possibility of restraining wages and asking for other concessions in return.

But there are great difficulties in the way of a thoroughgoing incomes policy. We are told that if the higher salaries are cut the 'best brains' in the country will be drained to the United States. I wish you joy of them.

In Western Europe, particularly in France, there are interesting experiments that have been going on. But in the USA an important new development during the age of growth is not at all favourable to labour's side in the class war. Here, business has always been able to play divide and rule with the work force at home – setting 'WASPs' against blacks and immigrants. Now that game is being played overseas as well. The diligent, dextrous workers of East Asia can be got at a cut price to make components for the sophisticated products of modern industry.

Uneven Growth

Another serious element of inherent vice in the age of growth was the unevenness of development of various capitalist nations. Differences in competitive power, whatever their origin, set up a spiral of divergence. A country such as West Germany, with growing exports, can maintain a high rate of investment and therefore of growing productivity which enhances its competitive power, and causes real wages to rise so that workers are less demanding; in the miserable United Kingdom, an increase in employment causes an increase in the deficit in the balance of payments so that every *go* has to be brought to an end with a *stop*. Thus strong competitors grow stronger so that the weak grow weaker.

Because of its mere size, the United States' overseas trade plays a small part in national income, but not a small part in the world market. It can move from deficit to surplus without much disturbance at home but with a great deal of disturbance to the other trading nations.

These disequilibria have set great strains on the international monetary system. According to the old rules of the gold-standard game, a deficit country could borrow to develop a source of exports that would service its debt; a lender could support a net outflow of capital no greater than its surplus on income account. Now, the UK has to go on borrowing because to cut imports would be an injury to foreign exporters. The USA was able to take advantage of the dollar being the world currency to run an ever greater outflow on capital account with an ever growing deficit on income account, until President Nixon suddenly tried to reverse the position by decree. A contributory cause to the great inflation was that the devaluation of the dollar in 1971 sent funds in search of liquidity to speculation in commodities and helped to drive up their prices.

Now it seems that gold after all is going to come back into the game, but lumps of metal will not establish rules of play that can bring modern chaos in the international money market into working order.

I said that the great rise in material prices was already under way before the 'oil crisis'. Certainly the sudden rise in the price of a commodity in inelastic demand helped to precipitate the recession. In the United States, the rise in consumers' expenditure on petrol, reflected in the large profits of the oil companies in 1973, was drawing purchasing power away from other goods and services. But I do not support the view that the change in the balance of monopoly power in the world market is a serious menace to the capitalist system. Modern capitalism suffers chronically from deficiency of demand. It can easily stand a depreciation in terms of trade. Expenditure of the oil money is useful to capitalist industry, especially the arms industry, and is one of the elements in the present recovery from the slump.

There used to be an old Soviet joke which today has rather a sour taste:

Q: What is the greatest problem facing the President of the United States?

A: Is it possible to have capitalism in one country?

I believe the oil sheiks are a great help to the United States in spreading capitalism hand over fist.

INVESTMENT AND SOCIAL CONTROL

The oldest element of inherent vice in the private enterprise system is still the most important, that is, the anarchy of unplanned growth. Keynes's last chapter was not so conservative after all, for he thought that it would be necessary to have a comprehensive social control of investment to overcome the short-period instability of capitalism. Its absence is even more serious in the long run. The textbooks teach us that in the free market economy demand 'allocates scarce means between alternative uses'. How are investible resources allocated?

Here, unfortunately, Keynes made an ill-considered remark, quite contrary to his main argument. He suggested that, provided governments make sure that there is enough investment to maintain full employment, 'the classical theory comes into its own again, from this point on'. Provided only that there is enough production, 'there is no objection to be raised against the classical analysis' of the determination of what in particular is to be produced and how the factors of production are allocated between different uses.

Here is the bastard Keynesian theory in its purest form.

But what does it mean? What theory has ever been advanced of how private self-interest directs *new* investment into the lines that best provide for the needs and desires of society as a whole?

It is true that there is nowadays a great deal of public support for certain lines of research and development. But whose needs is it designed to meet? Big money leads to an alliance of big science and big industry, which results in technological megalomania rather than a careful study of human needs. I will not be so unpatriotic as to refer to Concorde, or so ungracious as to remark that putting a man on the moon did nothing to make the earth more habitable. But I must add my voice to the protest that the great concentration upon atomic energy, not only here but in the Third World is largely due to the snobbery of being 'advanced', which attracts the scientists away from the search for safer, less costly, and so less glamorous ways of economizing and generating power.

In the sectors which are left to private enterprise, the great corporations, pursuing hoped-for profits, choose what lines to develop, and how the population is to be employed. A community grows up around the site where some corporation has found it convenient to install a plant, and is devastated when the corporation finds it convenient to shut the plant down.

As for the sovereignty of choice of the consumers, it rules only so long as they all choose the same thing. When a supermarket has killed off the neighbourhood shops, an individual housewife who regrets them cannot *reveal* her *preference* for buying from them any more.

The leading case of the dominance of production over consumers' tastes is, of course, the motor car. By taking away demand from public transport, raising its costs, and finally making it unable to exist, the motor-car industry increases its own market, until everyone who is not destitute is obliged to run a car, and those who are destitute have to stay at home.

Then television creates a whole new style of social life, and electronics, it seems, is creating a new style of politics.

Is all this what the free individual consumer chooses, or what he has been trapped into thinking that he needs?

The bastard Keynesian theory never even pretended to discuss the use of resources. It fell back upon the old defence of laisser-faire: what is profitable is right. The most remarkable application of this doctrine is now to the problem of pollution. The argument is that antipollution rules are hampering investment and reducing profits. Pollution should be allowed a little longer, so as to help recovery from the slump. Amenities and health have to be sacrificed to profits, because if we hinder the freedom of the corporations to employ the resources of the nation as they choose, they will not be able to employ them at all.

The workers in each industry line up with their employers. They do not *want* their children to be poisoned, but they are more anxious about losing their jobs.

Similarly with the problem of exhaustible resources. The great corporations must be allowed to go on chewing up the planet, else they will not be able to make profits and provide employment.

Now we are stuck with it. We must keep the show going. Private enterprise is wonderfully flexible in jumping from one profitable market to another, but it is very rigid in resistance to social control. Now that the authorities want employment to revive, they can only push industry further down the grooves that it has worn for itself. There is no point in thinking of what we really want, such as abolishing poverty and restoring peace. All we can ask for is what they choose to give us. We must keep the show going or else they won't give us anything at all.

13

REFLECTIONS ON THE
THEORY OF INTERNATIONAL TRADE

THE propositions which are taught as the orthodox theory of international trade are founded on the case which Ricardo made against protection. The development of the theory, to this day, runs in the narrow channel that was appropriate to Ricardo's demonstration of the principle of comparative advantage.

Models are usually set up in terms of two countries producing two commodities. Each commodity can be produced in both countries. This is an essential feature of the case for free trade. There is no need to argue against protection for a commodity which is useful and which cannot be produced at home. Professor Samuelson considered it fatuous to say 'the tropics grow tropical fruits because of the relative abundance there of tropical conditions'.[1] Trade theory applies only where potential imports and home-produced goods are alike.

This rules out the whole of what Adam Smith regarded as the main sphere of trade – exchanges between town and country, that is, between manufactures and primary products. (Modern exponents of free-trade theory do not hestitate to apply its dogmas to producers of primary products, but in fact it has nothing to do with their problems.)

Furthermore, the models imply trade between countries of equal weight and at the same level of development. This rules out imperialism and the use of power to foster economic advantage. In Ricardo's example, Portugal was to gain as much from exporting wine as England from exporting cloth, but in real life Portugal was dependent on British naval support, and it was for this reason that she was obliged to accept conditions of trade which wiped

---

[1] 'International trade and the equalisation of factor price', *Economic Journal*, June 1948, p. 182.

Lectures given at the University of Manchester, University of Manchester Press, 1974.

out her production of textiles and inhibited industrial development, so as to make her more dependent than ever.[2]

The British cotton industry grew up under protection from superior Indian imports. When it was sufficiently developed, free trade was imposed on India, but now that Indian textiles can once more undersell Lancashire, the British turn to protection again.

But let us leave these large questions aside and examine the 'pure theory' in its own terms.

1

PRICES OF COMMODITIES

Ricardo's argument is set out in the famous numerical example:

> England may be so circumstanced, that to produce the cloth may require the labour of 100 men for one year; and if she attempted to make the wine, it might require the labour of 120 men for the same time. England would therefore find it her interest to import wine, and to purchase it by the exportation of cloth. To produce the wine in Portugal, might require only the labour of 80 men for one year, and to produce the cloth in the same country, might require the labour of 90 men for the same time. It would therefore be advantageous for her to export wine in exchange for cloth. This exchange might even take place, notwithstanding that the commodity imported by Portugal could be produced there with less labour than in England. Though she could make the cloth with the labour of 90 men, she would import it from a country where it required the labour of 100 men to produce it, because it would be advantageous to her to employ her capital in the production of wine, for which she would obtain more cloth from England, than she could produce by diverting a portion of her capital from the cultivation of vines to the manufacture of cloth.
>
> Thus England would give the produce of the labour of 100 men, for the produce of the labour of 80 men.[3]

There are a number of points on which Ricardo's system is much easier to grasp than any that have followed – in particular, the determination of relative prices of commodities – though, as we shall find, his system is not complete.

[2] Cf. S. Sideri, *Trade and Power: Informal Colonialism in Anglo-Portuguese Relations*, Rotterdam, 1970.

[3] *Works and Correspondence of David Ricardo*, ed. Sraffa and Dobb, C.U.P., Vol. 1, p. 135.

Labour Value. Ricardo conducts his argument in terms of labour costs; in the example, he gives the numbers of men required to produce a unit of each commodity in each country. 'Constant returns' prevail in each industry in both countries. Although wine is used as an example, there are no scarce natural resources involved. The wage rate in terms of commodities is fixed in each country, and there is a uniform rate of profit on capital within each country.

Ricardo's theory of profits was not well understood until Piero Sraffa disinterred the simple 'corn' model from the complications with which it was overlaid in the course of Ricardo's search for an invariable standard of value.[4] When corn is the only wage good, and the corn-wage rate is given, the rate of profit on capital is determined by the technical conditions of production of corn. Output per man on marginal, no-rent land is a particular quantity of corn per annum; given the wage, the profit on employing a man is a particular quantity of corn. The investment required to employ a man is a quantity of corn in the barn after one harvest, sufficient to pay out the wage until the next harvest, along with the seed that is to be planted by a man (no other inputs are required). Then the corn profit per man over the corn invested per man is the annual rate of profit on capital.

Ricardo himself never quite succeeded in reformulating his theory of profits when the real wage consists of a number of different commodities, produced by various techniques, but we know from Sraffa and von Neumann that there is no difficulty in doing so. So long as the technique of production and the physical composition of the wage are given, there is one set of prices that will yield a uniform rate of profit on the value (at those prices) of the capital required in each industry.

Ricardo's example entails that prices, without trade, are proportional to labour values in each country. This implies that the technical requirements for inputs and the time patterns of production are such that, when there is a uniform level of wages and rate of profit in a country, the ratio of the value of capital to labour employed, and so the ratio of profits to wages, is the same for both commodities. Then the value of output per man, in any numeraire, is the same in both lines of production.

This is a convenient simplification. There is no particular presumption that the ratios of profits to wages should differ between commodities, in either country, one way or the other, and, if they did, it would mean only that the numerical examples would have to be somewhat more complicated.

Gains from trade. In Ricardo's example, output per man in Portugal is higher

[4] Ibid., Introduction.

than in England for both commodities. Presumably he set the example up this way in order to make it as striking as possible and in order to short-circuit the popular argument in favour of protecting home industry against low-cost imports.

But, properly speaking, the comparison in terms of 'men' is not relevant to the argument. A man may be an international unit in a moral sense, but, in strictly economic terms, a 'man' is not an international unit. The personal qualities of men of different countries may be different, and in any case climate, natural resources, the level of technology and the stock of equipment differ from one country to another. There is no meaning, in this context, in a direct comparison of output per man between countries. Indeed, this is really the point that Ricardo is making. His argument is that the benefit from trade springs from differences in the comparative advantages in the production of particular commodites within each country and has nothing to do with an absolute comparison between them.

Output per Portuguese man is higher than per Englishman, but the rate of profit on capital is not necessarily higher in Portugal than in England (though Ricardo seems to suggest that profits abroad are higher than in England).[5] The real wage per Portuguese man might be higher in a greater ratio than output, or some ingredient of the real wage in Portugal that does not enter into trade might have a higher cost in terms of Portuguese labour than that of the English real wage in terms of English labour, so that the rate of profit on capital in Portugal would be lower than in England. The rate of profit in each country is determined by its own technical conditions and its own real-wage rate; either one may be higher than the other, or by a fluke they might be equal.

Ricardo takes it for granted that there is no impediment to an industry either expanding or shrinking. England has an advantage in producing cloth compared to wine, and Portugal an advantage in producing wine. Each gains when trade increases (say, because import duties are abolished) by expanding the industry in which it has a comparative advantage and allowing the other commodity to be imported instead of producing it at home.

Nothing is said about difficulties or perturbations in making such a change. The argument is set out in terms of static comparisons of equilibrium positions. There is no account of a process of adjustment. However, since the position with free trade is later in time than the position with protection, we follow the convention of speaking of a *movement* from one to the other.

[5] Cf. below, p. 138.

For each commodity 'constant returns' prevail, so that costs are not affected by changes in the composition of output.

How does free trade influence outputs and prices? We can follow the logic of Ricardo's example, though he does not go into any detail himself. If the wine-price of cloth in the world market were the same as the ratio of costs in England, the wine-value of the output of cloth produced by an Englishman would be equal to the quantity of wine produced by an Englishman. There would be no inducement to move resources from one line to the other. Similarly if prices conformed to the cost ratio in Portugal.

To generate trade, the price ratio in the market must be, initially, somewhere between the cost ratios. Then the wine-price of cloth is higher in England and lower in Portugal than relative costs at home. Each country moves resources into producing its low-cost commodity and imports the other. Thus average output per head is raised for both commodities, so that, with the same employment in each country as before, total output is raised in the world as a whole.

But now labour-value prices cease to rule. Conditions of demand have to be brought into the story – the level and distribution of real income in each country and the tastes and habits of workers and capitalists in each. For instance, if the world demand for wine exceeded Portugal's capacity output, some high-cost wine, in the final position, would be produced in England, and the wine-price of cloth would settle at the English cost ratio. The gain to England would then consist in the wine-value of the additional output of cloth being produced there.

Ricardo was able to show that consumption has increased in both countries. In England, with no less cloth than before, more wine is consumed, and contrariwise in Portugal. (He did not think of the possibility of negative income elasticity of demand for either commodity.) But he did not enter into the question of how market prices would be determined or how the gain would be shared between households in the two countries.

Growth. A lower real cost of procuring wine in England does not affect the rate of profit on capital; it only increases the purchasing power of profit incomes. The whole advantage goes to the drinkers of wine. What Ricardo was really concerned about was to abolish the Corn Laws so as to lower the real cost of wage goods and raise the rate of profit. This rise in profits is not at the expense of wages, for the commodity wage is fixed in any case. An increase in profits leads to an increase in the rate of accumulation and so of the growth of employment, national income and wealth. This was the desideratum of the whole argument.

When accumulation is brought into the story, it is evident that Portugal is not going to benefit from free trade. Investment in expanding manufactures leads to technical advance, learning by doing, specialization of industries and accelerating accumulation, while investment in wine runs up a blind alley into stagnation.

Supply and demand. Marshall intended to improve on Ricardo by removing the assumption of 'constant returns', but the theory of the relative prices of commodities that underlies his analysis in terms of offer curves is not at all easy to make out.[6] His general argument turns on the concept of particular commodities 'obeying the law of diminishing returns' or 'of increasing returns'. The first 'law' involves static conditions –there is some scarce factor of production that causes the supply price of a commodity to rise as output rises. But increasing returns, for Marshall, is a dynamic concept. An increase in output leads to investment, training of labour and learning by doing. There does not seem to be any way of fitting these two 'laws' into the same time scheme.

We might perhaps rationalize Marshall's analysis by confining the argument to a case in which each particular commodity is produced 'under conditions of diminishing returns' because each requires some specialized ingredient that is in limited supply. Then there is a 'cost at the margin' for each commodity which is an increasing function of the amount produced. But we are told nothing about what cost consists of or how it is divided between wages and profits. A footnote in the *Pure Theory of Foreign Trade* promises an appendix which will explain the meaning of 'cost of production'[7] but Marshall evidently found it impossible to draft, and none of the innumerable textbooks that reproduce his offer curves has supplied the lack.

Perhaps we are supposed to forget about profits and think in terms of peasants from various hills and valleys exchanging their produce at a frontier town. Then, each individual calculates the cost of commodities in terms of his own labour time. Market prices are settled by supply and demand, and production is distributed over the whole territory in such a way that, wherever any two commodities are being produced side by side, labour costs at the margin (allowing for transport) are in the same ratio as market prices.[8]

A still further retreat from the conditions of capitalist production is the Walrasian model of pure exchange. Here each country has an endowment of ready-made commodities, and countries exchange them in just the same

[6] See Marhsall, *The Pure Theory of Foreign Trade*, Rare Tracts, No. 1, L.S.E., London, 1930.
[7] Op. cit., p. 2.
[8] Cf. Joan Robinson, *Exercises in Economic Analysis*, London, 1960, part III, 9.

way as prisoners of war swapping the contents of their Red Cross parcels.[9]

The very existence of prices determined by supply and demand impairs even the static case against protection, for it shows that a country can gain an advantage by restricting trade and so raising the price of goods it exports in terms of goods it imports. Marshall was aware of this difficulty and fell back on the argument that, in the long run, world supplies of goods are highly elastic.[10] But if supplies are elastic, what becomes of his theory of prices?

Factor prices. The model which is nowadays most fashionable is that which Professor Samuelson[11] derived from the work of Professor Ohlin, who derived it from the work of Professor Heckscher.

In this model there is no difference in technical conditions in different countries, and 'factors of production' are homogeneous over the whole world. The most essential point of Ricardo's argument, different conditions of production in different countries, is ruled out. The only distinction between countries is in their endowments of 'factors'.

In Professor Samuelson's model there are two countries, two commodities and two factors, land and labour. He is evidently relying on something like Wicksell's story of an economy where workers hire land or landlords hire workers and, in either case, when the whole labour force is working on the whole area of land, the wage is equal to the marginal product of labour and the rent per acre is equal to the marginal product of land, each paid in arrears out of the harvest, so as to eliminate interest on working capital.

The endowment of factors is such that one country has a higher ratio of land to labour than the other, and the technical conditions are such that one commodity requires a higher ratio of land to labour than the other.

These were the assumptions that permitted Professor Samuelson to enunciate his famous proposition, which can be stated in a less dramatic manner as follows: Trade may cause one or the other country to be specialized; the relative prices of the commodities are then determined by the ratio of marginal transformation costs in the country producing both. In the special case where both countries produce some of each commodity, the marginal productivities of the factors must be the same in both.

In this setting (as for Ricardo) the argument about protection involves a clash of class interests. The landlords in the country where land is scarce and

[9] Cf. Joan Robinson, *Economic Heresies*, Macmillan, 1971, pp. 4 et seq.
[10] *Memorandum on the Fiscal Policy of International Trade*, reprinted in *Official Papers of Alfred Marshall*, ed. Keynes, London, 1926.
[11] Op. cit.

the workers in the country where it is abundant would gain from restricting trade.

Professor Samuelson's model is not of much use for discussing trade between industrial countries. Many neo-neoclassical models seek to adapt it to the case where the 'factors' are labour and 'capital'. This runs into the question of what 'capital' means and how prices are determined in an industrial economy.

Sometimes 'capital' is taken to mean a stock of machines. The commodities that enter into trade are then either two consumption goods or a machine and a consumption good. If technology is the same in the two countries, each has identical input-output relationships in physical terms. 'Factor prices' are then independent of the level of production and have to be given from outside.

When there are two different real-wage rates in the two countries, then, in the general case, trade will cause at least one of them to be specialized. In the case of labour-value prices, the price ratio of the two commodities is independent of wage rates, and both countries may produce both commodities whatever the pair of real-wage rates may be, but then there is no gain from trade.

Sometimes Professor Samuelson's proposition is stated in terms of 'capital' consisting of a mythical substance called jelly, though he himself has repudiated this conception. The country which has the greater endowment of capital has a larger lump of jelly (relatively to its labour force) and a lower marginal productivity of jelly.[12]

This is intended to be a parable, but it does not illuminate reality. There is no everyday meaning of the concept of a greater endowment of capital that is associated in real life with a lower rate of profit. When the capital-to-labour ratio is compared between countries by any rough measure – dollars invested per man employed, horse-power per head, or even tons of steel – there is no presumption that where the ratio is highest (say, in the USA) the rate of profit on capital will be found to be lowest, although it is true that the rate of profit is exceptionally high in some low-wage countries, where, for that very reason, investment per man employed is also low.

Instead of widening the base of Ricardo's simple argument, modern developments have narrowed it to vanishing point.

[12] Ian Steedman has shown that Samuelson's proposition does no better if we interpret it in terms of a pseudo-production function (a variety of known techniques) and measure a quantity of capital in terms of its dollar value. See J. S. Metcalfe and Ian Steedman, 'Heterogeneous capital and the H.O.S. theory of trade', in J. M. Parkin (ed.), *Essays in Modern Economics*, London, 1973.

2

THE BALANCE OF TRADE

There is another huge gap in the orthodox theory. No explanation is offered for the assumption that the value of imports is equal to the value of exports for each country.

In Marshall's system there is said to be equilibrium at a point where the offer curves cut, so that trade balances for each country; the equilibrium is said to be stable if the curves cut the right way, so that an increase in the amount of any commodity offered would raise its supply price at home and reduce its demand price abroad. There is no possibility of international lending and borrowing. 'Exports pay for imports' was a dogma of neoclassical theory, and the neo-neoclassicals seem to have taken it over without question.

Ricardo, in his day, had postulated balanced trade, but he provided a reason for doing so. He maintained that international capital movements do not take place:

> If capital freely flowed towards those countries where it could be most profitably employed, there could be no difference in the rate of profit, and no other difference in the real or labour price of commodities, than the additional quantity of labour required to convey them to the various markets where they were to be sold.
>
> Experience, however, shows, that the fancied or real insecurity of capital, when not under the immediate control of its owner, together with the natural disinclination which every man has to quit the country of his birth and connexions, and intrust himself with all his habits fixed, to a strange government and new laws, check the emigration of capital. These feelings, which I should be sorry to see weakened, induce most men of property to be satisfied with a low rate of profits in their own country, rather than seek a more advantageous employment for their wealth in foreign nations.[13]

Since there are no flows of money between countries except those that pay for the goods traded, an excess value of exports leads to an inflow of gold, which raises prices; a deficiency leads to a loss of gold, which lowers prices. Gold movements continue until the relative levels of prices and relative real incomes of the countries establish balanced trade.

This is an explanation, but it is not a convincing one. Ricardo soon

[13] Op. cit., pp. 136–7.

turned out to be wrong in denying the possibility of international capital movements. Certainly, in Marshall's day, overseas investment was an important element in the British economy.

Moreover, monetary equilibrium does not require balanced trade. It requires harmony between the capital account and the income account. An outflow of gold, or its modern equivalent, occurs when a country is lending more abroad than its surplus of exports (including all sources of foreign income) or borrowing less than its surplus of imports. The net excess of a country's long-term foreign lending over its surplus of exports has to be offset, when the exchange rate is pegged, by attracting a net inflow of short-term finance – a position which cannot be maintained indefinitely.

There is, however, a price mechanism that acts on the balance of trade itself. In an industrial country the general level of the prices of manufactures depends, in the main, on the relation between output per man employed and money wage rates. When exchange rates are fixed, international trade tends to equalize the prices of exportable goods from different countries, and this comes about through the adjustment of the relative levels of money-wage rates to relative productivity. (There may be differences in the ratio of profit margins to prime costs in different countries, but these cannot be very large, while differences in levels of money wages are without limit.)

Competition in trade to some extent influences prices directly, but the main point is that it tends to correct discrepancies between costs in one capitalist country and another. In a country where money cost of labour per unit of output is relatively low, exports are extremely profitable. High profits and a high demand for labour drive up wage rates; even if trade unions are not demanding, firms able to expand output of export goods bid for labour from those supplying the home market and they have to defend themselves by raising wages too. Furthermore, an export surplus is more inflationary than home investment. It has the same immediate influence on effective demand as home investment, while it has less long-term effect in increasing productivity at home so as to mitigate the rise in prices.

Rising money-wage rates have the same effect as Ricardo believed would follow from an import of gold – checking exports and increasing imports so as to tend in the direction of restoring balance.

In a very broad way, this mechanism is evidently at work. Statistics such as those offered by B. S. Minhas[14] (though he tried to interpret them in terms of an inappropriate theory) show that between the industrial

[14] See B. S. Minhas, *An International Comparison of Factor Cost and Factor Use*, Amsterdam, 1963.

countries the overall rates of profit on capital do not vary very much, while there are wide differences in wage rates in terms of tradable commodities, corresponding to differences in productivity.

It is because 'factor prices' are not equalized that industrial countries are able to compete with each other over a wide range of closely similar products.

(It is this mechanism that accounts for the fact that 'the cost of living' is highest in the richest countries; housing, transport and services have to pay wages at the level set by productivity in export industries.)

If the price mechanism worked quickly enough, trade would normally be balanced for each country, just as in the text books, but it works slowly and imperfectly.

It may be helped out by changing exchange rates, but this is not an infallible expedient. A depreciation in a country's currency has much the same effect as an all-round cut in money-wage rates, reducing real wages in terms of tradable goods. For that very reason it may speed up the rise in money-wage rates so as to cancel out its effect. When one country has a competitive advantage over a wide range of tradable goods, because its relative level of money wages has not caught up with its relative level of productivity, its competitors complain that its exchange rate is undervalued, but only strong political pressure will induce its authorities to appreciate in order to reduce the advantage of its exporters.

The working of the price mechanism is impeded by differences in the strength of trade unions, attitudes of employers and the general political situation in different countries. It may happen that trade unions are most demanding where real wages are rising least and most complacent where they are rising fastest, so that money costs move in the opposite direction to that required for equilibrium.

The contrast between recent experience in West Germany and Japan on the one side and the UK on the other, as shown in the table overleaf, illustrates the point. It appears that the price mechanism works to a certain extent, since both in periods of mild and in periods of rapid all-round inflation, the order of the countries in respect to rising productivity and to rising wage rates is generally the same, but the mechanism is not strong enough to prevent money costs in the surplus countries from falling relatively to those in a deficit country.

Rather than proclaiming a natural tendency towards balanced trade, it would be more plausible to say that the differences amongst capitalist countries in rates of growth set up a tendency to imbalance which the price mechanism can only partially offset.

ANNUAL PERCENTAGE RATE OF INCREASE

	Output per Man Hour	Hourly Money Earnings	Money Cost of Labour
	1963–67		
Japan	10·2	11·0	0·8
West Germany	5·6	7·3	1·7
UK	4·1	6·7	2·6
	1967–71		
Japan	12·1	15·7	3·6
West Germany	4·9	9·4	4·5
UK	4·2	10·5	6·3

These figures are taken from a lecture (unpublished) delivered by Professor Kahn at Scarborough College, Toronto.

3

STATIONARY STATES

The way in which Ricardo set up his argument implied a comparison of the composition of output in each country when it was self-sufficient with the composition that trade brings about. As the theory developed, it was formalized in terms of comparisons of stationary states. Each country in isolation is in a stationary state with 'given resources' and, with trade, it is in a stationary state again with the same resources. This is quite foreign to the conceptions of the classical economists, who were concerned with accumulation and the growth of wealth of nations. For Ricardo a stationary state meant not equilibrium but stagnation. He used it as a horror story. With the Corn Laws in force, the labour cost of producing the necessary wage will rise, as the margin of cultivation is extended, till profits are reduced to the level at which accumulation is brought to an end.

Ricardo's argument starts from the position at a point in time and predicts a future path. In neoclassical theory there is no path, no process, no movement of any kind. An isolated country is in a stationary equilibrium and hey presto! trade puts it into a new equilibrium, with a different composition of output but resources, knowledge and tastes all the same. This has cut off the 'pure theory' from any relation to the trade that takes place in real life and has reduced it to an idle toy.

Keynes put everyone from Ricardo to Pigou in one box and called them 'classical' because they all believed in Say's law. It is true that there is no place for the problem of effective demand in Ricardo's system, but his argument is quite different from that of J. S. Mill and the neoclassicals. His views were elaborated in his dispute with Malthus. Malthus defended the expenditure of rent on the services of unproductive labour because it supported effective demand for the output of productive labour. Ricardo was quite baffled by this argument, which, indeed, was full of contradictions. In his scheme, wages were spent on necessaries, rents were spent on luxuries, and the excess of profits over the capitalists' modest household consumption was invested, so how could there be a deficiency of demand?

The neoclassical version of Say's law was based on the conception that 'goods are the demand for goods'. It is appropriate to an artisan economy rather than to capitalism. Each producer brings his goods to market and either swaps them for other goods or keeps them for himself.

Marshall combined both concepts in the saying that saving is a form of spending, while the Walrasians rely on the concept of 'market-clearing prices', though no one has ever said what this is supposed to mean in a monetary economy.

In modern teaching, Keynes is kept in a separate compartment. In that compartment it is permissible to discuss the relation of the balance of trade to the level of employment, but the so-called theory of international trade is still conducted in terms of comparisons of equilibrium conditions, with 'given resources' always fully utilized. Instead of following the path that Ricardo opened out and linking it up with Keynes, the modern theory never escapes from the blind alley of comparisons of stationary states. It is therefore worse than useless for a discussion of the problems of management of a national economy or the role of export-led growth and import-led stagnation in international competition.

4

FOREIGN INVESTMENT

Ricardo did not approve of overseas investment. He would be 'sorry to see weakened' the feelings which he expected to prevent it. For Ricardo the function of profits was to be saved and invested. Accumulation would increase employment and, when labour became scarce, raise real wages and promote productivity. To invest abroad would slow down the growth of the home economy.

The neo-neoclassicals' failure to distinguish between finance and physical means of production leads to a confusion between an export of capital goods (whether machines or jelly) and an export of capital in the sense of foreign lending. It is necessary to distinguish between lending in the sense of acquiring assets – bonds, securities or physical means of production – from the citizens of other countries, and foreign investment in the sense of a surplus on the balance of trade (including all items on income account).[15]

There is a particular means of acquiring foreign assets that is open to a country whose currency provides an international medium of exchange. Balances of the currency are held by central banks and by businesses all over the world. The growth of these balances, from year to year, represents interest-free loans to the country in question which enable its citizens and businesses to make corresponding purchases of foreign assets in excess of the county's balance in income account. From the point of view of the national economy these assets are paid for by cheques that will never be cashed; so long as confidence is maintained, the balances of its currency are held, and when confidence is lost, they cannot be sold.

Assets acquired in this way contribute to the wealth of the nation by interest and profits remitted and there is no reason why they should reduce investment at home, provided that the government is pursuing a full-employment policy. This kind of foreign investment, then, is clearly an advantage to the country that is able to carry it out at the expense of the rest of the world.

The benefit is not so obvious when an outflow of finance has to be matched by a surplus of exports. There is, certainly, a strategic advantage for an industrial country in securing its sources of raw materials. This was the effect of a great part of nineteenth-century investment, and it is still going on, notably by the USA in Canada and by Japan in Australia.

When the assets being acquired are securities or direct investment in foreign industry, there is still an advantage to owners of wealth and businesses (provided they are well informed), for the yield on securities and the prospects of profit from investment are higher abroad than at home, simply because they can pick and choose in a much wider field.

For the nation as a whole the advantage is more doubtful. The benefit

[15] A corporation whose headquarters are in one country is said to be carrying out investment abroad when it sets up a branch plant in another country. From the point of view of the national accounts of the headquarters country, the finance supplied to the branch is an outflow of capital or foreign lending. Expenditure on setting up the plant is gross home investment in the country where it takes place, which may be partly offset by imports of equipment, etc.

from owning foreign assets is a somewhat higher rate of profit, while the benefit of home investment also includes an increase of productivity or improved amenities at home. Provided that near-full employment is to be maintained in any case, a smaller surplus of exports, with less foreign lending and more attention to welfare at home, may be a preferable policy.

This argument is coming into fashion in Japan, where a competitive advantage in exports has been won partly by unbridled destruction of resources and serious damage to health at home.

What of the other side of the story – foreign borrowing? The conception of 'capital' as a factor of production leads to the idea that a capital inflow means acquiring real productive resources. (This is an aspect of the confusion between finance and capital goods.)

Foreign borrowing, in itself, does not provide any factors of production. It merely permits the borrowing country to run a deficit on its balance of trade. The rate of saving (private and public together) in a country is equal to its home investment minus the deficit in its foreign balance on income account. Foreign borrowing permits a lower rate of saving with a given rate of investment, that is, more consumption out of rent and profits or a greater budget deficit.

The borrowing has to be paid for by interest and dividends on securities or by the remission of profits to the headquarters of corporations that have set up branches in the borrowing country. This puts a strain on the future balance of payments. Both Canada and Australia at the present time are suffering from a feeling of the 'morning after' and wondering if they should not have done more of their saving for themselves.

A payment on securities is less onerous than remission of profits, for, over time, bonds can be redeemed or securities repatriated out of future surpluses, while branch companies have a permanent claim to remit profits. Moreover, the capital sum in respect to which profits accrue is often much larger than the original inflow. Part of the local investment may have been financed by bonds floated locally and the installations may be expanded out of profits made locally. The capital created in this way belongs to the foreign corporations just as much as that acquired by the original inflow of finance and is under the same obligation to remit profits.

In the so-called developing countries direct investment is said to be justified by bringing them know-how. Apart from the very latest inventions, the general technology of industry is a common heritage which can be tapped, by a process of education, of learning by doing, and purchasing patents, as the Japanese have shown. To take the short cut of importing foreign management along with investment has rather a tendency to keep the would-be developing country in a state of continued dependence.

But here we are touching on the large questions of imperialism and neo-colonialism which we ruled out at the start.

14

MARKETS

INTRODUCTION

The economics of the modern industrial system began with Adam Smith's dictum: 'The division of labour depends upon the extent of the market.' The factory system developed out of the trade in cotton textiles. Merchants, finding an apparently insatiable world-wide market, began to be interested in increasing production in order to have more to sell. The factory system led to an increase in productivity through specialization — each worker performing a single task separated out from those all combined in one by an independent artisan. From this came the use of power to supplement human muscle and the application of science to technology, which, in an ever accelerating spiral, has led to the enormous scope and complexity of modern industry. The growth of productivity itself led to the development of transport and communications, the spread of empire, and the growth of average consumption, which, together with the rise in population, created the enlargement of markets that made the growth of productivity possible.

A wide market leads to specialization even in natural materials, through fine grading, breeding varieties with particular characteristics and so forth; however, its greatest development is evidently in man-made products. Nowadays, with the elaboration of the commodities which are sold to the public, and the elaboration of equipment to produce them, there is a world-wide market for a great variety of semi-manufactures and components. For example, a particular model of a motor-car has a limited market but many of the ingredients that go into it are supplied to all the motor industries of the world. When there is a sufficiently large market for any specific item, it is worthwhile designing specialized equipment to produce it, and then equipment to produce equipment. Adam Smith did not distinguish between what are nowadays called 'economies of scale' and new inventions. He saw that the division of labour leads on to mechanization; both develop together with the extent of the market. Modern industry shows his principle working out beyond his wildest dreams.

A shorter version of this paper appeared in *Encyclopedia Britannica*, 15th edition, 1974.

A hundred years after Adam Smith, while his predictions were already being amply fulfilled, the centre of interest in economic doctrine shifted from growth and technical progress to the allocation of given resources between alternative uses; the concept of the market came to be treated in terms of the equilibrium of supply and demand. (Marx had developed the theories of the classical economists about production and accumulation along lines that were unacceptable to established orthodoxy; the neoclassicals of the latter half of the nineteenth century, instead of challenging him on his own ground, preferred to elaborate a problem that he had treated only sketchily – the determination of the relative prices of particular commodities).

Alfred Marshall (whose *Principles of Economics* was for long the bible of the English-speaking neoclassicals) setting out to define the concept of a market, quotes Cournot:

> Economists understand by the term *Market*, not any particular market place in which things are bought and sold, but the whole of any region in which buyers and sellers are in such free intercourse with one another that the prices of the same goods tend to equality easily and quickly.[1]

and Jevons:

> Originally a market was a public place in a town where provisions and other objects were exposed for sale; but the word has been generalized, so as to mean any body of persons who are in intimate business relations and carry on extensive transactions in any commodity.

Marshall adds, 'The more nearly perfect a market is, the stronger is the tendency for the same price to be paid for the same thing at the same time in all parts of the market.' This applies to standardized commodities; the concept of a market can be more loosely applied to heterogenous transactions – we speak of the market for real estate or the market for old masters and for contemporary paintings. We speak also of the labour market. Lenin defined capitalism as the system in which labour itself has become a commodity – that is a tradeable article.[2] Clearly a contract to work for a certain wage is not quite the same thing as the sale of a packet of goods; the connnecting idea in all these usages is the interplay of supply and

---

[1] *Principles* (8th edition) p. 324. Marshall gives the reference for Cournot to *Recherches sur les Principes Mathematiques de la Theorie des Richesses*, Ch. IV and for Jevons, *Theory of Political Economy*, Ch. IV.

[2] V. I. Lenin, *The Economic Teaching of Karl Marx*, p. 21.

demand; this certainly applies to labour in capitalist industry, though in a more complicated way than to the market for peanuts.

TYPES OF MARKETS

Except in the increasingly rare case of direct sales, such as from a farmer to a housewife, markets are formed by groups of intermediaries between the first seller and the final buyer. Intermediaries are of all kinds from the brokers in the great produce exchanges to the village grocer. They may be mere dealers with no equipment but a telephone or they may provide storage and perform important services of grading, packaging and so on. In general, the function of a market is to collect products from scattered sources and channel them to scattered outlets. From the point of view of the seller, dealers focus demand for his product and from the point of view of the buyer, they bring supplies to his reach.

There are two main types of markets in which the forces of supply and demand operate quite differently (with some overlapping and borderline cases). In the first, the producer offers his goods and takes whatever price they will fetch; in the second, the producer sets his price and sells as much as the market will take.

The first type is common among primary products, that is, those which depend upon animal, vegetable and mineral resources. Oil and some metals are controlled by powerful corporations, but the general run of agricultural commodities are produced under competitive conditions by relatively small-scale cultivators scattered over a large area. The final purchasers are also scattered and centres of consumption are distant from regions of production. The dealer, therefore, is indispensable and he is in a stronger economic position than the seller. This is markedly true where the producer is a peasant who is short both of commercial knowledge and of finance so that he is obliged to sell as soon as his harvest comes in; it is true also to a lesser extent of the capitalist plantation which has no source of earnings but its particular specialised product. In this kind of business, both demand and supply are inelastic in the short run – that is, a fall in price does not have much effect in increasing purchases and a rise in price cannot quickly increase supplies. Supplies are subject to natural variations, through weather conditions, pests and so forth, and demands vary with the level of activity in the centres of industry, and with variations in tastes and technical requirements. These markets, therefore, under a regime of unregulated competition, are tormented with continual fluctuations in prices and in the volume of business. Dealers may mitigate this to some extent, building up stocks when prices are low and releasing them when demand is high. But this involves speculation – that is guess work. Speculative dealings are stabilizing when the dealers have a clear view of what the normal price is expected to be. Thus under the gold standard when rates of exchange between national economies were confidently expected to be maintained, a small depreciation in one rate led to purchases and a small rise, to sales. But in commodity markets dealers cannot be certain of what the future holds; a fall in price may be a signal for sales and a rise for withholding, so that speculation exacerbates fluctuations.

In the longer run also, these markets are unreliable. A check to demand for a natural material due to the development of a synthetic substitute reduces proceeds quasi-permanently, for the producers who have become specialized may have no alternative line available and even if they had, have now little resources to invest; on the other hand a temporary check to supply, which produces high proceeds as long as it lasts, will often lead to an increase in productive capacity which will break the market as soon as it comes into bearing. At the same time a temporary scarcity may speed up the process of substitution, so that it is followed by a permanent reduction in demand. Thus in markets of this type, over a run of years, periods of low prices are likely to predominate over periods of relative prosperity.

This behaviour of markets is a serious matter where whole communities depend upon a single commodity for income, or for employment and wages. The agricultural communities which form part of an industrial economy are generally sheltered from the operation of supply and demand by various types of regulations, price-supports or protection; some attempts have been made to control world commodity markets, but these are more in talk than in performance; some primary-producing nations, such as Australia, could make enough profit from exports to be able to attract capital into the development of industry; on the other hand, most of the so-called developing countries find their export earnings insecure and insufficient to permit the diversification of production which would reduce dependence upon them. Their spokesmen complain that the world market system operates in such a way as to give the greatest benefit to the industrialized nations and least to those who need it most.

The other type of market prevails in the sphere of manufactured goods. The market for manufactures is what economists call 'imperfect,' because each company has its own style, its own reputation, and its own locations; and all of the arts of advertisement and salesmanship are devoted to making it even more imperfect by attracting buyers to particular brand names. Even small businesses that depend upon the services of dealers have the final say in what prices they will charge, and great corporations can differentiate their goods in order to create demand for them.

In this type of market, supply normally is very elastic — that is, responsive to demand — in the short run. Stocks or inventories are held at some point in the chain of distribution; while stocks are running down or building up, there is time to change the level of production, and once a price has been set, it is rarely altered in response to moderate changes in demand. Even in a deep slump, defensive rings may often be formed to prevent price cutting.

In the long run, as well as in the short, supply is responsive to demand in the market for manufactures. It is easier to change the composition of a firm's output than it is to change the production of a mine or a plantation. And when changes in demand are not too rapid, gross profits from one plant can be siphoned off and invested in something quite different. When business is good, moreover, there is continual new investment so that productive capacity is adapted to meeting changing requirements. Workers themselves may not even be aware of changes in the final commodities to which their work contributes, and the level of wages for any grade of factory labour is very little affected by the fortunes of a particular market.

MARKETS UNDER SOCIALISM

Markets were essential to the free enterprise system; they grew and spread along with it; the propensity to truck, barter and exchange one thing for another became exalted into a moral principle, since the doctrine of laisser-faire taught that the pursuit of self-interest by the individual would be to the benefit of society as a whole. In the USSR and other countries which claim to be building socialism, a different type of economy has been installed and a different ideology is dominant. There are two interlocking systems in the economy of USSR; the same pattern is followed, with variations, in other socialist countries. In industry all equipment and materials are owned by the state, and production is directed by a central plan. The payment to workers, looked at in a philosophical light, is not the purchase price for the commodity, labour; it is the individual's share in the total production of the economy; in practice, all the same, the system of wages is very much like that in capitalist industry, except that, in principle, rates are laid down by ⸱decree; the managers of enterprises have little scope for bargaining; workers can travel about to look for jobs but there is no 'labour market'; intermediate goods are distributed between enterprises by the plan (faulty planning leaves room for some kind of intermediaries to operate between enterprises, but this is not at all the same thing as the highly developed markets in materials, components and equipment which are an essential element in the development of capitalist industry).

Consumption goods, however, are distributed to households through the retail market. Some idealists of socialism, regarding money as the essence of capitalism, have advocated that it should be abolished altogether, but, in a large community, it is extremely convenient to provide incomes to individuals in the form of generalized purchasing power and to allow each to choose what he pleases from whatever goods are available to be bought. The advantage of this system is not so much the delicate balancing of relative marginal utilities against price ratios, which the academic economists claim for it, but rather the fact that it runs itself without bureaucrats or police to regulate it. Retail markets for manufactures, in the Soviets, however, are essentially different from 'commodity trade' in the full sense. The housewife who goes shopping is a *principal* in the sense that she is in charge of her own money and need account to no one for what she does with it. In the free-market system, the seller is also a principal, or an agent operating for a principal, who decides what he wants to offer. In the Soviet system, retailers and manufacturers are all agents of the same authority – the central plan. Instead of the seller making it his business to woo and cajole the customer, supplies are thrown into the shops in a somewhat arbitrary way and the customer has to search for what he wants.

A second basic difference is that there is no relation between earnings of an individual and the market for the goods that he is concerned with producing or retailing. (There are certain incentives and bonuses for production but they do not depend upon the prices of the commodities being produced.) Money incomes, in the large, are settled by wage rates and total employment. The main requirement in planning prices is to adjust the overall value of goods available to be sold in relation to the overall flow of purchasing power directed to buying them. It appears to have been Soviet practice to keep prices a little low in relation to incomes so that there is always excess demand; this makes life easy for the seller and tiresome for the buyer.

Agriculture was organized on quite different principles. (In recent times it seems that state farms, organized as socialist enterprises, are growing in importance.) The original collective farms, though managed in an authoritarian way, were like cooperatives in respect to their relations to the rest of the economy – that is, members shared in the income of the farm in respect to the work points that each could earn. The value of a work point was thus affected by the prices set for the products of the farm. The terms of trade between agriculture and industry were politically determined in setting the prices of produce and of manufactures. In the Western industrial economies, also, there is a political element in setting agricultural prices; there, generally, the problem is to prevent excess production from driving prices too low. For the Soviets, the problem was the opposite. Agricultural output failed to expand to keep step with the growth of urban employment. Prices were kept down in order to prevent the terms of trade being too unfavourable to the industrial sector. At the same time, there is a free market where individual members of the collective farms can sell the products of the private plots of land that they are allowed to cultivate, mainly fruit, vegetables, milk, etc. In this market there is commodity trade in the full sense for the seller, in effect a peasant, is as much a principal as the buyer. Official prices of foodstuffs in the shops are usually below free market prices, but supplies fresh from the country offer other attractions.

In all the Western socialist countries there is some element of peasant production and therefore some trade on market principles.

In China the cooperative farms, organized in communes, are much more genuinely cooperatives. There is commodity trade in vegetables, etc., supplied to the cities, but it is organized through a kind of socialist wholesaling. The city authorities place contracts with neighbouring communes, specifying prices, varieties, quantities and delivery dates, and direct the supplies to retail outlets which are part of the socialist economy.

A similar system controls trade in manufactured consumption goods. Through the retail shops the authorities keep a finger on the pulse of demand and guide supply as far as possible to meet it by the contracts placed with the socialist enterprises. By adapting to its own requirements a particular element in the market system – wholesale trade – the Chinese economy seems to have avoided some of the difficulties in which the Soviets find themselves.

The most complete case of non-market socialism was seen in the early days of the kibbutzim in Israel. Here a group of cultivators took over a piece of land and shared the proceeds of their work without any distinction of individual incomes. (A kibbutz could trade with the surrounding market economy so that its members were not confined to consuming only the produce of their own soil.) At first some carried the objection to private property so far that a man who had sent a shirt to be washed took back a shirt – no matter who had worn it last. To dispense with market relationships altogether is possible only in a small community where everyone knows each other and where all share a common ideal. Moreover, it is unlikely to outlast the heroic period of struggle with hardship. The austere standards of the original kibbutzim have naturally softened somewhat with growing prosperity, but they still maintain a small-scale example of economic efficiency without commercial incentives.

The Market in Economic Doctrine

The concept of the market in the economic theory which became dominant with the neoclassicals of the late nineteenth century, and is still influential in academic teaching, was highly abstract. It was primarily conceived as an exchange of goods for goods between individuals differing amongst themselves in their particular 'endowments' and their particular 'tastes' but standing in symmetrical economic relations to each other. The concept was most systematically worked out in the general equilibrium system of Walras. It is now known that Leon Walras took over the basic idea from an engineer, A. A. Isnard (1749–1803), who treated demand, supply and price for a set of commodities on the analogy the balance of mechanical forces. This was an ingenious argument, but there are two serious limitations of the mechanical analogy; it leaves out time and the effect upon behaviour today of expectations about the future and it ignores the consequences to the human beings concerned of the distribution of purchasing power amongst them that the market throws up. There is one very special case to which the Walrasian analysis applies pretty well: that is the market in a prisoner-of-war camp. The men receive parcels from the Red Cross which contain a variety of commodities. They set up a market for exchanging them, using cigarettes as a unit of account and a medium for three-cornered transactions. The contents of the parcels are not tailored to the tastes of the recipients, so each can gain by swapping what he wants less for what he prefers. Thus all are subjectively better off than they would be if each could consume only his own parcel. Here the limits to the validity of the mechanical analogy are of minor importance. Time does come in to some extent through the effect on demand today of speculation about when the next lot of parcels will arrive, but demand here and now is strongly predominant. Secondly, the endowment (his parcel) of each man is more or less equivalent to that of every other. Distribution of benefits is effected by the way the market goes; for instance the Sikhs, who do not smoke, are at an advantage because their ration of cigarettes is pure purchasing power, while for others it meets an urgent need for consumption. But these are minor considerations compared to the situation of primary producers depending upon the world market, for whom movements of prices are literally a matter of life and death.

The extension of the Walrasian system to an economy in which production is going on is made by postulating trade amongst owners of 'factors of production', areas of land, machines, materials etc. fully specified in physical terms, and labour power. Owners of the factors hire them out for production and buy consumer goods from each other. In equilibrium, each factor is being used in such a way that it could not get any better return in any other line and each consumer is using his purchasing power in such a way that he would not get more satisfaction by using it any other way. The prices and amounts produced of each commodity are thus determined by the incomes and the tastes of consumers, the prices of factors are derived from the prices of commodities and the incomes of the consumers are derived from the prices and amounts of the factors that they own. Thus the circle of interacting forces is complete. The requirements of equilibrium are carefully examined in the Walrasian argument but there is no way of demonstrating that a market which starts in an out-of-equilibrium position will tend to get into equilibrium, except by putting further very severe restrictions on the already highly abstract argument.

It is to be noted that in this scheme the labour power of a worker is a factor of production completely on a par with, say, a stock of copper or a meadow. There is an equilibrium wage at which everyone is doing as much work as he chooses to do for that rate of return (though special assumptions have to be put in to ensure that earnings are not below the level of subsistence).

Economists generally salve their professional conscience by admitting the abstract nature of their arguments (Marshall, in particular, had many hesitations and reservations) but the doctrine generally accepted as orthodox teaching was that the free play of market forces tends to bring about full employment and the optimum allocation of scare means between alternative uses. This doctrine was still influential in the great depression of the thirties, when it was commonly believed that unemployment could be caused only by wages being too high.

The change in view that became known as the Keynesian Revolution was largely an escape to common sense. In an industrial economy, the wage bargain is necessarily made in terms of money; real wages emerge from the relation of money prices of commodities to money-wage rates. The overall demand for labour by employers depends upon the overall demand in money terms for their products. The amount of consumption goods that the public will buy depends mainly upon their incomes. Most consumption goods are purchased to be used up over the near future, but investment in industrial installations and housebuilding are aimed at profitability over a long time ahead. Investment therefore depends upon expectations. Unfavourable expectations of profit tend to fulfil themselves, for when outlay on investment falls off, workers are unemployed, incomes fall, therefore purchases fall, therefore unemployment spreads to the consumption good industries, therefore receipts are reduced all the more. The essential operation of the market principle generates instability. This principle has in recent years been operating in the other direction. A high level of effective demand leads to a scarcity of labour; rising money-wage rates raise both cost of production and incomes in money terms, so that there is a general tendency to inflation.

At the same time as Keynes was attacking the concept of equilibrium in the market as a whole, the notion of perfect competition in the market for particular commodities was also being undermined. In order to adapt the Walrasian concept of relative prices to industrial production it was necessary to introduce the idea of a group of firms operating in a perfect market for a single commodity. For each (providing a small part of the whole supply) the price of the commodity is given by the market and each maximizes its current profits by selling as much as makes marginal cost equal to price – that is to say, so much that to produce a little more would add to costs more than to proceeds. This means that each firm is working its plant up to capacity in the sense that output is limited by rising costs. This is quite contrary to the general run of business experience, and particularly in the slump, under-capacity working was prevalent. If marginal cost can be identified with prime cost for wages, materials, power, etc., it is generally found to be roughly constant or even falling as output approaches capacity. Thus, so long as prices exceed prime cost when plant is working below capacity, competition is evidently not perfect in the economist's sense. A formalistic theory of imperfect competition was introduced to reconcile the principle of profit-maximization with under-capacity working.[3] This in its turn was attacked as unrealistic. The upshot of the debate was that strict profit maximizing is impossible in conditions of uncertainty, that prices of manufactures are generally formed by adding a margin to prime cost, which is calculated to cover overheads and yield a profit at less than capacity sales, and that an increase in capacity generally has to be accompanied by some kind of selling costs to ensure that it will be used at a remunerative level.

The analysis of imperfect competition was conceived as an attack upon orthodoxy. Another line of approach to the same field was opened up by Professor Chamberlin in the theory which he developed under the title of

[3] See 'After Forty Years', *Economics of Imperfect Competition*, second edition.

Monopolistic Competition. He concentrated upon the problem of oligopoly, that is, a situation where two or three powerful firms are manoeuvring in a single market, and upon product differentiation and advertisement as modes of non-price competition. He was reluctant, however, to draw the conclusion that the market system cannot perform the function of an ideal allocation of resources when it is being manipulated by salesmanship.

Once it is recognized that competition is never pure and perfect in reality, it becomes obvious that there is great scope for individual variations in the price policy of firms. No precise generalization is possible. The field is open for study of what actually happens and much exploration of it is going on. Meanwhile, however, textbook teaching often seeks refuge in the illusory simplicity of conditions of perfect competition, correct foresight and general equilibrium in the markets for commodities and factors of production.

ORIGIN AND DEVELOPMENT OF MARKETS

History and anthropology provide many examples of systems of exchange which were not commercial. An exchange of gifts between communities with different resources may have economic consequences similar to trade, in diversifying consumption and encouraging specialization in production, but subjectively it has a different meaning. Honour lies in giving; receiving imposes a burden; competition is for who can show the most generosity not for who can make the biggest gain. (There are vestigial remnants of such a system in our own society in the custom of standing drinks or giving parties.) We know that in neolithic times there was an exchange of flint axes from the British Isles for amber from the Baltic, but it is unlikely that we shall ever know whether it took the form of commerce or whether the peoples concerned thought of it in terms of ritual, honour, or of duty to gods or men.

Another kind of non-commercial exchange which is still very much with us is the payment of dues to a political authority, from which expenditure proceeds. There have been examples of great elaborate and wealthy civilizations in which it seems that commerce was almost entirely unknown. In the Babylonian empire, evidence suggests that procurement of a great variety of commodities was carried out by a network of official agents of the state, at fixed prices, passed forward with a fixed margin, and redistributed from the centre as salaries and gifts, for what is now called 'defence expenditure', as investment in tombs and palaces and as finance for imports. It seems likely that some private business developed side by side with the organized flows of commodities, but the main source of supply for the cities was through the official channels. The succeeeding empire may have operated on similar principles, for Herodotus remarks that the Persians have no market places.[a]

The hall-mark of commerce is that goods are offered, not as a duty or for prestige or for neighbourly kindness, but in order to acquire purchasing power. A sale is different from a swap in that the seller is not obliged to spend his receipts until he chooses. The Walrasian conception of market transactions as an exchange of goods for goods is essentially misleading. Even in the prisoner-of-war camp, cigarettes were used as currency. Money as a medium of exchange naturally arises from trade in diverse goods; any one that is durable and in fairly general demand will serve. There is some evidence that the neolithic axes in time became recognized as money. It is clearly a convenience to all parties to have a single generally established currency-commodity. Once a commodity is acceptable as money, its use as a store of purchasing power overshadows its use for its original purpose; it ceases to be a commodity like any other and becomes the very embodiment of value.

The development of markets as centres of commerce seems to have had three separate points of origin. The first is in local fairs in a rural economy. The cultivator, in the typical case, provides the main food supply for his own family and pays the landlord and the usurer from his chief crop. He has some sidelines which provide saleable products, and he has needs which he cannot satisfy at home. It is then convenient to hold a market at a known time and place where many can meet to sell and buy. The catchment area from which trade can be drawn depends upon the means of transport and the time that can be spared from productive labour. Already at this simple stage, Adam Smith's principle is at work; the larger and the better off are the group of families that can be represented at a single market, the larger is the volume of business and the greater the scope for specialization in handicrafts or cultivation of varieties of animal and vegetable products. From the local market, also, grows the business of itinerant dealers who carry from fair to fair articles of which the value in relation to weight makes long-distance trade profitable.

The second growing point of the market was in serving the landlords' requirements. Rent was essentially paid in grain even when it was transposed into money, for sales of grain were necessary to supply the cultivator with funds to meet his dues. Payment of rent was a one-way transaction, imposed if necessary by force. The landlord supported warriors, clients and artisans by disbursing the rent. In peaceful conditions, with growing wealth, towns sprang up as centres of trade and production and an urban class developed with a standard of life which enabled them to enjoy each other's services and goods as well as providing them to the landlords and officials.

The third, and most influential, origin of markets was in international trade. From early times there were merchant adventurers (the Phoenicians, the Arabs), who risked their lives and their capital in carrying the products of one region to another. Warring nations might both gain from the trade of third parties; from this came the institution of ports of trade, in seacoasts or on caravan routes, where self-regulating enclaves were respected and left in peace by the belligerents for their mutual advantage. Commercial cities developed into independent political powers, later to decay when trade routes changed, or to be absorbed into expanding empires.

The importance of international trade for the development of the market system was precisely that it was carried out by third parties. Within a settled country, commercial dealings were restrained by considerations of rights, obligations and proper behaviour. After specialist production was already far advanced in Medieval Europe, dealings were partly regulated by the concept of the 'just price', that is, a system of valuations which would enable the producers and merchants to maintain life at a level suited to their respective positions in society. But in trade where the dealer is not subject to any obligations at either end, there are no holds barred; purely commercial principles have free play. It was from trade (for instance, the export of English wool to the weavers of Italy) that the commercial principle undermined feudal conceptions of rights and duties in Medieval Europe. As Adam Smith foresaw, it took a great leap when trade released the forces of industrial production.

The relations between the trader and the producer are constantly shifting with the development of technique and of the economic power of the parties. The nineteenth century was the heyday of the import-export merchant. Merchants, from a metropolitan country, could establish themselves in a particular foreign centre, become experts on its needs and possibilities and deal with a great variety of producers and customers each on a relatively small scale. With the growth of the giant corporations, the scope of the merchant narrows; his functions are largely taken over by the sales departments of the industrial concerns. Nowadays it is common to hold international fairs at which industrial products can be displayed by their makers for inspection by customers. This is a grand and glorified version of the village market. The business, however, here consists in placing orders rather than buying on the spot and carrying merchandise home.

Similarly the function of the independent wholesaler shrinks as great retail businesses grow to a scale where they can deal direct with manufacturers; but specialized exchanges, for instance for wheat, for cocoa, tea and such like crops of small-scale producers are still of great importance.

Side by side with the growth of trade in goods has gone a proliferation of dealing in finance. Any marketable commodity is potentially an object of speculation. The dealer who has stocks on his hands must take a view about the best moment to sell – that is, he must take a view about the future course of the price. When prices fluctuate there are profits to be made by dealing purely for speculation. Trading in futures is a convenience for the producer and the user who want certainty of prices at the dates when payments will be due and speculators 'make a market' for them by dealing for future delivery. The market offsets contrary risks against each other and at the same time attracts finance from those who are prepared to bet on their own judgement against the market. A Stock Exchange is a market for finance itself. In the early days of capitalism, the 'adventurer' had to provide funds of his own or of a backer and had to take the full risk of his operations. The system of limited liability was introduced in order to facilitate the supply of finance to industry – it tapped the resources of owners of wealth who would not risk many eggs in one basket and attracted their funds out of real property or gilt-edged bonds into the purchase of shares. This led to a great development of business at second hand. Nowadays dealings in securities which came into being long ago greatly predominate over dealings in new issues, while the greater part of industrial investment in financed by retention of profit in the firms that make it. Instead of serving mainly as a channel for lending to industry, the chief function of a Stock Exchange is to provide a convenient way for owners of property (inherited or newly saved) to place their wealth in income-yielding form, and to improve liquidity and security for them by making a market in which financial assets can readily be realized or redeployed. Dealings in a commodity market as we have seen, necessarily contain a speculative element, but there is, so to say, a solid bottom in the real demand and supply of the commodity. In the market for securities, there is only money for money; their expected future prices overshadow all other characteristics. The art of speculation is 'to anticipate what average opinion expects average opinion to be.' The notorious instability of Stock Exchanges, reacting upon the availability of finance for business and on the nominal wealth of shareholders, can be extremely disturbing to the whole market for real goods and services.

The 'money market' is not a definite organized exchange. The phrase refers rather to the general supply of finance, particularly short-term finance, from many sources both for industry and commerce and for financial dealings themselves. Originally the prime source of short-term finance was from banks. The special characteristic of a bank is that its liabilities (notes or deposits made with it) are a convenient form of currency. The banking system 'creates money' in the sense that the greater is the sum of its total liabilities, the greater is the supply of liquid assets in the hands of the public (firms and households together). A modern money market is made up of complex and variegated sets of intermediaries dealing in credit, that is, borrowing from one source and lending to another. In this business, in a certain sense, demand creates supply, for when times are good and prospects of profit hopeful, the credit of borrowers is felt to be sound and loans are offered more readily than in times of slack. A *fall* in prospective profits destroys credit which may produce a disastrous shrinkage in the supply of finance. At any moment, the monetary authorities (say the Bank of England or the Federal Reserve Board) have some power to restrict lending by the banks and through them by other sources of credit; by doing so they may frustrate schemes of investment that would have been carried out if finance were available and check sales of consumer durables on hire-purchase. Thus they can restrict real productive activity and cause employment and incomes to fall. This reduces current profits, dims expectations and so curtails the supply of credit by destroying the credit-worthiness of borrowers. Over the longer run, however, the more the authorities attempt to exercise their powers, the faster the money market develops new organs for bringing lenders and borrowers together and new types of transferable obligations that are 'almost money', in order to escape from control.

The two sides of the market economy, industry and finance, are necessary to each other but their interests are partly in conflict. The managers of an industrial corporation value above everything their freedom to carry on business as they think fit. They are, of course, interested in profits, but they are not obliged to pursue pecuniary gain at all costs. Some draw the benefit for their independence in slackness and inefficiency or gentlemanly leisure; some shine for technical excellence beyond commercial advantage; most, nowadays, are concerned in some degree to keep good relations with their employees. The viewpoint of finance, on the other hand, regards profit as the only aim of industry and the ruling criterion of success. The great corporations are powerful enough, especially in good times, to keep financial interests at bay, but a smaller company which is found to be doing less well for its shareholders than it might can be taken over (through dealing in its shares) behind the back of its directors. The threat of takeover is a means of keeping a check upon the independence of managers who are not sufficiently adept at 'maximizing profits'.

An inflationary situation of rising prices, so long as it does not get out of hand, is generally favourable to industry, since costs are incurred some time before sales and so at a lower level in money terms. The world-wide fraternity of bankers is strongly opposed to inflation and regards unemployment as a lesser evil, not because they gain from a slump but because it is a matter of principle for them to assert the authority of finance over industry.

Problems of Welfare

The department of academic doctrine that goes under the title of the Economics of Welfare is nowadays generally taught by setting out the presumption in favour of laisser faire and free competition, then following it by a list of reservations and exceptions that destroy its validity.

The original doctrine was derived by Pareto from the general equilibrium system of Walras. It has nothing to do with Adam Smith's principle of expansion and technical progress. It is confined to a situation where there is a particular group of individuals, each with his tastes for a predetermined list of specific commodities, predetermined endowment of labour power, a list of physically specified equipment and stocks, and a predetermined body of technical knowledge.

In these conditions there is a 'production possibility surface' showing the outer bound of the quantities of the commodities that can be produced in every possible combination. When production is taking place at a point on this surface it is impossible to produce any more of one commodity (with the given resources and the given know how) without producing less of another. At each point on the surface there is a pattern of prices which shows the opportunity cost of each commodity in terms of the rest – that is to say, the minimum sacrifice of other things necessary to permit a small ('marginal') increase of any one to be produced. The argument requires that atomistic competition between the individuals regarded as producers, each following his own commercial advantage, will carry the system as a whole to the production-possibility surface.

On the other side of the market are the same individuals in their capacity as consumers. If their tastes are all alike, there is an indifference surface, showing the subjective valuation of different combinations of commodities, expressed in terms of the relative prices corresponding to their relative 'marginal utilities'.

There is assumed to be a unique set of prices at which the two surfaces are tangential to each other so that relative opportunity costs correspond to relative marginal utilities. This point is the optimum in the sense that any move away from it would reduce the total of utility being enjoyed.

When different consumers have different tastes, the argument is not so simple. At any one pattern of prices established in the market (at a point on the production possibility surface) each consumer can adjust his purchases so that his relative marginal utilities are equated to relative prices. Then, starting from that set of prices, it can be shown that no one consumer could be made better off, by changing the composition of output, without making some other worse off. This is a powerful argument for the status quo wherever it may happen to be. At every other point, there would be a different *status quo*, suiting some consumers better and some worse than the point which was chosen at the beginning of the argument.

The first general objection that is now admitted to this scheme (over and above some technical points within its own terms) is that it is purely static. Actual life is lived in the stream of time. In any economy, tastes, commodities, resources and know-how are continuously changing and modifying each other.

Secondly, there is a deep-seated inconsistency in the assumptions. When every individual is pursuing his own advantage, atomistic competition cannot persist, for any group of sellers or of buyers can secure a monopolistic or monopsonistic gain by acting together and share the benefits among individual members of the group. Perfect competition, like free trade amongst nations, can persist only when there is some rule of behaviour which overrides pure self interest.

Thirdly, we must consider the distribution of consumption between the individuals who make up the market. The purchasing power of each is limited by the receipts that he draws from sales. His receipts depend on the amount of his original endowment and the price that it will fetch. The importance of this consideration is revealed dramatically by the 'rule of free goods'. In order to ensure that there is an equilibrium pattern of prices for any arbitrarily given set of commodities and means of production, it is necessary to allow that there will be a zero price for anything for which supply consistently exceeds demand; in such a case a specialist seller receives zero income. (Labour power is as much subject to this rule as any other input.) In less extreme cases, it is still obvious that distribution of the benefits of the market between individuals is quite arbitrary and that it may often happen that a particular group amongst them would be far better off at some sub-optimum position (established by limitation of supplies) than on the productivity-possibility surface.

When this objection to the scheme is admitted, it is often said that inequalities should be corrected by a system of bounties and taxes, but there is no explanation of how the mechanism of the system – ruthless competition – is to work when an individual's income does not depend upon his own pursuit of individual advantage.

A fourth set of objections, which are coming very much into prominence at the present time, were treated by Pigou under the head of differences between private and social costs. He gave the mild example of the smoke nuisance, which imposes costs upon the public that the factory concerned cannot be charged for. Under the name of pollution, examples of this phenomenon on a devastating scale are now daily coming to notice. On the other side, very great advantages may follow from activities for which it is impossible to collect adequate payment in a society of unequal wealth and income – not only performances of grand opera, but the whole of education and the health service.

Thus the doctrine that the free play of individual interests in a competitive market maximises welfare for society as a whole has been demolished by its own practitioners. Yet these notions still have an important influence on the formation of ideology. The argument grew out of the hedonistic calculus, which regards all human life as governed by the pursuit of pleasure and avoidance of pain. Then it identifies pleasure with consumption, leaving out of account the whole sphere of the conditions in which work is carried out, and finally it reduces consumption to terms of spending money, so that the whole of economic basis of life is reduced to terms of commercial transactions.

> The current economic situation is a price system. Economic institutions in the modern civilized scheme of life are (prevailingly) institutions of the price system. The accountancy to which all phenomena of modern economic life are amenable is an accountancy in terms of price; and by the current convention there is no other recognized scheme of accountancy, no other rating, either in law or in fact, to which the facts of modern life are held amenable. Indeed, so great and pervading a force has this habit (institution) of pecuniary accountancy become that it extends, often as a matter of course, to many facts which properly have no pecuniary bearing and no pecuniary magnitude, as, e.g., works of art, science, scholarship, and religion.[b]

Nowadays the very word *economic* has come to mean commercial. Those who want to campaign for some public purpose, say clean air, find it necessary to make their case in terms of the loss in money value of saleable output attributable to ill health.

POLITICAL ECONOMY

The doctrines of laisser faire were very attractive, not only to those who gained most directly from the market system. If the economy is a self-regulating mechanism and economics a system of scientific laws, moral and political problems are excluded from it. Questions of social justice do not arise, all the operations of public administration are to be strictly neutral between interested parties. Ethics can be discussed on Sunday. It is considered unsound, soft-headed and unpatriotic to bring it in to week-day business. As soon as we recognize that the market, by its very nature, is necessarily a scene of conflicting interests, every element in it (such as we saw above, the price of cocoa beans) becomes a moral and political problem. This is tormenting because there are no longer any 'principles of economics' to provide safe and simple rules for finding the correct solutions.

The intrusion of politics into economic affairs increased dramatically in all the Western nations after 1945. We are now living in the era of *modern capitalism*, which has certain characteristics that distinguish it from all former systems. There were many contributory causes of this mutation in the free-market economy. Perhaps the most important was the experience of the great slump. After the super-full employment of war time, public opinion, business interests, politicians and administrators were united in resolving that a relapse into massive unemployment, declining output and financial ruin must never be allowed to recur. Indeed, the strongest adherents of laisser faire were now the greatest supporters of policies to maintain full employment, in order to prove that it was not an exclusive prerogative of the Soviets.*

A government which is committed to preserving near-full employment finds its sphere of operation ramifying throughout the economy. Some observers of modern capitalism maintain that the sole object of policy is to maintain profitability for the great corporations, but, even so, if near-full employment is maintained as a by-product, the results are important for all classes.

In spite of the great change in ideology which is required for national policies concerned with economic stability and growth, the doctrines of the neoclassical economists are still influential. Keynes himself, after ripping the

* This was written before the Age of Growth had come to an end.

theories of the neoclassicals (whom he called classicals) to pieces, turned round and gave them his blessing.

> Our criticism of the accepted classical theory of economics has consisted not so much in finding logical flaws in its analysis as in pointing out that its tacit assumptions are seldom or never satisfied, with the result that it cannot solve the economic problems of the actual world. But if our central controls succeed in establishing an aggregate volume of output corresponding to full employment as nearly as is practicable, the classical theory comes into its own again from this point onwards. If we suppose the volume of output to be given, i.e. to be determined by forces outside the classical scheme of thought, then there is no objection to be raised against the classical analysis of the manner in which private self-interest will determine what in particular is produced, in what proportions the factors of production will be combined to produce it, and how the value of the final product will be distributed between them.[c]

But this view derives from sentiment more than logic. It is impossible to have a policy designed to maintain effective demand in the abstract. Every policy must have some concrete content. The instruments in the hands of an administration – monetary policy, the exchange rate, taxation, government expenditure impinge in specific ways upon specific interests. Taxation may be designed to foster either investment or consumption; if consumption, it may be on the principle to him that hath shall be given, that is by a proportional reduction in direct tax rates, or it may be used to make transfers in one way or another to the lower income groups. Still less can there be a neutral programme of government investment. There is no simple rule to allocate outlay between say, armaments and infant schools in a neutral manner.

But while economic affairs grow ever more overtly political, at the same time commercial influences spread into new spheres. Continuous inflation and rapid technical change make it necessary for every group to defend itself against the erosion of its relative income and status, so that the method of organizing strikes spreads from industrial trade unions to the professions. Old notions of loyalty, service and proper behaviour are undermined by commercial principles.

Twenty-five years of near-full employment has been a new experience for capitalism; while we have been enjoying its benefits, it has been developing internal contradictions that may be going to make the next twenty-five years more uneasy.

At the same time, in the Soviet sphere, also, new problems were coming to the surface. The Soviet style of administration and ideology was formed in the struggle for rapid and massive industrialization, under Stalin's five-year plans, and a great part was to do over again because of wartime destruction. Now that the Soviet economy is over the hump and has become the second industrial and military power in the world, it is time to enjoy the fruits of struggle and sacrifice in leisure and comfort. Moreover the Soviet economists, who were happy to despise the free-market system as long as it was wallowing in the great slump, now have to admit that capitalism is (at least for the time being) providing its working class with near-full employment, a rising level of real earnings and an enticing variety of goods and services in which to enjoy it. Some of these economists, in Russia and the People's Democracies, reading Western textbooks, came to the conclusion that the secret of the success of capitalism lay in the price mechanism and the interplay of supply and demand. The notion of 'market socialism' thus came into vogue. Now, the rigid, over-centralized administration of industry by a system of instructions had, admittedly, led to considerable waste and inefficiency, and sometimes to a total lack of elementary common sense. There was therefore great scope for improvements in management. But the notion (first propagated in Russia by Libermann) that a general solution could be found by introducing the criterion of profitability into Soviet enterprises turned out to be illusory. The secret of private enterprise (both for good and ill) is that it is private enterprise – the manager of a capitalist concern acts as a principal and uses initiative and judgement. A socialist manager who is told to make profits is still an agent acting under instructions, necessarily anxious to seem correct and avoid responsibility. The instructions in terms of profits may be somewhat less confusing and contradictory than the old multiform plan indicators, but they are still arbitrary instructions; moreover profitability depends upon prices; a system of prices fixed by decree would certainly lead to a new crop of anomalies not much less idiotic than those that it replaced, while freedom for the enterprise to set its own prices (as in Yugoslavia) would import the anomalies of imperfect competition and instability of markets. As the Hungarian economist, Kornai, has said, changes in methods of administration must be made in such a way as to develop the 'advantageous aspects of our economic mechanism further, rather than endangering them.'[d] It seems that reforms, similar to those which were frustrated in Czechoslovakia in 1968 or which have withered in Poland, are being carried out in Hungary with a sophisticated appreciation of the need to adapt of the relations administration to the mechanism of the economy.

There is one element in the Walrasian scheme that ought to be of use in a planned economy – that is, the very concept of physical efficiency and opportunity cost. When planning is clumsy, numerous situations arise where industry is operating well within the production possibility surface, that is when it would be possible (with given resources) to produce more of one good and more of others as well. The Soviet mathematician, Kantorovich, devised the powerful tool of linear programming to provide solutions for the Walrasian problem in concrete reality. There is a school of thought which holds that the way ahead for the Soviet economy lies, not in less planning, but in more – in improving efficiency by intelligent application of devices that a brilliant group of mathematical economists have already worked out in theory. But mathematical methods can apply only in the strictly limited sphere of using pre-existing resources for pre-determined ends. The mathematicians cannot instruct the planners in what products to produce. It still remains to find some means (as has to a great extent been found in China) of bringing the needs and tastes of would-be consumers to bear upon the design and composition of the flow of production intended for their benefit.

Meanwhile many nominally independent nations in the Third World find that the opening up of their resources and their markets to commercial and financial operations turns out, as is natural, to be more convenient for businesses already experienced and already powerful than for struggling newcomers. The slow pace of domestic capital accumulation and the great inequality in the distribution of the proceeds where accumulation does take place, combined with an unprecedented growth in numbers, leads to a situation in the so-called developing countries that does not give much support to the doctrine that the free play of market forces can be relied upon to maximize human welfare.

[a] Karl Polanyi. *Primitive, Archaic and Modern Economies*.

[b] Thorstein Veblen. 'The Limitations of Marginal Utility' in *The Place of Science in Modern Society*, p. 245. Viking Press, New York, 1919 and 1960.

[c] Keynes, *General Theory* (JMK) Vol. VII, p. 378.

[d] Janos Kornai. *Overcentralisation in Economic Administration*, Oxford, 1959.

SECTION THREE

15

WHAT HAS BECOME OF
THE KEYNESIAN REVOLUTION?

1

WHAT was the dominant orthodoxy against which the Keynesian revolution was raised? *The General Theory of Employment Interest and Money* was not published till 1936 but the revolution began to stir in 1929, lurched forward in 1931 and grew urgent with the grim events of 1933.

In those years British orthodoxy was still dominated by nostalgia for the world before 1914. *Then* there was normality and equilibrium. To get back to that happy state, its institutions and its policies should be restored – keep to the gold standard at the old sterling parity, balance the budget, maintain free trade and observe the strictest laisser-faire in the relations of government with industry. When Lloyd George proposed a campaign to reduce unemployment (which was then at the figure of one million or more) by expenditure on public works, he was answered by the famous 'Treasury View' that there is a certain amount of saving, at any moment available to finance investment, and if the government borrows a part, there will be so much the less for industry.

In 1931, when the world crisis had produced a sharp increase in the deficit on the U.K. balance of payments, the appropriate remedy (approved as much by the unlucky Labour government as by the Bank of England) was to cut expenditure so as to balance the budget. These were the orthodox views that prevailed in the realm of public policy.

In the realm of economic theory, orthodox doctrine comprised two distinct branches – *Principles* and *Money*. In the department of Principles, the main topic was the behaviour of markets under the influence of supply and demand and the determination of the relative prices of commodities and the relative earnings of 'factors of production'. In so far as there was anything that would nowadays be called a macro theory, that is, an analysis of the

---

Presidential Address, Section F, British Association, 1972. Reprinted in *After Keynes*, Basil Blackwell, 1973.

operation of the economy as a whole, it was dominated by the conception of a natural tendency to equilibrium under the free play of market forces. *General* unemployment was a contradiction in terms.

Marshall had a foxy way of salving his conscience by mentioning exceptions, but doing so in such a way that his pupils would continue to believe in the rule. He pointed out that Say's Law – supply creates its own demand – breaks down when there is a failure of confidence, which causes investment to fall off and contraction to spread from one market to another. This was mentioned by the way. It was not meant to disturb the general faith in equilibrium under laisser-faire.

The department of monetary theory was quite different. This dealt with the general price level and had to include awkward subjects like inflation and the trade cycle. According to this theory movements in prices were determined by changes in the quantity of money. It is a strange fact that, when it came to pronouncing on public affairs, the economists everywhere derived their advice from the department of Principles and forgot all about Money. In those days (unlike now) the leading symptom of a recession was a fall in prices. If all that was needed to raise prices, and so get production going again, was to print some bank notes, why did not the economists advise their governments to do so at once? No. The money cranks were saying: It can all be done with a fountain pen, but the orthodox economists thought them very wrong. The orthodox line was that nothing can be done, that nothing should be done; that in good time, equilibrium will be restored.

Keynes started life as a monetary economist. When he was working on his *Treatise on Money*, he thought that he had to be concerned strictly with the general price level. He rejected the suggestion that his subject was connected with the problem of unemployment. But in 1929 he had descended from this high theoretical plane to practical policy, supporting Lloyd George's campaign for public works. The pamphlet which he wrote with Hubert Henderson, *Can Lloyd George Do It?*, sketches out the theory that investment generates saving, so that a budget deficit can reduce unemployment without generating inflation.

The analysis is very sketchy. R. F. Kahn took it up, worked out the theory of the multiplier in a more coherent manner, and persuaded Keynes that he and Henderson had been perfectly right. The ink was not dry on the first copies of the *Treatise* before Keynes began to acknowledge that employment was after all the central point. The quantity of money fell into place in the theory of interest rates. Changes in activity were seen to be governed by changes in expenditure on investment and the purchase of consumption goods. The price level had nothing to do with banking policy, it depended on money-wage rates. So the old dichotomy was broken down and 'monetary theory' was absorbed into the analysis of output as a whole.

Meanwhile the Nazis had been proving Lloyd George's point with a vengeance. It was a joke in Germany that Hitler was planning to give employment in straightening the Crooked Lake, painting the Black Forest white and putting down linoleum in the Polish Corridor. The Treasury view was that his unsound policies would soon bring him down. But the little group of Keynesians was despondent and frustrated. We were getting the theory clear at last, but it was going to be too late.

2

There will soon be an account in the latest volume of the *Collected Writings of John Maynard Keynes* of the upheavals and reformulations that led from the *Treatise* to the *General Theory*. It will be seen that there were moments when we had some trouble in getting Maynard to see what the point of his revolution really was, but when he came to sum it up after the book was published he got it into focus.[1]

On the plane of theory, the revolution lay in the change from the conception of equilibrium to the conception of history; from the principles of rational choice to the problems of decisions based on guess-work or on convention.

In traditional teaching, it was assumed

> that the amounts of the factors of production in use were given and that the problem was to determine the way in which they would be used and their relative rewards.

Keynes' contemporaries

> like their predecessors were still dealing with a system in which the amount of the factors employed was given and the other relevant facts were known more or less for certain. This does not mean that they were dealing with a system in which change was ruled out, or even one in which the disappointment of expectation was ruled out. But at any given time facts and expectations were assumed to be given in a definite and calculable form; and risks, of which, though admitted, not much notice was taken, were supposed to be capable of an exact actuarial computation. The calculus of probability, though mention of it was

[1]'The General Theory of Employment', (JMK) Vol. XIV.

kept in the background, was supposed to be capable of reducing uncertainty to the same calculable status as that of certainty itself.

Keynes drew a sharp distinction between calculable risks and the uncertainty which arises from lack of reliable information. Since the future is essentially uncertain, strictly rational behaviour is impossible; a great part of economic life is conducted on the basis of accepted conventions.

> Knowing that our own individual judgment is worthless, we endeavour to fall back on the judgment of the rest of the world which is perhaps better informed. That is, we endeavour to conform with the behaviour of the majority or the average. The psychology of a society of individuals each of whom is endeavouring to copy the others leads to what we may strictly term a *conventional* judgment . . . Being based on so flimsy a foundation, it is subject to sudden and violent changes. The practice of calmness and immobility, of certainty and security, suddenly breaks down. New fears and hopes will, without warning, take charge of human conduct. The forces of disillusion may suddenly impose a new conventional basis of valuation. All these pretty, polite techniques, made for a well-panelled board room and a nicely regulated market, are liable to collapse. At all times the vague panic fears and equally vague and unreasoned hopes are not really lulled, and lie but a little way below the surface . . .
>
> Though this is how we behave in the market place, the theory we devise in the study of how we behave in the market place should not itself submit to market-place idols. I accuse the classical economic theory of being itself one of these pretty, polite techniques which tries to deal with the present by abstracting from the fact that we know very little about the future.

The existence of money is bound up with uncertainty, for interest-earning assets would always be preferred to cash if there was no doubt about their future value. In this light, the nature of interest becomes clear. Keynes was able to resolve a deep-seated confusion in traditional teaching by emphasizing the distinction between the rate of interest, as the price of finance, and the rate of profit expected on an investment, for which he unfortunately devised a new term – *the marginal efficiency of capital*.

It is uncertainty that accounts for

> the liability of the scale of investment to fluctuate for reasons quite distinct (a) from those which determine the propensity of the

individual to *save* out of a given income and (b) from those physical conditions of technical capacity to aid production which have usually been supposed hitherto to be the chief influence governing the marginal efficiency of capital.

Once we admit that an economy exists in time, that history goes one way, from the irrevocable past into the unknown future, the conception of equilibrium based on the mechanical analogy of a pendulum swinging to and fro in space becomes untenable. The whole of traditional economics needs to be thought out afresh.

After the war, Keynes' theory was accepted as a new orthodoxy without the old one being rethought. In modern text-books, the pendulum still swings, *tending* towards its equilibrium point. Market forces allocate given factors of production between alternative uses, investment is a sacrifice of present consumption, and the rate of interest measures society's discount of the future. All the slogans are repeated unchanged.

How has this trick been worked? First of all, simplifications in Keynes' own exposition, which were necessary at the first stage of the argument, have been used to smooth the meaning out of it. Keynes sometimes talked of total output at full employment as though it was a simple quantity. Obviously, the maximum output that can be produced in a given situation depends on the productive capacity in existence of plant and equipment for labour to be employed with, and productive capacity exists in concrete forms available for producing particular kinds of output. The notion of 'the level of investment that will ensure full employment' presupposes the existence of productive capacity for investment and consumption goods in the right proportions.

Moreover, it presupposes a particular ratio of consumption to investment. But the level of consumption from a given total income depends upon its distribution between consumers, and this depends on the distribution of wealth among households, the ratio of profits to wages, relative prices of commodities and the system of taxation.

All this is ignored in the vulgarized version of Keynes' theory. At any moment, the text-book argument runs, there is a certain amount of saving per annum that would occur at full employment. Let the government see to it that there is enough investment to absorb that amount and then all will be well.

So we return to the classical world where accumulation is determined by saving and the old theory slips back into place. But here there is a difficulty. Investment every year is to be just enough to absorb the year's savings. What about the new equipment that it creates? Will that be just enough to employ the labour then available, when investment is absorbing saving next year? The long-period aspect of investment, that it creates capital goods, must be considered as well as the short-period aspect, that it keeps up effective demand.

Never mind! Never mind! cry the bastard Keynesians. We can pretend that capital goods are all made of putty. They can be squeezed up or spread out, without trouble or cost, to give whatever amount of employment is required. Moreover, there is no need to worry about mistaken investments or about technical change. Not only the putty added this year, but the whole lot, can be squeezed into any form that is needed so as to re-establish equilibrium instantaneously after any change.

There has been a lot of tiresome controversy over this putty. The bastard Keynesians try to make out that it is all about the problem of 'measuring capital'. But it has nothing to do either with measurement or with capital; it has to do with abolishing time. For a world that is always in equilibrium there is no difference between the future and the past, there is no history and there is no need for Keynes.

3

The other half of the Keynesian revolution was to recognize that, in an industrial economy, the level of prices is governed primarily by the level of money-wage rates.

To clear some details out of the way, let us first look at Keynes's theory of the behaviour of prices with given wage rates. First, he accepted the idea of competitive market prices. Neither Roy Harrod nor I could get Maynard to take an interest in 'marginal revenue'. He therefore had to find an explanation of the obvious fact that prices do not immediately fall to the level of average prime cost whenever sales are below full capacity output. This was the point of 'user cost'. The modern concept of gross profit margins as a mark-up on prime cost would really have suited him much better. Second, following Marshall's notion of 'cost at the margin', he took it for granted that there is a tendency for prices to rise somewhat with an upswing in activity and to fall in a recession, when money-wage rates do not change. This was a question of empirical fact that had no particular logical importance in the theory; it led to unnecessary complications in the definition of 'involuntary unemployment' and it led to the view that a rise in employment normally leads to a fall in the level of real-wage rates, which Keynes had to emphasize was by no means the same as the view that a fall in real wages causes an increase in employment. Thirdly, in the *Treatise* Keynes made a great point of the shift to profit that occurs when effective demand rises. He did not deny this in the *General Theory* but there he generally dealt with a rise in incomes overall without much emphasis on distribution.

These are all minor points compared to the main argument, that the level of prices in terms of money is a reflection of the level of money-wage rates.

This was a greater shock to notions of equilibrium even than the concept of effective demand governed by volatile expectations. The level of money wages in any country at any time is more or less an historical accident going back to a remote past and influenced by recent events affecting the balance of power between employers and trade unions in the labour market.

Then there is no meaning whatever in the idea of an equilibrium value of money. This was such a blow to orthodox ideas that almost all those who were ready to welcome the Keynesian diagnosis of unemployment somehow refused to take it in until it became too painfully obvious to be ignored any longer.

I believe that the extraordinary revival of the quantity theory of money in recent years (in an even more hollow form than of old) must be accounted for by the longing to have some kind of theory that provides something to tether the value of money to, some defence against the horrid thought that under laisser-faire the private-enterprise system does not tend towards equilibrium in any way at all.

There was another attempt to tame Keynes's theory of prices and bring it into the orbit of a mechanical analogy – that was the late-lamented Phillips curve. It is obvious enough that a *rise* in wage rates occurs more often after a recent *rise* in the level of employment than after a fall. When employment has recently risen, bargaining power of trade unions has improved, there has been an increase in profits, and often an increase in the cost of living. In a buoyant market, employers are reluctant to lose output through a strike and are confident of being able to recover costs by raising prices if they have to grant a rise in wages. On the other hand, in a deep slump, when there is heavy unemployment and at the same time real-wage rates for those in work have recently improved because of reduced prices of primary products, wage rates rarely rise and may even be cut in some cases.

From a hasty run over of the statistics reflecting this historical experience is derived an econometric *law* relating the level of unemployment (not changes in it) to changes in wage rates. From this can be read off the amount of unemployment associated with a constant level of prices, and then policy can be framed in terms of the 'pay off' between unemployment and inflation.

The simplicity of this faith in the econometrician's magic numbers is matched by the remarkable cynicism of the proposals derived from it.

Perhaps the publicity given to the Phillips curve contributed to falsifying its predictions. It was natural for the trade unions to resolve to demonstrate that it is not true that when a certain proportion of their members are unemployed they are incapable of demanding higher wages. However that may be, it is clear enough that the 'pay off' is a cheat. We can have a recession and say goodbye to full employment without inflation being any the less.

Already before the war, Keynes was pointing out that wage-bargaining in conditions of continuous near-full employment was going to present an extremely awkward political problem. Now everyone agrees with the theory, but the political problem has not become any easier to solve.

4

What about the influence of the *General Theory* on practical affairs?

There is a kind of simple-minded Marxist who has a great resentment against Keynes because he is held responsible for saving capitalism from destroying itself in another great slump. This is often made an excuse for not understanding the theory of effective demand, although Michal Kalecki derived pretty well the same analytical system as Keynes from Marx's premises. Moreover it implies that capitalists are so stupid that they would fail to learn from their experiences during the war that government outlay maintains profits, unless they had Keynes to point it out to them.

But what was the political tendency of the *General Theory*? Keynes himself described it as 'moderately conservative' but this was intended as a paradox, for the whole book is a polemic against established ideas. His own mood often swung from left to right. Capitalism was in some ways repugnant to him but Stalinism was much worse. In his last years, certainly, the right predominated. When I teased him about accepting a peerage he replied that after sixty one had to become respectable. But his basic view of life was aesthetic rather than political. He hated unemployment because it was stupid and poverty because it was ugly. He was disgusted by the commercialism of modern life. (It is true he enjoyed making money for his College and for himself but only as long as it did not take up much time.) He indulged in an agreeable vision of a world where economics has ceased to be important and our grandchildren can begin to lead a civilized life.

At the time when the *General Theory* was being written, Keynes, projecting the situation of the slump into the future, threw out the suggestion that the need for accumulation could be overcome in thirty years of investment at the full-employment level, provided that wars were avoided and population ceased to grow. (He was taking an insular view. The Third World had not yet come to mind.) Alvin Hansen took this up and turned it into a horror story. With the closing of the frontier in North America, there would not be sufficient outlets for the saving that capitalism generates and chronic stagnation will set in. This was not Keynes's attitude. He welcomed the euthanasia of the rentier. He was only afraid that the prospect might be spoiled by failure to get the rate of interest to fall fast enough. This part of the argument in the *General Theory* is not at all clear. It seems to contain an undigested lump of what Keynes called classical theory. In a long-run sense the 'marginal efficiency of capital' means both prospective profits to a business and the real usefulness of investment to society. There is no hint that these might not always be the same thing. But, in any case, Keynes is arguing that, if a private-enterprise system cannot deal with potential abundance, we must turn it into a system that can. Certainly, the last chapter of the *General Theory* tries to make out that such a change could be easy and painless but it does not suggest, like Hansen, that if capitalism is incompatible with plenty, plenty ought to be sacrificed to keep capitalism going.

Of course, it has all turned out to be a daydream. The twenty-five years after the war that passed without a major recession has been called the Age of Keynes, but it was not much like his vision. It turned out closer to Kalecki's sardonic description of the regime of the political trade cycle.

Unemployment is a reproach to a democratic government. When it gets too big, steps are taken to reduce it. Besides, unemployment is associated with low profits. But when unemployment falls too low, inflation sets in. So policy is always alternating between go and stop. This is not using resources for rational ends; it is making employment, or rather avoiding *much* unemployment, an end in itself.

When we were up against sound finance and the Treasury view, we had to argue that any expenditure is better than none. Dig holes in the ground and fill them again, paint the Black Forest white; if men cannot be paid wages for doing something sensible, pay them to do something silly.

'To dig holes in the ground', paid for out of savings, will increase, not only employment but the real national dividend of useful goods and services. It is not reasonable, however,' Keynes adds 'that a sensible community should be content to remain dependent on such fortuitous and often wasteful mitigations when once we understand the influences upon which effective demand depends.[2]

As it has turned out, employment has been kept up by expedients that are not just silly. The self-styled Keynesians in the United States boast of having overcome the rule of sound finance. The consequence has been to facilitate deficit expenditure on armaments; it has helped to keep up the cold war and promoted hot wars here and there around the world.

Now, it seems that the bastard Keynesian era is coming to an end in general disillusionment; the economists have no more idea what to say than they had when the old equilibrium doctrine collapsed in the great slump. The Keynesian revolution still remains to be made both in teaching economic theory and in forming economic policy.

[2] *General Theory*, p. 220.

16

SMOOTHING OUT KEYNES

THE subtitle of this book is *The Life, times, thought and triumph of the greatest economist of our age.* The story leads up to the tax cuts of 1965 and ends with the suggestion that the United States will live happily ever afterwards in Keynesian full employment.

The life is pieced together from Harrod's biography and other memoirs and reminiscences; the development of Keynes' thought from quotations from his works up to the time of the *General Theory.* Already at this stage in the book a kind of mollifying process is at work, smoothing out contradictions. Keynes had a high degree of intellectual detachment but he frankly admits to an emotional ambivalence. Morally and aesthetically, capitalism disgusted him, while at the same time he felt that the system was the 'best in sight' and must be defended. Robert Lekachman quotes only the defensive passages. From the analysis of the pre-1914 world in *Economic Consequences of the Peace* he gives us the description of the capitalists: 'Like bees they saved and accumulated, not less to the advantage of the whole community because they themselves held narrower ends in prospect' but not:

> the labouring classes accepted from ignorance or powerlessness, or were compelled, persuaded or cajoled by custom, convention, authority, and the well-established order of Society into accepting a situation in which they could call their own very little of the cake, that they and Nature and the capitalists were co-operating to produce.[1]

From the *Short View of Russia* he gives us the oft-quoted phrase about 'preferring the mud to the fish' but not the analysis of Communism as a new religion:

> At any rate to me it seems clearer every day that the moral problem of our age is concerned with the love of money, with the habitual appeal

[1] *Economic Consequences of the Peace*, p. 17.

Review of *The Age of Keynes*, by Robert Lekachman, The New York Review of Books, 26 January, 1967.

to the money motive in nine-tenths of the activities of life, with the universal striving after individual economic security as the prime object of endeavour, with the social approbation of money as the measure of constructive success, and with the social appeal to the hoarding instinct as the foundation of the necessary provision for the family and for the future.[2]

What appealed to Keynes in Russia (in spite of the mud) was the hope of a society built on other motives.

This ambivalence runs through the *General Theory* itself. The hard argument demolishes the orthodox defence of the private-enterprise system and the bravura passages are full of devastating irony; yet at the end the 'social philosophy towards which the General Theory might lead' turns out to be 'moderately conservative'.[3] It is the end that our author finds appealing; he does not have much to say about the rest.

The mollifying treatment is most marked in the account of Keynes' relations with the United States at the end of his life. Even respectable opinion is now coming round to the view that Keynes' Clearing Union was a more intelligent conception than the International Monetary Fund advocated by the US and finally adopted after much debate. The situation today, when the trading world is threatened by a totally unnecessary crisis because of the inadequate and unreliable supply of international liquidity, underlines the advantages of Keynes' conception of a super-central bank which could regulate the world's monetary system on the same principles as a national central bank manages its own currency. In any case, no one could deny that his argument was clearer and his style more persuasive than Harry White's. But England (without yet noticing it) had finally come to the end of her age of dominance. Keynes had no force behind him to oppose the weight of American wealth and power. His wit only irritated slower thinkers. He had to be careful what he said, which he was not used to at home. Moreover, a loyal public servant, he had to defend the botched-up agreement at home as though he really believed in it. (He had submitted himself to the sarcasm of his old Bloomsbury friends by accepting a peerage the better to play the part of a respected national figure, but his old role of *enfant terrible* still suited him best.) Finally, when lend-lease was abruptly cut off, he had to return to Washington to beg and was obliged to accept the humiliation of agreeing to terms – an early return to convertibility of sterling – which he knew to be impossible to fulfil.

[2] *Essays in Persuasion*, (JMK) Vol. IX, p. 308.
[3] *General Theory of Employment, Interest and Money*, ch. 24.

'What should this mean?'
'It is the god Hercules, whom Anthony loved, now leaving him.'

This great historical scene naturally has a different emotional colour
when viewed from different sides of the Atlantic, but, either way, it was a
historical scene: it is a shame to smooth it over with complacent phrases.

The major part of the book is concerned with the influence of Keynesian
ideas on American economic policy. Lekachman points out that the New
Deal was a mixed bag, containing restrictive as well as expansionary
elements. The halting recovery from 1933 to 1937 gave little evidence,
either way, of the effectiveness of deficit spending as a remedy for
unemployment. The sharp slump of 1937 due to a return to 'sound finance',
however, was an experimental test providing a dramatic illustration of the
main thesis of the General Theory, which made many converts. After this
experience, it could no longer be argued that a budget deficit was
necessarily inflationary, or that cutting outlay and increasing taxes, when
there was already unemployment, would not make the situation worse.

The most influential popularizer of Keynes in the US was Alvin Hansen,
who put the new doctrine out in the form of the stagnation thesis according
to which the cessation of population growth and the 'closing of the frontier'
had dried up the outlet for investment and would lead to chronic depression
because of a lack of market demand to make production profitable. There is
a great difference between Keynes' version of the long-term implications
of the General Theory and the moral that was drawn from it by Hansen.
Keynes maintained that, with peace and a more or less constant population,
it would be possible for the industrial nations (he did not look beyond) to
saturate the need for capital accumulation within thirty years, so that, from
then on, saving would cease to be necessary, and the resources released
could be used to cultivate the arts of agreeable living. (He did not distinguish between public and private investment so that he did not have to
distinguish between *useful* and *profitable* capital equipment.) This held out
the promise for a genuinely civilized life in the future, but it would require
great changes in our institutions and ideas if it was not to run to waste in
unemployment and stagnation. The social justification for inequality of
income, as a restraint on mass consumption, would have disappeared and
the anarchy of private enterprise would have to give way to the planned use
of resources for the benefit of society as a whole.[4] The thirty years was one
of Keynes' wild guesses, but we cannot tell how far out it was, for we have

[4] The clearest statement of this point of view is in Keynes' Galton Lecture, *Eugenics
Review*, 1937.

had neither peace, constant numbers, nor full employment maintained by useful investment, since he spoke.

For Hansen, a decline in outlets for profitable investment appeared not as a glorious opportunity but as a threatening disaster. He did not conceive, or preferred not to utter, dangerous thoughts about the need to change our institutions and ideas.

The war, which expanded *civilian consumption* in the US by 50 per cent, was a crude lesson in the principles of the General Theory. The devotees of private enterprise, sensing danger, put up a great resistance to the Keynesians after the war; the Employment Act of 1946 was a vague and feeble remnant of the Bill that they had proposed. All the same, for fifteen years stagnation was fended off; recessions were relatively mild. Keynes seemed unnecessary.

Three problems were emerging under the surface of near-enough stability. The first was inflation. Lekachman implies that this was an unforeseen danger that lay outside the scope of Keynes' argument. But the English Keynesians deduced from the General Theory, even while the slump was still with us, that a successful employment policy would lead to a chronic spiral of wages and prices. (Lekachman associates this phenomenon with the growth of large oligopolistic businesses, but it would be even more marked in a regime of unrestricted competition.) The incompatibility of continuous full employment with stable prices they saw as the unsolved problem of the future as, indeed, it still is.

Keynes did not maintain that everything would be easy once the principles of employment policy were understood, or that simple automatic regulators could be fitted into the system of a private enterprise economy that would dispense with the need for wise judgment. The main message of the General Theory was negative. It struck off the shackles of laisser-faire ideology. Keynes knew that new freedom would raise fresh problems and require fresh solutions. He certainly did not see himself as a quack peddling a panacea.

The second problem, which Lekachman touches upon only lightly, was the disequilibrium in the balance of payments. The huge surplus of income in the USA balance of payments (arising from an excess of exports over imports and from receipts of interest and profits from overseas investments) was gradually proving insufficient to support both the overseas expenditure of the Government and the outflow of profit-seeking finance which laisser-faire permits.

The third problem of the Fifties in the USA was the growth of 'non-Keynesian' unemployment lasting for long periods. The stabilization of the economy kept total output more or less constant, or slowly growing. Technical progress, including automation, was raising output per head. Consequently the demand for labour failed to keep up with the growth of the labour force. The growth of small-scale service businesses provided 'disguised unemployment' for many, while open unemployment drifted up from 4 per cent to nearly 6 per cent of the available labour force. The concentration of unemployment upon the young, particularly young Negroes, created horrifying social dislocation.

Lekachman opens the discussion of automation with the question:

> Even after it is conceded that Republican programs administered less stimulus than the economy required, there remains a crucial question: Why did the economy require the stimulus in the first place? Why weren't the impulses of private spending strong enough to employ men and machines fully?

To put the question this way seems to betray a lingering belief in laisser-faire equilibrium. Why should we expect private spending to be at the right level? And if it were, is *private* spending the best use for the resources that technical progress releases? Does not the present scene reveal a disastrous failure in *public* spending, particularly on education? Lekachman refers somewhat patronizingly to Galbraith; he fails to remark that Galbraith alone has drawn the moral from the General Theory – once we accept the idea that there ought to be full employment, the question follows what should employment be for.

But in the sixties in the USA the argument was still at the primitive stage. The idea whose triumph Lekachman celebrates was the idea that massive unemployment ought not to be allowed. He describes how the economists converted President Kennedy to the view that budget deficits were not only permissible but actually advantageous to an under-employed economy, how the idea of tax cuts was resisted by public opinion (to the amazement of the rest of the world), and how, taken over by President Johnson, they suddenly became respectable.

Lekachman is well aware of the limitations of the new policies, but he believes, as Keynes did in his day, that once the primitive stage of the argument has been won, unbounded possibilities open up.

> What can be achieved by the consensus of the major interest groups in the United States is very substantial. The flood of legislation in 1965 verified the possibility of moderate improvement within the fiscal limits set by business predominance in the administration coalition. In

short, conservative expansionism is really capable of making American society tolerable for most Americans. Nevertheless, its limitations are such, its powerful tendencies to favor the prosperous are so dominant, and its suspicion of the public sector is still so strong that it will take a more vigorous path of government action, the road of liberal intervention, to convert even an enlightened commercial community into a Great Society – to move from Keynesian fiscal policy to the Keynesian vision of a rational community.

In all this there is one very striking omission. I could find only two or three passing references in the whole book to armaments expenditure (cold or hot) as a booster to employment and profits.

> Theoretically, however, it is just as possible to stimulate a sluggish economy by reducing taxes as by enlarging social welfare programs, or, for that matter, military spending.

and

> What would happen to the economy if peace broke out and military expenditure declined from $50 billion to $1 billion per year?

And it is shown that the Republican regime, in spite of a doctrinal belief in sound finance, ran budget deficits to maintain outlays required by the exigences of cold war diplomacy'.

Many well-meaning US citizens become extremely indignant (though others are cheerfully cynical) when the dependence of prosperity in the United States upon armaments is remarked on. There is no need, however, to inquire whether the cold war, the 'missile gap' and the crusade against Communism in Asia were conceived, deliberately or unconsciously, as a means of fending off depression without drastic political or social change. Attribute them to whatever noble motives you please – that has clearly been their effect. Even while this book was in the press, tax cuts were proved unnecessary and visions of the Great Society were bundled into storage while the 'exigencies' of a hot war provided more than sufficient stimulus to the economy.

In a well-known passage, Keynes sarcastically maintains that useless expenditure is even more effective for maintaining demand than productive investment. 'Two pyramids, two masses for the dead, are twice as good as one; but not so two railways from London to York.' Two stocks of bombs, two little nations blitzed, are twice as good as one. We are indeed living in the age of Keynes, but it is not turning out so well as he expected.

17

MICHAL KALECKI

1

IN the natural sciences it is common enough for the same discovery to come almost simultaneously from two independent sources. The general development of a subject throws up a new problem and two equally original minds find the same answer, which turns out to be validated by further work. In the history of economic thought, there is one notable example of this phenomenon, the discovery of the theory of employment by Maynard Keynes and Michal Kalecki. In the social sciences, experiments are not made in laboratories but thrown up by history. The problem to which they were both searching for an answer was the breakdown of the market economy in the great slump of the 1930s.

The orthodox economists were still reiterating the old doctrine of a natural tendency to equilibrium under the free play of market forces and enunciating the proposition that the central problem of economic analysis is the allocation of scarce means between alternative uses, as though the whole nation was a single peasant farmer deciding what to grow to feed his family. (This doctrine, in a garbled form, has been revived and, even today, is taught in the leading American textbooks.) It was not possible, in 1932, to deny that millions of workers were unemployed or that, in the United States, national income had fallen to half its value of three years before, but these phenomena were attributed to 'frictions' that held up the working of market forces, to the folly of trade unions in preventing wages from falling further, or to a scarcity of gold that was constricting the monetary system.

Unshakeable faith in equilibrium was derived from a conception that ran deep into the heart of orthodox theory – the notion that the growth of wealth for society as a whole, like that of a single family, depends on saving. 'Saving is a form of spending'; whatever an individual does not spend on consumption (giving employment in producing commodities for sale) is

---

Michal Kalecki Memorial Lecture, reprinted from the *Oxford Bulletin of Economics and Statistics*, February 1977.

devoted to investment (giving employment in creating additional productive capacity in the form of capital equipment and stocks). The simple and obvious point, that occurred independently to Keynes and to Kalecki, is that in a modern capitalist economy, accumulation is not controlled by household saving but by the investments of profit-seeking firms. In the situation of the slump, investment was low because prospects of profit were weak and uncertain. Because investment was low, employment was low and incomes were low. Because incomes were low, expenditure was low. Therefore business was working below capacity and there was little demand for new investment goods (capital equipment and stocks).

Government expenditure on public works would create jobs and raise incomes. The wages, and later, profits would be spent, so that incomes and employment would increase. Each increase would lead to further spending. The total increase in income would be related by a 'multiplier' to the original outlay, while savings would be increased by as much as the original government expenditure.

To accept this point of view meant to admit that there is an inherent defect in the laisser-faire system, that the concept of a natural tendency to equilibrium is mis-conceived, and that household saving is a consequence rather than a cause of capital accumulation. Since this went to the heart of orthodox doctrine, a stout resistance was put up. The Keynesian argument was still in dispute when war broke out in 1939. After the war, government policy in the capitalist world could not return to the prescription of complete laisser-faire, but academic teaching (especially in the USA) resisted every attempt to reconsider the orthodox position. Keynes' version of the new theory was emasculated and wrapped up again in equilibrium and Kalecki's version was simply ignored.

2

In England the argument started, in 1929, with a debate about the case for Government loan expenditure on public works as a means of reducing unemployment. On the academic plane, Keynes was still working on his *Treatise on Money*. As soon as it was published, a great storm of argument broke out in Cambridge. By 1933 it was clear that what Keynes was looking for was not a theory of 'money' but a theory of the determination of output as a whole. In the summer of 1934 the main lines of the *General Theory of Employment, Interest and Money* had become clear, but the book was not published until 1936. I had been writing some essays drawing a number of riders from the main theory,[1] holding them back to be published when the *General Theory* was out. One of these appeared in the *Economic Journal* in June 1936.

Soon afterwards I received a letter, evidently from a foreigner visiting England, who said that he was interested in my article as it was close to some work of his own. I thought this very strange. Who could claim to be doing work that was close to this – the first fruits of the Keynesian revolution? When Michal Kalecki turned up, I was still more astonished. He cared little for party manners or small talk and plunged directly into the subject. He was perfectly familiar with our brand new ideas and he had invented for himself some of Keynes's fanciful concepts, such as the device of burying bank notes in bottles and setting off a boom in mining them.[2] As we talked, I felt like a character in a Pirandello play, I could not tell whether it was I who was speaking or he. But he could challenge a weak point in Keynes' formulation and quickly subdued my feeble attempt to defend it.

He told me that he had taken a year's leave from the institute where he was working in Warsaw to write the *General Theory*. In Stockholm someone gave him Keynes' book. He began to read it – it was the book that he intended to write. He thought that perhaps further on there would be something different. No, all the way it was his book. He said: 'I confess, I was ill. Three days I lay in bed. Then I thought – Keynes is more known than I am. These ideas will get across much quicker with him and then we can get on to the interesting question, which is their application. Then I got up.'

Kalecki did not make any public claim to his independent discovery of the *General Theory*. I made it my business to blow his trumpet for him but I was often met with scepticism. In the USA, only Laurence Klein recognized (in the *Keynesian Revolution*, 1947) that Kalecki's system of analysis was as complete as Keynes's and in some respects superior to it.

At the end of his life, Michal told me that he felt he had done right not to make any claim to rivalry with Keynes. It would only have led to a tiresome kind of argument. Perhaps scepticism about my claim for him was due to the difficulty of believing that anyone was capable of taking this high line in our degenerate age.

The only reference Kalecki ever made to the question is in the preface to a selection of essays, published, alas, posthumously:[3] 'The first part includes

---

[1] Some of these are republished in *Collected Economic Papers*, Vol. IV.

[2] *General Theory*, p. 129.

[3] *Selected Essays on the Dynamics of the Capitalist Economy, 1933–70*. Cambridge University Press, 1971.

three papers published in 1933, 1934 and 1935 in Polish before Keynes' *General Theory* appeared, and containing, I believe, its essentials.'

These papers establish, without any doubt, the fact of Kalecki's independent discovery of what is now known as Keynes' theory. Moreover, it was not only in Polish that he had publication priority over Keynes. He read a paper to the Econometric Society, in October 1933, on 'A Macro-dynamic Theory of Business Cycles'[4] which contains the basic elements of the theory of saving, investment and employment. At the same date I published a piece on 'The Theory of Money and the Analysis of Output'[5] which was a kind of interim report on how far the Keynesians had got by that time and it is now evident that Kalecki had got much further.

When Kalecki came to Cambridge in 1936, we told Keynes about him, but he was not much impressed. His own ideas were in full spate (he was thinking about rewriting the *General Theory* in a completely different way) and he had not patience with anyone else's. He picked on a phrase in the *Econometrica* paper that seemed to him too 'monetarist', though in fact it contained a point of view which he later came to himself. Keynes did not sympathize with Kalecki's political presuppositions and by background and temperament they could not have been further apart. I commented on this once, saying 'oil and vinegar would not mix'. Some critic objected that they are mixed every day, but that needs constant stirring. Neither of these two characters was easy to stir. However, Keynes took the trouble to get a research project set up to provide Kalecki with a job. (This was just before the war and nothing much came of it.)

Although Michal behaved in public with a kind of scholarly dignity which is nowadays all too rare, he was naturally disappointed at lack of recognition. He said to me once: 'In the economics profession, no one notices the difference between good work and rubbish'. (I have been disappointed by this myself.)

3

The important question is not about priority, but about the content of the theories. In several respects, Kalecki's version is more robust than Keynes'.

Theory of prices. Keynes' treatment of the prices of particular commodities was rather vague. Orthodox teaching was that of Pigou – under competitive conditions, each firm produces such an output that marginal cost equals price, provided that price exceeds average prime cost.

[4] *Econometrica*, No. 3, 1935.
[5] Reprinted in *Collected Economic Papers*, Vol. I.

This can be illustrated by a diagram. In the short-period case, with given plant, Pigou's U-shaped curve can be reduced to a reversed L, with constant average prime cost (APC) up to capacity output.

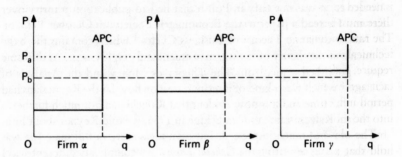

When the price of the commodity being produced is OP_a all three firms are producing it. When it is at OP_b, the two low cost plants continue to produce and the high cost plant (firm γ) has been put into moth balls.

This theory requires that any plant that is working at all is working to capacity, but in the slump, obviously nearly all plants were working part time, and yet prices did not fall to equality with prime cost. Profit margins held up, even when marginal cost was no greater than average prime cost. The 'marginal revenue' concept was brought in to explain this phenomenon, but Keynes did not use it. He introduced the idea of 'user cost', (the loss of value of equipment due to using it rather than leaving it idle) to reconcile competition with the evident fact that a profit margin entered into supply price even in a deep slump. This theory does not correspond to business behaviour. His elaboration of it did not take root and it has faded out in the post-Keynesian tradition.

Kalecki opened up a more promising line. He divided the price system into two parts. In the trade in raw materials, supply and demand rules. In manufacturing industry, prices are set by the producer; the profit margin that he is able to enjoy (the excess of price over average prime costs) depends upon the 'degree of monopoly' in the market where he sells.

The expression degree of monopoly has been misunderstood. Kalecki has been accused of reducing it to circularity by defining the degree of monopoly as the ratio of the gross margins to prices. What it means is the absence of price competition (there are other forms of competition in salesmanship, product differentiation etc.). The weaker is price competition in any market, the greater is the freedom of firms to set prices in excess of costs. The ratio of margins to prices is a symptom of the degree of monopoly.

Kalecki at first advanced his theory in strictly short-period terms and he argued that the overall degree of monopoly in industry as a whole is all that is needed to account for the shares of wages and gross profits. I objected that there must be some long-period element in the relation of prices to costs. The ratio of overheads to prime costs, which varies between industries for technical reasons, must have some influence on the gross profits that they require. Kalecki met this by suggesting that firms with high overheads act in tacit agreement to 'protect their profits'. This was an admission of long-period influences on the formation of prices but it was not well integrated into the short-period analysis.

The old 'full cost' doctrine went to the other extreme. It appeared to hold that prices of manufactures are determined solely by average cost, which would imply that prices fall when demand increases because overheads are spread over a larger output. This argument was put forward in ideological terms to defend businessmen from the implication that they behave monopolistically. The modern theory of administered prices is closer to Kalecki's view, for it means that producers set prices in advance of knowing sales, but it admits a long-period element into the process in the sense that firms are assumed to take account of average costs for a standard output. The realized net profit varies with the relation of actual to standard output.

The latest view advanced, for instance by Adrian Wood[6] and A. S. Eichner,[7] is that large firms set prices in such a way as to abstract from the market as much net profit as they need to finance the investment that they plan to carry out (taking account of the retention ratio and the gearing ratio that they maintain).

Such theories can never be quite convincing for motivation in business is multi-dimensional and cannot be squeezed into a simple formula; moreover in modern conditions a market does not exist independently of the commodities which innovating firms choose to offer for sale. The question of the formation of profit margins still needs more investigation.

Unfortunately, it will never be possible to get a knock-down answer, for investigation is concerned with *ex post* results, not with *ex ante* decisions. But in any case, it was the principle of the 'degree of monopoly', that is the absence of price competition, that opened up the question.

The importance of the determination of profit margins as an influence in

[6] *A Theory of Profits*, C.U.P., 1975.
[7] *The Megacorp and Oligopoly*, C.U.P., 1976.

the level of real wages, which Kalecki stressed, is now generally recognized, and so is the influence upon industrial prices of the fluctuations in the markets for raw materials, governed by supply and demand. (As OPEC reminds us, the degree of monopoly has to be brought into the theory of that kind of market as well.)

The importance of Kalecki's line of argument was in integrating the analysis of prices with the analysis of effective demand. Before Keynes, they were kept in two separate boxes; in America now the division between micro and macro theory is more complete than ever; but no progress can be made with either until they are united in a truly general theory.

Savings and investment. A powerful simplification that Kalecki introduced into the theory of distribution is the assumption that earned income is generally spent week by week as it is received, while expenditure out of unearned income (rent, interest and dividends) does not immediately react to a change in receipts (moreover, changes in profits are not immediately passed on in dividends).

He was then able to sum up the whole theory of effective demand as follows:

> We may consider first the determinants of profits in a closed economy in which both government expenditure and taxation are negligible. Gross national product will thus be equal to the sum of gross investment (in fixed capital and inventories) and consumption. The value of gross national product will be divided between workers and capitalists, virtually nothing being paid in taxes. The income of workers consists of wages and salaries. The income of capitalists or gross profits includes depreciation and undistributed profits, dividends and withdrawals from unincorporated business, rent and interest. We thus have the following balance sheet of the gross national product, in which we distinguish between capitalists' consumption and workers' consumption:

Gross profits	Gross investment
Wages and salaries	Capitalists' consumption
	Workers' consumption
Gross national product	Gross national product

If we make the additional assumption that workers do not save, then the workers' consumption is equal to their income. It follows directly then:

Gross profits = Gross investment + capitalists' consumption.

What is the significance of this equation? Does it mean that profits in a given period determine capitalists' consumption and investment, or the reverse of this? The answer to this question depends on which of these items is directly subject to the decisions of capitalists. Now, it is clear that capitalists may decide to consume and to invest more in a given period than in the preceding one, but they cannot decide to earn more. It is, therefore, their investment and consumption decisions which determine profits, and not vice versa.[8]

Nowadays, so much stress is laid upon retained profits as the source of finance for investment that we are in danger of slipping back into a new kind of Say's Law, and forgetting that saving cannot take place without investment to generate an excess of income over consumption. Last year's retained profits may be financing this year's investment, and this year's retentions may be going to finance investment next year, but the profits accruing this year are the result of this year's expenditure on investment and capitalists' consumption.

Kalecki's way of setting out the essential principle of effective demand avoids two weak points in Keynes' formulation. The first is the concept of the 'propensity to consume'. Keynes relies upon a psychological law that men are disposed to increase their consumption as their income increases, but not by as much as the increase in their income. Kalecki separates the 'men' into workers and capitalists and incomes into wages, which will be fully spent as they are received, and profits, of which a proportion will be handed over to rentiers (with a time lag) and partly spent by them. For Keynes, 'men' and their incomes are undifferentiated, while for Kalecki the overall relation of national income to consumption is strongly influenced by its distribution between work and property.

The second point of difference with Keynes concerns the proposition that 'savings equals investment', over which we made very heavy weather in the early stages of the Keynesian revolution. Kalecki simply asserts that a rise in the rate of investment will increase the flow of wages, which will be spent, and if the accompanying rise in profits causes an increase in spending out of dividends, profits will rise by so much the more. Thus there is an increase in retained profits equal to the increased outlay on investment.

After working out the pure model, Kalecki brings back the budget, the foreign balance and intermediate incomes which combine earning and saving. This provides all the essential elements of the theory of effective

[8] *Selected Essays*, op. cit. pp. 78 et seq.

demand, but it lacks the exposition of the multiplier, which makes the
Kahn-Keynes version more persuasive.

The monetary aspect of the theory was much more fully elaborated by
Keynes, but Kalecki was the first to emphasize that finance has to be
available before investment begins, while saving comes afterwards. This
was the point over which Keynes stumbled when we showed him the
Econometrica article.

Money-wage rates. Kalecki joined with Keynes in attacking the then
prevalent view that cutting wages was the best way to increase
employment. Keynes argued that an all-round cut in money-wage rates
would reduce prices more or less equally, so that real wages would not fall,
but the burden of debt would be increased and investment discouraged,
Kalecki argued that if prices did *not* fall, real wages would be cut, and
unemployment would increase because of the fall in demand for wage-
goods. Kalecki was not very keen on pressing the reverse argument, that
rising money-wage rates raise prices and fail to raise real wages. He was
very suspicious of those who use the problem of inflation to attack the trade
unions. The last essay that he published is an analysis of 'Class Struggle and
Distribution of National Income'.[9]

The short-period theory of distribution. There are two elements in
Kalecki's analysis of profits: the share of gross profit in the product of
industry is determined by the level of gross margin, while the total flow of
profits per annum depends upon the total flow of capitalists' expenditure on
investment and consumption.

Combining these two theories, we find the very striking proposition
that firms, considered as a whole, cannot increase their profits merely by
raising prices. Raising profit margins reduces real wages and consequently
employment in wage-good industries. The *share* of profit is increased but
the total profits remain equal to the flow of capitalists' expenditure. (Kalecki
argued that the mere expectation of higher profits will not increase
expenditure, for the firms would wait to see if more profits were going to
accrue, and, for firms as a whole, they will not.)

This argument is illustrated as follows:

The x axis measures employment and the y axis prices. BC represent
employment in the investment sector, and OW·BC its wage bill. Profit on
the sale of consumption goods is represented by a rectangular hyperbola
subtending an area equal to OW·BC, above the WF line (consumption out
of profits is omitted for simplicity).

When the competitive price level, OP, rules, employment in the

[9] *Selected Essays*, op. cit.

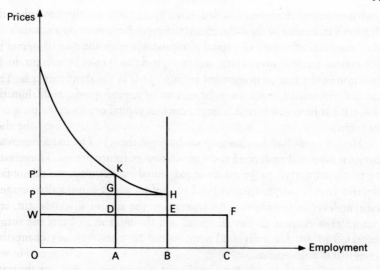

consumption sector is OB; at the price level OP′, employment in that sector is OA and unemployment AB, if employment in the investment sector remains unchanged.

In this way, Kalecki was able to weave the analysis of imperfect competition and of effective demand together and it was this that opened up the way for what goes under the name of post-Keynesian economic theory.

The trade-cycle. Kalecki provided the first coherent model of the mechanism of a self-repeating trade cycle (Kaldor, Goodwin and many others have built on his foundations). The clue to his analysis is the distinction between investment decisions and actual investment outlay. Today, plans are being laid for investment in the light of expectations held today. If prospects are such that investment plans exceed current investment, then current investment will be higher in the next period; consequently profits will be higher, expectations will be brighter, and so the 'self winding up' process of a boom is under way. Meanwhile the stock of productive capacity is gradually growing, and when the growth of capacity overtakes the growth of current production, utilization falls, prospects of profit are dimmed and the boom collapses.

As with all such models, the theory of an automatic recovery from a slump was rather weak, and Kalecki later gave up the search for a 'pure' trade cycle and sought for an analysis combining fluctuations in activity with accumulation over the long run.

The marginal efficiency of capital. The distinction between investment

and investment decisions enabled Kalecki to clear up the confusion in
Keynes's treatment of the inducement to invest. Keynes set up a schedule of
the 'marginal efficiency of capital' (comparable with the rate of interest),
for various levels of investment, and he argued that it must be a diminishing
function of the rate of investment because, *first*, in the short run, a higher
rate of investment raises the relative cost of capital goods, and, *secondly*,
when it has been completed, a larger stock of capital depresses the prospect
of profits.

Here Keynes had lost his grip on his own theory. The inducement to
invest is supposed to depend upon *expectations* of future profits. These must
be partly subjective, in the minds of individual businessmen, and they must
depend largely on the current level of profits, which is influenced by the
current level of investment. An increase in the rate of investment today
would raise current profits all round and the influence of this in raising
expected profits for individual firms would far outweigh any change in
costs that it might cause.

Keynes' schedule of m.e.c. collapses future time into the present
moment, confusing the forward-looking expectations of profits of
individual firms with the profits that will be realized for industry as a
whole. Moreover, he projects the argument into the long run and assumes
that a larger stock of capital will entail a lower rate of profit, thus relapsing
into the 'classical' theory he intended to combat.

Kalecki sorts the analysis out; conditions today influence investment
decisions being taken, and they will affect the conditions that prevail in the
future when they are being carried out.

Keynes fell into another confusion. He argues that the rate of
investment, at any moment, will be such as to equate the marginal efficiency
of capital (that is, the expected rate of profit) to the rate of interest. This is a
fudge to begin with, because marginal efficiency of capital is related to the
rate of interest by an allowance for risk which varies with the state of
confidence. Letting that pass, how can it be true that the amount of
investment firms plan to make, over the immediate future, is limited only
by the cost of borrowing? The amount of finance that a firm can command,
as Kalecki pointed out, depends upon its liquidity and its credit standing.
The distribution of borrowing power between firms depends upon their
existing capital and their past success. The rate of investment is not
regulated by *the* rate of interest which is the same for everybody.

Kalecki was free from the remnants of old-fashioned theory which
Keynes had failed to throw off. He could see through these confusions at the
first glance. His amendments are completely in line with the main argument

of the *General Theory*. Kalecki gets Keynes back onto the rails where his 'classical' education had led him astray.

The political trade cycle. The most famous of all Kalecki's insights into the economics of capitalism is contained in a short article published in 1943 on 'Political aspects of full employment.'[10] He predicted that, when governments understand how they can maintain full employment by budgetary policy, they will not really want to do so, because continuous full employment would undermine the power of business leaders to control the workers and to keep down wages. On the other hand, too much unemployment is not popular with the electorate. Thus he predicted that after the war we should experience a political trade cycle with alternating *stop* and *go*.

The final paragraphs of the article make sad reading after 30 years experience of how accurate Kalecki's prediction turned out to be:

> Should a progressive be satisfied with a regime of the 'political business cycle' as described in the preceding section? I think he should oppose it on two grounds: (i) that it does not assure lasting full employment; (ii) that Government intervention is tied down to public investment and does not embrace subsidizing consumption. What the masses now ask for is not the mitigation of slumps but their total abolition. Nor should the resulting fuller utilization of resources be applied to unwanted public investment merely in order to provide work. The Government spending programme should be devoted to public investment only to the extent to which such investment is *actually needed*. The rest of Government spending necessary to maintain full employment should be used to subsidize consumption (through family allowances, old age pensions, reduction in indirect taxation, subsidizing of prices of necessities). The opposers of such Government spending say that the Government will then have nothing to show for their money. The reply is that the counterpart of this spending will be the higher standard of living of the masses. Is not this the purpose of all economic activity?
>
> 'Full employment capitalism' will have, of course, to develop new social and political institutions which will reflect the increased power of the working class. If capitalism can adjust itself to full employment a fundamental reform will have been incorporated in it. If not, it will show itself an outmoded system which must be scrapped.
>
> But perhaps the fight for full employment may lead to fascism? Perhaps capitalism will adjust itself to full employment in *this* way?

10 *Political Quarterly*, No. 4, 1943.

This seems extremely unlikely. Fascism sprang up in Germany against a background of tremendous unemployment and maintained itself in power through securing full employment while capitalist democracy failed to do so. The fight of the progressive forces for full employment is at the same time a way of *preventing* the recurrence of fascism.

Long run growth. From the first, Kalecki was trying to broaden the theory of investment to include a theory of accumulation over the long run, but he was never satisfied that he had got to the bottom of it.

In the preface referred to above he wrote:

> It is interesting to notice that the theory of effective demand, already clearly formulated in the first papers, remains unchanged in all the relevant writings, as do my views on the distribution of national income. However, there is a continuous search for new solutions in the theory of investment decisions, where even the last paper represents – for better or for worse – a novel approach.

I had a running argument with Michal on this subject. He regarded my use of the concept of 'animal spirits' as somehow irrational (though to me it was only a modification of the Marxian imperative: 'Accumulate! Accumulate! That is Moses and the Prophets'). He maintained that new inventions raise prospects of profit and stimulate investment. I pointed out that, according to his own theory, if steady accumulation is maintained, the rate of profit on capital will be constant.

In the end we compromised on the view, set out in this last paper, that inventions raise the prospect of profit for the technically progressive firms that make innovations, not the average realized profit for industry as a whole.

Though Kalecki liked to express his ideas in neat formulae, he was always conscious of the limitations of that style of exposition, and set his arguments against the background of history, politics and institutional change.

In the United States, Keynes' theory was melted down and moulded into a 'neoclassical synthesis', but Kalecki proved indigestible and was simply ignored. Now that disillusionment with the synthesis is setting in, perhaps he will get a hearing at last.

18

WHAT HAS BECOME OF EMPLOYMENT POLICY?

with Frank Wilkinson

THE wartime coalition government of the UK published a White Paper, *Employment Policy* (Cmnd. 6527, 1944), which boldly declared that it is the responsibility of government to maintain a high and stable level of employment. Sure enough, from 1945 to 1966 (with the exception of the hard winter of 1947) unemployment in Britain, as represented by official statistics, never rose above 2·5 per cent of the labour force, and in some years hovered around 1 per cent. This was quite a surprise. Sir William Beveridge (Beveridge, 1944) estimated that the attainable minimum would be an average of 3 per cent, varying between 2 and 4 per cent from time to time, and Keynes thought this much too optimistic (Kahn, 1975). The expected post-war slump never came. Twenty years of near-full employment was something new in history. Indeed, in some capitalist countries demand for labour overtook supply and foreign workers flooded in.[1] It seemed that the ghost of the trade cycle of the pre-war variety had been exorcised, apart from accidental disturbances such as the Korean war boom and slump. Continuous prosperity began to be taken for granted. Workers came to expect real-wage rates to rise from year to year and shareholders began to look forward to unending capital gains.

Over the period as a whole, annual growth rates in *per capita* income in the rest of western Europe and in Japan ranged between 4 per cent and 10 per cent. Average real consumption per head grew at more or less the same pace but, since inequality was, if anything, slightly reduced, there was probably a greater rise in the level of consumption for the broad mass of the population (see Table 1, p. 208). Even in the poorest third world countries,

[1] For instance, the proportion of foreign workers in the West German labour force increased from less than 1 per cent in the 1950s to some 10 per cent in the 1970s (Böhning and Maillet, 1974).

per capita GNP grew at 1 or 2 per cent per annum, but there it was associated with growing inequality and a great increase in misery.[2]

In the USA *per capita* growth from the early 1950s to the mid-1960s was only 2·5 per cent per annum, but starting from a higher base, mass consumption swelled prodigiously, which made poverty all the more annoying for those who did not get much of it. The UK was at, or near, the bottom of the league table, with a growth rate slightly less than that of the USA, but even so, the general standard of life was indubitably rising. Disgruntled elements in the middle class began to be annoyed to see workers' families encroaching on their former privileges, such as private cars and holidays in Spain, but conservative views were generally supported by the experience of prosperity. The spokesmen for capitalism were saying, in effect: we have to admit that the unemployment that prevailed before the war was a serious defect in the free-market system. Now we are giving you capitalism with full employment, so what have you got to complain of?

In the inter-war period, while capitalism was wallowing in the slump, full employment and rapid growth were being maintained in the USSR. (Perhaps it was the desire to avoid a repetition of this contrast that made conservative opinion accept the Keynesian doctrines, which were formerly considered subversive.) Now the boot was on the other foot; the spectacle of luxury consumption spreading among industrial workers in the West aroused envy and doubt in the socialist world.

In Great Britain, 1966 was disconcerting – a so-called Labour government deliberately causing unemployment in order to maintain the exchange value of sterling (and thereafter failing to do so). But British troubles were put down to special circumstances or to peculiarities in the national character.[3] In the capitalist world as a whole, activity revived after

[2] In the third world countries, during the period 1950–2 to 1964–6, the growth rates of product *per capita* averaged about 1·7 per cent for Africa, 1·8 per cent for America, 1·6 per cent for South Asia, 2·6 per cent for the Far East and 4·4 per cent for the Middle East (as compared with 5·0 per cent in western Europe over the comparable period) (see OECD national accounts). Recent empirical studies have established substantial support for the hypothesis that relative inequality increases in the early stages of development (Ahluwalia, 1976; Chenery, 1974). Ahluwalia's evidence suggests that 'the stronger hypothesis of declining absolute incomes for large sections of the population is not so unequivocally established by cross-country data as to be uncritically accepted as one of the "stylized facts" about development' (p. 135). However, this stronger hypothesis does seem to hold, for example, in the case of the Indian economy, where the percentage of rural people below the 'poverty line' increased from 38 per cent in 1960–1 to 45 per cent in 1964–5 and to 54 per cent in 1968–9 (Bardhan, 1974).

[3] See, for example, Caves (1968), especially Chapters 7 and 8.

a setback, and ran high for another seven years (see Table 1). Belief in perpetual prosperity was restored.

While prosperity ruled, the deeper insights of the Keynesian revolution were lost to view. The bastard Keynesian doctrine, evolved in the United States, invaded the economics faculties of the world, floating on the wings of the almighty dollar. (It established itself even amongst intellectuals in the so-called developing countries, who have reason enough to know better.) The old orthodoxy, against which the Keynesian revolution was raised, was based on Say's law – there cannot be a deficiency of demand. Spending creates demand for consumption goods, while saving creates demand for investment goods such as machinery and stocks. Keynes pointed out the obvious fact that investment is governed by the decisions of business corporations and public institutions, not by the desire of thrifty householders to save. An increase in household saving means a reduction in consumption; it does not increase investment but reduces employment.

According to the bastard Keynesian doctrine, it is possible to calculate the rate of saving that households collectively desire to achieve; then governments, by fiscal and monetary policy, can organize the investment of this amount of saving. Thus Say's law is artificially restored, and under its shelter all the old doctrines creep back again, even the doctrine that a given stock of capital will provide employment for any amount of labour at the appropriate equilibrium real-wage rate. If so, unemployment occurs only because wages are being held above the equilibrium level. (In the third world, it is just too bad, because the equilibrium wage corresponding to full employment is far below the level of subsistence.)

Keynes was diagnosing a defect inherent in capitalism. Kalecki, who developed the same theory independently, went much further and held that without radical change capitalism was incapable of rectifying the defect. But the bastard Keynesians turned the argument back into being a defence of *laisser-faire*, provided that just the one blemish of excessive saving was going to be removed.[4]

---

[4] Thus, typically, Samuelson argues:

The finding of our macroeconomic analysis rejects both the classical faith that *laisser-faire* must by itself lead to utopian stability and the pre-World War II pessimism that classical microeconomic principles have become inapplicable to the modern world. Instead we end with the reasoned prospect that appropriate monetary and fiscal policies can ensure an economic environment which will *validate* the verities of microeconomics – that society has to choose among its alternative high-employment production possibilities, that paradoxes of thrift and fallacies of composition will not be permitted to create cleavages between private and social virtues or private and public vices.

By means of appropriately reinforcing monetary and fiscal policies, a mixed

Against this background, the slump of 1973–4 was a considerable shock. We were told, in early 1976, that a revival was gathering momentum and that soon the United States and West Germany would be pulling us all up into a new boom. At best, then, we appear to be getting back into the clutches of the old trade cycle;[5] perpetual steady growth has proved to have been a daydream. The bastard Keynesian economists are quite disconcerted and the spokesmen for capitalism have got their brief muddled up.

The complacency of the age of growth covered up what, in the legal phrase, may be called *inherent vice* in the free-market system, which has now broken out in the unprecedented combination of inflation with unemployment, along with increasing tension in international economic relations and growing distress at the social consequences of unregulated capitalist accumulation.

1

A major point in the analysis of Keynes and Kalecki, which the complacent economists seem to have overlooked, is that there is no meaning to be attached to the concept of equilibrium in the general level of prices. The Keynesian revolution began by refuting the then orthodox theory that there is a natural tendency in a market economy to establish equilibrium with full employment. If men in fact were out of work, on the orthodox view, it must be because wages were above the equilibrium level and profits were too low. Unemployment on this view was 'voluntary' because trade unions could easily get rid of it by accepting lower wage rates. Keynes agreed that a rise in profits would increase employment, but he argued that a general cut in money-wage rates would reduce the price level more or less in proportion, so that neither profits nor employment would increase. If this argument is correct, it must follow that to raise money wages will increase prices, even if there is unemployment.

economy can avoid the excesses of boom and slump and can look forward to healthy progressive growth. This being understood, the paradoxes that robbed the older classical principles dealing with small-scale 'microeconomics' of much of their relevance and validity will now lose their sting. The broad cleavage between microeconomics and macroeconomics has been closed by active public use of fiscal and monetary policy (Samuelson, 1970, p. 348).

By 1976, Samuelson's faith in macroeconomic policies (but not in the verities of microeconomics) had been badly shaken. Compare the passage quoted above with the corresponding passage in the tenth edition of his textbook (p. 373).

[5] See Table 1. The old trade cycle was associated with actual reductions in GDP, whereas, as is well known, cyclical downturns in the period since World War II in most industrial countries have merely meant a slowing down of the rate of growth of output.

It was easy to predict that a long run of high employment and high profits, without any change in the mechanism and psychology of wage bargaining, would lead to continuously rising prices. Keynes foresaw that it would be a difficult political problem to prevent free wage bargaining from generating inflation in conditions of continuous high employment (see Robinson, 1973), but he did not suggest how to solve it. Orthodox economists do not like to discuss politics. The old-fashioned monetarist doctrines enabled them to ignore the political causes and consequences of inflation. They held that the level of prices is regulated by the quantity of money. Wage rates are prices like the rest. When there is an excessive creation of money, wages are bound to rise whether trade unions demand increases or not. The simple cure for inflation is to regulate the quantity of money correctly. This theory had a great success with central bankers, but even many bastard Keynesians found it too much to swallow. They prefer to discuss inflation in terms of demand pull and cost push.

The appearance of symmetry between demand and costs is deceptive. A sudden rapid increase in effective demand, with given productive capacity, runs output into bottlenecks and, even if prices do not rise, there is a sharp increase in profits. By itself, this does not cause continuing inflation, though it may set off a rise in wage rates which thereafter continues to feed on itself. A pure cost push – wages being raised, so to speak, in cold blood, without any preceding rise in profits – is logically possible though hard to distinguish in practice.

By the mid-1950s, however, the link between high employment and wage increases had become obvious and Professor Phillips' econometric study (Phillips, 1958) reduced this relationship to a simple formula. His analysis of the causal link between high employment and the rate of wage inflation was widely accepted, despite the doubtful quality of much of his data, and pressure in the labour market was brought to the fore as an explanation of inflation.

This view has now been embodied in a new form of monetarism. According to this doctrine, with non-inflationary equilibrium in the labour market, there is a certain amount of *voluntary unemployment*, of workers who prefer not to work at the ruling level of real wages. If government attempts to lower unemployment below this *natural level* by increasing the money supply, labour market pressures increase money wages. The increased prices which result are built into wage claims via workers' expectations of inflation and the rate of price increase accelerates. To cure inflation the increase in the money supply has to be adjusted so as to raise unemployment to the natural level – even beyond that if there is a large element of expectations in wage claims. When money wages continue to increase while unemployment is rising, this only shows that equilibrium in the labour market has not been reached and that unemployment should be further increased. By emphasizing the importance of voluntary abstentions from the labour market as an explanation for unemployment, the new monetarists have arrived back at the point where Keynes started.[6]

One of the oddest notions produced by bastard Keynesians is that trade unions suffer from 'money illusion' because they do not bargain in real terms. In fact, negotiations about wages can only be conducted in terms of money. When inflation is already going on, the rising 'cost of living' is brought into the argument, but there is no way in which trade unions can operate directly on the level of real wages. Moreover, there is no point in preaching to workers that to raise the general level of money wage rates merely raises prices, so that they get no benefit from it. Any group of workers which secures a rise ahead of others does get higher real wages for some time, and any who fall behind suffer a permanent loss.

A rise of prices normally leads to a demand for a compensating rise in wages and a rise in wages leads to rising prices again. However, the ability of any group of workers to maintain their standard of life in an inflationary period depends on collective action. In industries where workers are strongly organized, trade unions are effective in protecting their members' interests and every rise in living costs quickly leads to increased wages. In other sectors, where organization is weak or trade union leaders complacent, wages lag behind prices, so that real wages fall.[7] For a time, this helps to slow down inflation, since the rise in the aggregate wage bill for industry as a whole is less than proportionate to the rise in the level of prices. But for this very reason, organization grows stronger and rank-and-file pressure on leaders grows more insistent. Soon, wages are following prices more quickly and inflation accelerates.[8]

[6] For example, 'In one sense all employment could be regarded as voluntary because there is some wage level at which almost any individual could price himself into a job' (Brittan, 1975, p. 30). Brittan's list of reasons for voluntary unemployment includes trade unions, minimum wage and equal pay legislation and social benefits. It is worth noting that this list is remarkably similar to that in Pigou (1933), the book singled out by Keynes as 'the only detailed account of the classical theory of unemployment which exists' (Keynes, 1936, p. 7). See also Laidler (1975).

[7] However, in some relatively unorganized sectors, such as domestic service and shorthand typing, wages have risen sharply, apparently in response to demand for labour.

[8] Research being undertaken by one of the authors indicates that the upsurge in militancy among important groups of workers, e.g. hospital ancillary workers, local government manual workers, teachers and, particularly, the miners in the late 1960s and early 1970s, was preceded by a period in which real take-home pay fell sharply. Moreover, a fairly common

It is commonly said that trade unions cause inflation: however that may be, it is quite clear that inflation causes trade unions. In Britain for the last decade, organization has been spreading not only among previously ill-organized manual workers and among the clerical grades, but also among the professional classes. Now respected servants of the public, physicians and judges, have to struggle, just like dustmen, to prevent their living standards from being undermined by the successful struggles of others.

There is, however, another aspect of wage bargaining which certainly does cause inflation. The trade union movement regards itself as charged with the right and duty to maintain for its members a proper share in the growing productivity of industry. In prosperous times, it is performing a useful function for capitalism. In the absence of trade union pressure, real wages would not rise in line with the increasing productivity due to technical progress, and stagnation would be induced by the failure of mass consumption to rise in step with productive capacity. The struggle over the relative share of wages in the product of industry interacts with the struggle over the relative wage rates of different bargaining groups. The strong technically progressive firms do not much object to granting money wage increases as real wage-costs fall. Prices for their products may remain more or less constant. Additional purchasing power from their wage bill tends to raise the demand for other commodities. Workers in the less progressive industries and services are now at a double disadvantage. Their share in consumption has been reduced and their relative position in the hierarchy of wage rates has been pushed down. They must demand rises and, to defend profits, their employers must put up prices.

Though this is the effect of their traditional function, trade union leaders bitterly resented the accusation that they were causing inflation and for a long time refused to admit that rising wage rates had anything to do with it. After all, they were behaving quite correctly in trying to keep wage rates, each for their own members, from falling behind the cost of living. The British trade union movement had inherited a proud tradition and its central principle was the demand for freedom in wage bargaining. It was hardly their fault if modern capitalism could not accommodate itself to their using the strength that they had managed to build up over two centuries.

---

pattern of development of this militancy emerges; a rapid increase in unofficial strikes and other forms of industrial action was eventually followed by official strike action. The situation, therefore, is the opposite of the popular image of the militant leaders pushing the silent, and often reluctant, majority; in fact the militant majority tend to push the silent, and frequently reluctant, leaders (R. J. Tarling and S. F. Wilkinson, 'Wage Differentials and Incomes Policy: an Inter-industry Study', *British Journal of Industrial Relations*, forthcoming).

Moreover, it is not fair to say that trade unions have always ruthlessly followed their sectional interests at the expense of everyone else. Both leaders and members have demonstrated from time to time their willingness to co-operate with government policy, particularly when the Labour party is in power. In 1948, the trade union movement accepted a wage freeze and maintained it more or less intact for two years. Again in 1966, the movement broadly accepted the need for wage control. Both these efforts succeeded in securing their short-term objectives of improving the balance of payments and mitigating inflation for a time, but both soon collapsed into rapid inflation, mainly because of the government's inability to provide an adequate quid pro quo.

The violent inflation of 1974, running up to an annual rate of 27 per cent in 1975, gave everyone a fright. This time the efforts of the trade unions to co-operate with a Labour government to check inflation have been more convincing than before. But, so far, union involvement has been largely confined to tinkering with the process of wage determination; in other spheres of government policy it has been narrowly limited. It was this failure to extend the influence of the unions beyond wage control that proved fatal to previous attempts at co-operation.

In 1943 Kalecki, looking forward, sceptically, to the possibilities of the post-war world, wrote:

> 'Full employment capitalism' will have, of course, to develop new social and political institutions which will reflect the increased power of the working class. If capitalism can adjust itself to full employment a fundamental reform will have been incorporated in it. If not, it will show itself an outmoded system which must be scrapped (Kalecki, 1943).

2

Class war was not the only element of inherent vice in the free-market system to disturb the age of growth. There were also the problems generated by the unevenness of development amongst various capitalist nations and the economic and political relationships between industrial countries and primary producers, particularly those in the third world.

The pre-Keynesian theory of international trade required the balance of imports and exports for each country to be maintained by movements in relative price levels. After experiencing the attempt to return to the gold standard in 1925 (see Keynes, 1972), Keynes adopted the view that depreciating the exchange rate was much to be preferred to attempting to depress the price level. At the end of his life, feeling obliged to defend the Bretton Woods agreement against his better judgement (Kahn, 1976), he lapsed into arguing that, *in the long run*, market forces would tend to establish equilibrium in international trade (Keynes, 1946). He had forgotten his old crack, that in the long run we are all dead.

As it turned out, market forces generated disequilibrium. Differences in competitive power, whatever their origin, set up a spiral of divergence. A country such as West Germany, with growing exports, could maintain a high rate of investment and therefore of growing productivity, which enhanced its competitive power, and allowed real wages to rise so that workers were less demanding. In the United Kingdom, any increase in employment caused an increase in the deficit in the balance of payments so that every hopeful *go* had to be brought to an end with a despairing *stop*. Thus strong competitors grow stronger and the weak, weaker.

Because of the size and strength of the United States and its overseas economy, trade plays a small part in national income, but not a small part in the world market. The USA can move from deficit to surplus without much disturbance at home, but with a great deal of disturbance to the other trading nations. Moreover, it was able to take advantage of the dollar being the world currency to run an ever greater outflow on capital account with an ever growing deficit on income account, until President Nixon, with the dollar devaluation of 1971, suddenly tried to reverse the position with a stroke of the pen. All this laid great strains on the international monetary system.

Keynes worked out the structure of the *General Theory* mainly in terms of a closed economy. When it is extended to take in the operation of international economic relations, a missing link appears in the argument. The rate of interest was to be used to regulate home investment, and Keynes believed that a secular fall in interest rates was both necessary for this purpose and desirable in itself. Exchange rates were to offset differences in relative labour costs. Then nothing would be left to regulate short-term capital movements. Traditionally this was the function of relative interest rates. Britain, and other countries with chronically weak payments balances, could not indulge in cheap money however much home conditions required it, and had to follow the interest rates of other countries up whenever they happened to rise. This was one more turn in the spiral of weakness weakening itself.

Over and above the strains set up by the uneasy relationships amongst the industrial nations themselves, there were the strains involved in the relations of the industrial countries as a whole and the third world. The formation of prices in the free-market system is in two parts – cost-plus in manufacturing industry and supply and demand for primary products.[9] A rise in the level of production and consumption in industrial countries normally increases demand for all kinds of primary products. When prices of materials rise, while money wage rates are constant, real wages fall and so generate a demand for rising money wages, which adds to the original rise in costs. Thus favourable terms of trade reduce class conflict in the industrial countries and unfavourable terms exacerbate it.

Commodity prices responded sharply to the pressure of demand during the Korean war boom, but this was soon over and during the 1950s the terms of trade moved in favour of industrial countries. However, the long boom, swollen by the Vietnam war, financed by the USA on the principle of guns *and* butter, caused an acceleration in the rate of increase in commodity prices and finally sparked off the great inflation of 1973.

In an economic model, it is possible to analyse the consequences of any one change by keeping other things constant. In real life a lot of things happen at once. During the long boom, an excess of demand over growth of capacity led to shortages of one commodity after another. The demonetization of the dollar in 1971 drove speculative funds into commodity markets. The Moslem oil producers, temporarily bound together by hostility to Israel, suddenly realized the extent of their monopoly power. Inflation at what now seems a mild and acceptable rate had been going on for years all over the capitalist world, setting up expectations that inflation would continue and undermining the conventional belief that a dollar is a dollar. Injected into this situation, the sudden rise in the costs of materials, especially oil, blew the inflation sky high.

This concatenation of circumstances has been described as a historical accident. But it is the inherent vice in the free-market system of international trade which creates the setting for such 'accidents', from which it has no means to defend itself except by destroying prosperity and depriving the primary product sellers of their favourable terms of trade.

3

The hopes which accompanied the Keynesian revolution, of reforming capitalism so as to ensure continuous prosperity with full employment, are

[9] See Robinson (1962); K. J. Coutts, W. A. H. Godley and W. D. Nordhaus, *Industrial Pricing in the United Kingdom*, Cambridge, CUP, forthcoming.

now all but extinguished. The slide into crisis in the capitalist world has re-established the pre-Keynesian orthodoxy as the conventional wisdom in economic policy-making at both national and international levels. The inevitable consequence of this is a much higher general level of unemployment and recurrent crises, involving a massive waste of resources and considerable human misery.

Important changes in the world economy have taken place over the last two decades, which have ended the era of near-full employment and exposed the inadequacies of the conventional Keynesian analysis. One of the most important of these developments has been the relaxation of tariffs and exchange controls and the resulting large increase in international trade[10] and capital movements; this has increasingly exposed national economies to the ravages of uncontrolled capitalist competition, in the way that they were exposed before the 1930s.

While the USA remained the predominant world economic and political power, and effectively acted as the world central bank, some semblance of order in international economic relations was retained. The use of the dollar as a reserve currency and the eagerness of the USA to lend abroad allowed international liquidity to expand to meet the needs of the growing volume of trade and facilitated post-war reconstruction and structural adaptation in the capitalist world. But with the emergence of Japan and western European countries as strong competitors to the USA, and the deterioration of the USA's balance of payments, unhindered capital movements became a major destabilizing force. The IMF proved totally inadequate to its appointed task of protecting national economies from external shocks and assisting the correction of more permanent imbalances in payments. In fact, by establishing rules which threw the burden of adjustment mainly onto deficit countries, the IMF institutionalized an important element in the process of unequal development among capitalist countries.

Faced with growing international pressures, the governments of debtor countries have been obliged to adopt the deflationary policies acceptable to their creditors (including the IMF); policies which conflicted with the avowed aim of maintaining full employment and with the real-wage demands of the working class. Thus democratically elected governments of debtor countries, where the working class is well organized, have walked a knife edge between the international and internal disapproval of their economic policies. But the frequently imposed deflationary policies

[10] Exports of OECD countries as a whole increased from 11 per cent of GDP in 1954 to almost 17 per cent of GDP in 1973.

progressively weakened the competitive position of such economies, increasing their indebtedness and reducing the opportunities for advances in real wages. Unable to meet either internal or external demands, economic policy vacillated wildly; consequently growing economic crisis has been accompanied by increasing political instability and further destabilization of the international economy.

The world market system has run into a second, and much more general, impasse, caught between two interlocking conflicts – the demands of workers in the industrial countries for higher real wages and the demands of the third world for improved terms of trade.

So long as unemployment and slow growth continue, the relative prices of raw materials are kept down and this somewhat mitigates inflation in industrial countries. As soon as a revival begins, prices of raw materials and foodstuffs begin to go up and real wage demands become harder to resist; the authorities nervously pull back and the revival is checked. The orthodox economists, still repeating incantations about equilibrium, encourage the authorities to pursue these deflationary policies – the very same that Keynes in the thirties used to describe as sadistic.

It is ironic that after the great technical achievements brought by the age of growth, all we are offered is a return to large-scale unemployment and poverty in the midst of plenty, in an age of frustration. Kalecki was right to be sceptical; the modern economies have failed to develop the political and social institutions, at either domestic or international level, that are needed to make permanent full employment compatible with capitalism.

RATES OF GROWTH OF PER CAPITA
GROSS DOMESTIC PRODUCT AND CONSUMPTION
OECD and selected OECD countries, 1954–75 (constant 1970 prices and exchange rates)

Annual compound rates of growth	Gross Domestic Product			Consumption		
	1954–66	1966–73	1973–75	1954–66	1966–73	1973–75
USA	2·5	2·7	−2·7	2·6	3·1	−0·7
Canada	2·6	3·5	0·4	2·5	3·8	3·6
Japan	8·4	9·1	−0·6	7·2	7·4	2·4
Germany	5·5	3·9	−1·5	5·6	3·9	n.a.
France	4·3	4·9	0	3·8	4·6	n.a.
UK	2·3	2·5	−0·5	2·3	2·5	−0·7
OECD Total	3·2	3·7	−1·6	3·1	3·7	n.a.

Sources: *National Accounts of OECD Countries 1953–69* and *1962–73*, OECD, Paris
   Main Economic Indicators, OECD, Paris, 1976
   Manpower Statistics, 1954–64, OECD, Paris, 1965
   Labour Force Statistics, 1963–74, OECD, Paris, 1976
Note: GDP growth rates were adjusted to a *per capita* basis using population statistics from OECD sources.

BIBLIOGRAPHY

Ahluwalia, M. S. 1976. 'Income Distribution and Development: Some Stylised Facts', *American Economic Review* (Papers and Proceedings)

Bardhan, P. K. 1974. 'On the Incidence of Rural Poverty in India in the 1960's, in *Poverty and Income Distribution in India*, ed. P. K. Bardhan and T. W. Srinivasan, Calcutta, Indian Institute of Statistics

Beveridge, W. 1944. *Full Employment in a Free Society*, London, Allen & Unwin

Böhning, W. R. and Maillet, D. 1974. *The Effects of the Employment of Foreign Workers*, Paris, OECD

Brittan, S. 1975. *Second Thoughts on Full Employment Policy*, London, Centre for Policy Studies

Caves, R. E. and associates 1968. *Britain's Economic Prospects*, London, Allen & Unwin

Chenery, H. *et al.* 1974. *Redistribution with Growth*, Oxford, OUP

Cmnd. 6527, 1944. *Employment Policy*, London, HMSO

Kahn, R. 1975. 'Unemployment as seen by Keynesians', in *The Concept and Measurement of Involuntary Unemployment*, ed. G. D. N. Worswick, London, Allen & Unwin

Kahn, R. 1976. 'The Historical Origins of the IMF', in *Keynes and International Monetary Relations*, ed. H. P. Thirlwall, London, Macmillan

Kalecki, M. 1943. 'Political Aspects of Full Employment', *Political Quarterly*, Vol. 14

Keynes, J. M. 1936. *The General Theory of Employment, Interest and Money*, London, Macmillan

Keynes, J. M. 1946. 'The Balance of Payments of the United States', *Economic Journal*, Vol. 56

Keynes, J. M. 1972. 'The Economic Consequences of Mr. Winston Churchill', in *Collected Writings of John Maynard Keynes*, Vol. 9, *Essays in Persuasion*, London, Macmillan

Laidler, D. E. W. 1975. 'The End of "demand management". How to Reduce Unemployment in the late 1970s', in M. Friedman, *Unemployment versus Inflation?*, London, Institute of Economic Affairs

Pigou, A. C. 1933. *The Theory of Unemployment*, London, Macmillan

Phillips, A. W. 1958. 'The Relationship between Unemployment and the Rate of Change of Money Wage Rates in the UK, 1861–1957,' *Economica*, Vol. XXV, no. 100

Robinson, J. 1962. 'Philosophy of Prices', in *Collected Economic Papers*, Vol. 2, Oxford, Blackwell

Robinson, J. 1973. *Collected Papers*, Vol. 4, Oxford, Blackwell

Samuelson, P. A. 1970. *Economics*, 8th edition, New York, McGraw-Hill

19

KEYNES AND RICARDO

To me, the expression *post-Keynesian* has a definite meaning; it applies to an economic theory or method of analysis which takes account of the difference between the future and the past.

When Keynes replied to his critics in 1937,[1] he examined the nature of the basic difference between his theory and those that he was opposing. He showed that the difference lay in his recognition of the fact that, at any moment of time, the future is unknown. 'It is generally recognized', he wrote 'that the Ricardian analysis was concerned with what we now call long-period equilibrium.'[2] It is characteristic of a position of equilibrium that it is fulfilling expectations (as to prices, flows of output, profits, etc.) which were held in the past and is therefore recreating expectations that will be fulfilled in the future. In reality, this situation is never realized. 'Thus the fact that our knowledge of the future is fluctuating, vague and uncertain, renders wealth a peculiarly unsuitable subject for the methods of the classical economic theory.'[3]

The Short-Period

The notion of *getting into* equilibrium is 'a metaphor based on space to explain a process which takes place in time.'[4] In space, it is possible to go to and fro and correct misdirections, but time goes only one way.

> The Moving Finger writes; and, having writ,
> Moves on: nor all your Piety nor Wit
> Shall lure it back to cancel half a line,
> Nor all your Tears wash out a Word of it.

[1] 'General Theory of Employment', *JMK*, Vol. 14, pp. 109 et seq.
[2] Loc. cit., p. 112.
[3] Ibid.
[4] See Joan Robinson, 'A Lecture Delivered at Oxford by a Cambridge Economist', 1935. Reprinted in *Collected Economic Papers*, Vol. IV, Oxford, Blackwell.

This is why equilibrium cannot be achieved by a process of trial and error.

Whenever equilibrium theory is breached, economists rush like bees whose comb has been broken to patch up the damage. J. R. Hicks was one of the first, with his IS/LM, to try to reduce the *General Theory* to a system of equilibrium. This had a wide success and has distorted teaching for many generations of students. J. R. Hicks used to be fond of quoting a letter from Keynes which, because of its friendly tone, seemed to approve of IS/LM, but it contained a clear objection to a system that leaves out expectations of the future from the inducement to invest.[5]

Forty years later, John Hicks[6] noticed the difference between the future and the past and became dissatisfied with IS/LM but (presumably to save face for his predecessor, J. R.) he argued that Keynes's analysis was only half *in time* and half in equilibrium.[7]

The *General Theory* is set in a strictly 'short-period' situation. A short-period is not a length of time but the position at a moment of time. Fixed capital, stocks, the organization of business, the training of workers and the habits of consumers are all whatever they are. In such a situation, a particular level of effective demand determines a particular level of output and flow of incomes; a change in effective demand at that moment brings about a particular change in output. Thus, in that situation, there is a short-period supply curve or utilization function, expressing the relation of the amount of employment to the level of effective demand.

Keynes inherited from Marshall the notion of rising short-period marginal costs but this is inessential; the modern treatment of the subject would have suited him better. Taking money-wage rates as given:

> Fixed or 'sticky' prices are found in manufacturing and distribution, where products are not homogeneous and labour costs are constant or decreasing up to the limits of capacity. The result . . . is that productivity in industry increases with short-run increases in output, while prices are sticky.[8]

Rising marginal costs are associated with fixed natural resources.

A state of expectations, controlling a given level of effective demand, is given only momentarily and is always in course of bringing itself to an end.

---

[5] *JMK*, Vol. XIV, p. 80.

[6] For the change of signature, see 'Revival of Political Economy, the Old and the New', *Economic Record*, September 1975.

[7] 'Some Questions of Time in Economics', in *Essays in Honour of Nicholas Georgescu Roegen*, 1976.

[8] R. Kahn, 'Malinvaud on Keynes', *Cambridge Journal of Economics*, December 1977.

Perhaps it was a misnomer to describe such a position as equilibrium, but without a concept of the character of an existing short-period situation it is not possible to say anything at all. John Hicks, once his eyes had been opened, ought to have been able to see in what sense Keynes used the concept of equilibrium and not made it an excuse to provide an apology for J. R. Hicks's distortions.

RICARDO VIA SRAFFA

Keynes hardly ever peered over the edge of the short period to see the effect of investment in making addition to the stocks of productive equipment. He used to say: The long period is a subject for undergraduates. He dealt only with forward-looking expectations of profits which would never be exactly fulfilled. All the same, he hankered after the concepts of a normal rate of profit and value of capital though he could not get them clear.[9] Here it was Ricardo who could have helped him out.

All the time that the explosions of the Keynesian Revolution were going on overhead, Piero Sraffa was sapping and mining away to prepare a revolution of his own. He first broke surface in 1951 with the *Introduction* to Ricardo's *Principles*.[10] Ricardo was concerned with the distribution of the product of the earth between the classes of the community. Leaving rent aside, this is the question of the relative shares of wages and profits in net national income. The classical theory that had come down to Keynes through Marshall was a travesty of Ricardo. There is a kind of ghost of a long-run normal rate of profit on capital in Marshall's *Principles*, but it is expressed only in terms of departures from it with unexpected changes in demand and it was tied up with the moralizing concepts of 'profit as the reward of enterprise and interest as the reward of waiting'. Marshall did not commit himself to the notion of 'the marginal productivity of capital' but his doctrine that the 'real costs' of production are the 'efforts' of the workers and the 'sacrifices' of the capitalists lent itself to being vulgarized in that way by J. B. Clark. Keynes knew very well that this would not do, but he had nothing to put in its place. Sraffa replaced it by re-establishing Ricardo's theory that the rate of profit is determined by the technical conditions of production in physical terms and the share of wages in net output.

Ricardo himself got lost when he departed from a one-commodity

[9] Cf. Murray Milgate, 'Keynes on the "classical" theory of interest', *Cambridge Journal of Economics*, November 1977.

[10] *Works and Correspondence of David Ricardo*, Vol. I.

economy in which all inputs and outputs are quantities of corn. In *Production of Commodities by Means of Commodities*, Sraffa set up a multi-commodity input-output system and showed that, corresponding to any share of wages, there is a particular pattern of normal prices that yields a particular uniform rate of profit on capital valued at those prices.

The book was not published until 1960. Sraffa had shown a draft to Keynes in 1928. Keynes evidently did not make much of it and Sraffa, in turn, never made much of the *General Theory*. It is the task of post-Keynesians to reconcile the two.

Keynes was right in showing that Ricardo was blind to the nature of effective demand but it was not right to throw him into the same box as Pigou in timeless equilibrium. Ricardo was observing a historical process of accumulation going on through time and, like Keynes, he was applying what he believed to be a realistic analysis of the actual situation to problems of policy. His stationary state was not an equilibrium, but an awful warning. If they did not abolish the Corn Laws so as to reduce the real cost of wages, which were fixed in terms of bread, the rate of profit would go on falling as employment in agriculture increased with 'diminishing returns' until, sooner or later, accumulation would be brought to an end.

Ricardo overlooked the possibility of a deficiency of effective demand; he supposed that both workers and landlords would spend all their incomes currently as they were received while capitalists would devote most of their profits to financing additions to stock. Thus he made saving govern investment. This became the orthodox dogma of J. S. Mill and of Marshall (though he had some reservations)[11] and it needed the whole force of the Keynesian revolution to overturn it.

There was another stumbling block to Ricardo's system. He took the real-wage rate to be given in physical terms. Therefore distribution was determined entirely by the technical conditions of production and there was no room for bargaining power, monopoly or the needs of accumulation to influence relative shares.

Marx, at one level of his thinking, postulated a given real wage. He maintained that labour power, like any other commodity, is exchanged for its *value*. The *value* of labour power is a real-wage rate sufficient to maintain the customary standard of life. But as his argument goes on, the *rate of exploitation*, which governs relative shares, may be pushed up or down with the fortunes of the class war.

Sraffa's system was designed precisely to show that technical conditions

[11] See *Principles*, 8th edition, p. 711.

do *not* determine relative shares, thus knocking out the 'marginal productivity of capital' as the determinant of the rate of profit.

The neo-neoclassics cannot give up marginal productivity because of its deep roots in the moralizing ideology of J. B. Clark. They resort to all kinds of sophistries to defend it, including abolishing the difference between the future and the past by making machines malleable. The post-Keynesians must make use of Sraffa to build up a type of long-period analysis which will prevent neoclassical equilibrium from oozing back into the General Theory.

THE SHARE OF PROFITS

Confining the argument to a 'pure' capitalist economy, without foreign trade or government activity, where can we find a post-Keynesian theory of relative shares? Keynes himself did not say much about it but Kalecki showed that, in a simple two-class society in which workers spend all their wages currently as they are received, the flow of gross profit per annum is equal to the value of gross investment plus capitalists' consumption.

The same flow of profits is compatible with different levels of profit margins, a higher level being consonant with lower real wages, less employment and a lower level of utilization of the plant in existence. Each firm is assumed to reckon its costs on the basis of a standard ratio of utilization of its plant. The short-period level of effective demand is then in balance with the long-period situation when all equipment throughout industry is being utilized at its standard ratio and prices have been set at the level at which the corresponding outputs can be sold. This is not a position of equilibrium, for if effective demand happened to move away, there is nothing to bring it back to the point of balance.

Such a situation could exist only if there had been correct expectations of what the situation would be like while investment was being undertaken to create the equipment now in use. This is the link between the future and the past which is required for long-period analysis.

Long-period balance could be continuously maintained only on a steady growth path where confident expectations about the future can be maintained, continuously fulfilled and so renewed. This is not something that actually happens. It might be called a subject for graduate students. But, as we shall see, it has interesting implications.

THE RATE OF PROFIT AND TECHNICAL CHANGE

When we have accounted for the share of profit in the flow of value of output, in a steady state, we still have not found the rate of profit on capital, for that involves the value of the stock of means of production in existence. Here we come upon the problem of technical change, for accumulation never takes place without innovations.

The Sraffa model represents a strictly one-technique economy. Inputs used up in production are continuously replaced in kind and there is a clear physical distinction between gross and net output. The great controversy that the book aroused unfortunately went chasing after the red herring of 'reswitching'. This arises in the context of a pseudo-production function, comprising alternative techniques. Each technique must have had its appropriate stock of inputs built up by past accumulation. There is no way of switching from one to another unless we could go back into the past and rewrite history, or go into the future with a long course of investment and disinvestment to change one stock into another.

Different stocks, appropriate to different techniques, do not coexist in time and space. Change takes place by inventions and discoveries which cause innovations to be introduced successively through time. Now, the principal requirement for steady growth is that each round of innovations should be neutral to the last. This means that new best-practice techniques require the same 'degree of mechanization' as before. Then, at a constant rate of profit, the capital to output ratio, in wage units, remains constant while the capital to labour ratio rises at the growth rate.

When accumulation and innovations are raising productivity at a steady rate, to maintain balance, the real wage rate must be rising at the same rate. Here is where bargaining power and the class war come into the argument. When real wages fail to rise sufficiently, effective demand fails to absorb the growth of production and the economy sinks into stagnation.

It is also necessary that the supply of money and of finance in general expands in such a way as to keep the rate of interest constant.

Assuming steady growth to be maintained, then at any moment there are a number of vintages of equipment in use, each being operated at standard utilization. The oldest, which is just about to be scrapped, can barely cover its costs at the wage rate ruling at that moment; the latest is yielding the highest quasi-rent. The distance between them, corresponding to the share of gross profits in proceeds, determines the length of service life of a vintage, and so the number of vintages in use. The higher is the share of profit the lower is the real wage rate at any point on the path and therefore the longer the tail of older, less efficient vintages in use.[12] But the share of gross profit is determined by the short-period relationships – gross investment and rentier consumption. Thus technical conditions and the

[12] Cf. Joan Robinson, *Economic Heresies*, pp. 129 et seq.

share of profit determine the level of real wages at any moment, the value of the stock of capital, the rate of profit and the prices of all inputs and outputs (in any numeraire) as Sraffa has shown.

Is this all just a rigmarole? I think not, for it helps to illuminate a problem of urgent importance. When technical progress is neutral, older plant is continually being replaced by new which employs the same amount of labour at normal utilization, producing a higher rate of output. The overall level of employment is then maintained provided that the real-wage rate, the level of consumption and gross investment are all rising at the same rate as output. The rate of profit and the ratio of value of capital to value of output are then both constant, and the capital to labour ratio is rising at the same rate as output per man employed.

What if innovations take on a capital-using bias so that, over a certain range, the capital to labour ratio is rising faster than output?

Marx believed that rising organic composition of capital would cause a fall in the rate of profit, but no one has ever succeeded in making this comprehensible. Ricardo held the opposite opinion, that the introduction of machinery was not against the interests of the capitalists but might be against the interests of the workers. His argument is the more cogent. When the same ratio as before of gross investment to the value of the stock of capital is being maintained when innovations take on a capital-using form, then the new plant that is being created requires less employment at normal utilization than that which is being replaced. It would need a sharp increase in gross investment to prevent this from happening but there is nothing in the situation to cause gross investment to rise.

The condition of increasing long-period unemployment seems to be prevalent at the present time. This cannot be prevented by operating on effective demand; it requires fundamental structural remedies. On top of it a short-period, Keynesian recession has reduced the level of utilization of plant.

Post-Keynesian theory has plenty of problems to work on. We now have a general framework of long- and short-period analysis which will enable us to bring the insights of Marx, Keynes and Kalecki into a coherent form and apply them to the contemporary scene, but there is still a long way to go.

20

INFLATION WEST AND EAST

IN the West, nowadays, inflation is treated as Enemy Number One. It appears as something unexpected and disconcerting. The public turn to the economists for an explanation and, apart from some revival of monetarist superstition, the economists have nothing to say.

The old orthodoxy of laisser-faire, against which the Keynesian Revolution was raised, taught that the free play of market forces could be relied upon to establish equilibrium with full employment and balanced trade. The new school, which came into a position of dominance in the USA after 1945 (spreading its influence in India and everywhere else) taught that full employment can be established by means of government policy, and balanced trade by means of manipulating exchange rates, while at the same time reiterating the doctrines of laisser-faire, and the adulation of the free market economy. The general burden of their song was that all the old problems had been overcome and now we would have a perpetually growing economy, in harmony and content.

The Keynesian revolution in economic theory can be summed up in two main propositions: First, the level of employment, at any moment, in a capitalist economy, depends upon the level of investment and the share of wages in national income (because saving comes mainly from non-wage incomes). Second, the level of prices in an industrial economy depends primarily upon the level of money-wage rates in relation to output per man employed.

The bastard Keynesian doctrine, developed in the USA, included a version of the first proposition but totally ignored the second.

It was an obvious corollary from the Keynesian theory of prices that a successful policy of maintaining near-full employment, without any other change in the industrial system, entails money-wage rates rising faster than output per head and therefore a chronic tendency to rising prices.

It is a sad kind of satisfaction to say I told you so, but for the honour of the true Keynesian tradition it is necessary to point out that we were well aware of this problem from the first.

In 1936, when recovery from the great slump was by no means complete, I published a contribution to the Keynesian theory of employment.

> The general upshot of our argument is that the point of full employment, so far from being an equilibrium resting place, appears to be a precipice over which, once it has reached the edge, the value of money must plunge into a bottomless abyss.[1]

In 1943, looking forward to the promise of full employment after the war, I argued:

> Unemployment in a private-enterprise economy has not only the functions of preserving discipline in industry, but also indirectly the function of preserving the value of money. If free wage-bargaining, as we have known it hitherto, is continued in conditions of full employment, there would be a constant upward pressure upon money wage-rates. This phenomenon also exists at the present time, and is also kept within bounds by the appeal of patriotism.[2]

During the 1950s, the era in England of 'you never had it so good', when unemployment rarely reached a statistical level of 2 per cent, I emphasized the hidden menace.

> In formulating the theory of employment, Keynes uncovered another problem. His argument showed that unemployment is not just an accidental blemish in a private-enterprise system – it has a function. The function of unemployment in the laisser-faire system is to preserve the value of money.
>
> The main determinant of the purchasing power of money over goods and services of all kinds is its purchasing power over the labour that produces them – in other words, the general price level depends upon the level of money-wage rates relatively to the productivity of labour. But the price level itself influences the level of money wages. Starting from any given position, a rise in prices raises the cost of living and reduces real wages, which strengthens the demand of workers for higher money wages and weakens the resistance of employers against

[1] 'Full Employment', reprinted in *Collected Economic Papers*, Vol. IV.
[2] 'Planning Full Employment', *Collected Economic Papers*, Vol. I.

granting them. This is the famous vicious spiral which gives an inherent instability to the value of money in a private-enterprise system.[3]

The problem of inflation came into official consciousness in Great Britain through the balance of payments. With a slower rate of growth of productivity than in other industrial countries, and falling behind in design and quality of new sophisticated products, rising money-wage rates were raising relative costs and destroying the competitive position of British industry. For a time, a belief in exchange-depreciation as a remedy was still dominant; but for a country which imports food, depreciation raises the cost of living and throws oil on the fire of rising money-wage rates, so that the competitive advantage is soon wiped out.

Then the notion of *just a little* unemployment as a remedy against inflation came into fashion.

It was a fairly obvious generalization of historical experience that wage rates rise faster when unemployment is falling than when it is rising – falling unemployment means booming conditions when prices are rising and profits are high. At such a time, trade unions consider it their duty to ask for an upward revision of rates and employers are in a weak position to refuse. From this historical association, Professor Phillips distilled a *law*, by means of some very slap-dash econometric analysis, that the level (not the rate of rise) of unemployment determines the movement of money wage rates. The conception of a 'pay-off' between unemployment and inflation was influential both in the USA and in Great Britain.

I commented upon this view:

> Some observers draw the conclusion that full employment with a stable value of money is unattainable, and that the only possible policy is to keep a sufficient margin of unemployment to discipline the unions, and a sufficiently slack market to make employers anxious to avoid raising costs. They would be content with a mild rate of progress in real production in order to enjoy the benefit of a stable or rising value of money. Those who support this kind of view are generally of the most respectable and conservative kind, but they seem to me to be making propaganda for Communism. They seem to agree with the Marxists that capitalism cannot preserve employment and that it has reached the stage of being a fetter upon progress.[4]

[3] 'Full Employment and Inflation', *Collected Economic Papers*, Vol. II, p. 278.
[4] Ibid.

However, the policy of controlling the level of wages by unemployment turned out to be unsuccessful. Kalecki foresaw the regime of the political trade cycle under which we lived for twenty-five years after the war. Before each election, the government in power courts popularity by a boost to the economy, reducing unemployment, and whichever party wins introduces a stern policy of restraint to try to undo the damage.

In the last three years, both in Great Britain and the USA, the political trade cycle has been revolving faster and wider than before, but during the period of restraint, prices have continued to rise and powerful trade unions have still succeeded in defending their members from suffering a fall in real wages, so that the vicious spiral still revolves, though with a more and more unequal effect between various groups in society. Meanwhile, the boom in commodity prices (now beginning to subside) and the discovery by OPEC of their monopoly power has thrown a fresh lot of oil onto the inflationary fire.

At last it begins to be recognized that 'incomes policy' is the only real remedy, but now the political setting in which it might have been introduced has long since dissolved.

There was a successful control of money incomes in the Netherlands for a decade after the war. The yearly percentage growth of national income in real terms was worked out, and that percentage addition was made to all money-wage rates for next year. Prices remained almost constant and the Dutch economy enjoyed a great advantage in trade, since money costs were rising everywhere else.

The success of this system required two essential conditions. First, that everyone accepted without question his status in society and his relative share in national income; second, that total national income was rising fast enough to give everyone an appreciable improvement in his family's standard of life. Both these conditions are very far from being fulfilled in the Western world today. In an industrial country, the pattern of relative wage rates and the general level of prices govern the distribution of income. In a time of inflation everyone has to fight to maintain his share. Inflation is an expression of the class war. It can be avoided in a case of social harmony, as in the Netherlands for a time, or it can be overcome by brutal means as in Brazil.

In the Indian economy, the industrial sector is a small part of the whole. Within that sector, the vicious spiral operates as in the West, the initiating cause of rising prices coming from the rise in the price of grain. Mrs. Ghandi's new deal appears to be to break the power of the trade unions, offering as a compensation a promise to make the urban middle class pay their taxes. But this is a very small corner of the problem. In India the price that determines the distribution of income is the price of grain and the class war is between those who own land (even two bigars) and the rest.

In India, there is 'Keynesian' inflation in the industrial sector and 'Keynesian' unemployment due to the industrial slump, but Keynesian analysis has a narrowly limited relevance in India. The main problem is the growth of the potential labour force relatively to the stock of means of production. Even if all the bright hopes of successive plans had been fulfilled, the growth of industry could have made only a small dint in this problem. The main means of production is cultivable land.

The function of unemployment of this kind is not to keep money wages from rising but to keep real wages down to a starvation level. This problem is so formidable that the mind boggles at it. The economists in India, for the most part, avert their eyes and spend their time making beautiful mathematical models of a pie in the sky or developing the logic of the pure theory of choice.

But if they did not, what would they be able to say?

21

THE GUIDELINES OF ORTHODOX ECONOMICS

THE so-called mainline teaching of economic theory has a curious self-sealing capacity. Every breach that is made in it by criticism trying to let in some air from reality is somehow filled up by admitting the point but refusing to draw any consequences from it, so that the old doctrines can be repeated as before. Thus the Keynesian revolution was absorbed into the doctrine that, 'in the long run', there is a natural tendency for a market economy to achieve full employment of available labour and full utilization of equipment; that the rate of accumulation is determined by household saving; and that the rate of interest is identical with the rate of profit on capital. Similarly, Piero Sraffa's demolition of the neoclassical production function in labour and 'capital' was admitted to be unanswerable, but it has not been allowed to affect the propagation of the 'marginal productivity' theory of wages and profits.

The most sophisticated practitioners of orthodoxy maintain that the whole structure is an exercise in pure logic which has no application to real life at all. All the same they give their pupils the impression that they are being provided with an instrument which is valuable, indeed necessary, for the analysis of actual problems.

An interesting example of the attempt to apply the orthodox approach to an important real-life situation is the UNIDO *Guidelines of Project Evaluation*[1] which purports to advise economic advisers to Third World countries on how to set about their task. This was compiled in 1972, long after the Sraffa revolution (not to mention the Keynesian revolution), but its whole argument is built up on orthodox foundations, whose conclusions it attempts to modify to some extent by orthodox methods. (One of the authors, however, has since recanted.)

The question to be discussed is the appraisal of projects for investment which have been proposed in a would-be developing country. There is one

---

[1] *Guidelines for Project Evaluation*. United Nations Industrial Development Organisation. UN, 1972.

very useful concept in the orthodox system – that is, the idea of opportunity cost. When national resources are fully employed, it is not possible to organise an increase in any one line of production without drawing resources away from others; when national investible resources are limited, a plan to carry out any one project must entail stinting of others. Appraisal of the benefits from any plan (when the criteria have been accepted) consists in comparisons of it with other possible plans. The opportunity cost of any one consists in the benefit from others that will be foregone if this one is chosen.

The *Guidelines*, however, are drawn up for use in countries where there is massive unemployment and much of the potential surplus is running to waste. In such countries, generally something is better than nothing. The argument starts off on a false trail by implying that it is possible to appraise a single project by assessing benefits and costs absolutely, rather than in comparison with possible alternatives. This causes considerable confusion, which runs throughout the argument.

The criteria for assessing the benefits to be expected from a project are an important and an admittedly problematical element in economic theory.

At the first step, benefits in the *Guidlines* are assessed as the contribution a project will make to aggregate consumption per head. (This is taken to be a measure of the country's standard of living.) Aggregate consumption is evaluated according to 'willingness to pay', that is, at market prices.

But this is only the first step. Leaving aside for the moment the question of the flow of consumption through time, a number of modifications are suggested. First, consumption per capita is an average for rich and poor. It may be that consumption of the rich should be given a smaller weight in the calculation of benefits than that of the poor. 'Such detailed corrections are, however, not easy to make, and refuge may be taken by the project evaluator in the use of some rough methods as may be practicable.'

In the main argument there is some discussion of inequalities between different regions in a would-be developing country, but almost none of inequalities of income between families. 'Willingness to pay' remains the criterion for the value of consumption.

Other objectives of development are the level of employment, the degree of self-reliance of the national economy and particular 'merit wants' that are undervalued in the market, such as the education of girls.

Next, these various criteria have to be combined into a single calculation. This, we are assured, 'is not very difficult'. All that is necessary is to write down the various types of benefit as B_1, B_2, etc., and then apply weights to them, and so arrive at the total benefit to be expected from an investment. (This is a prize example of the inanity of economic theory.)

Later, it is observed that the evaluator cannot himself determine the weights. He must find out, by a process of dialogue, what are the weights attached to various benefits by 'those who are politically responsible and politically accountable for their stewardship of the national interest'. Technicians must not intrude their own judgement. They must 'carry out the will of their political masters and thereby the will of the people'. Presumably this is the attitude of the economists from Chicago who are advising General Pinochet in Chile.

The authors of the *Guidelines* are not actually so naïve as they have to pretend to be. Remarks here and there indicate that they know very well how planning in Third World countries is carried out under the pressures of particular interests, but this is outside their professional competence. The model in which orthodox theory is expressed does not permit of any discussion of the structure of society, or of the formation of classes (heaven forbid!). It depicts a number of undifferentiated 'transactors' who exchange with each other both commodities and 'factors of production' in a perfect market, without any distinction between property and work or between employers and employed. The authors' intelligence, common sense and knowledge of the world has to be squeezed into the limits set by orthodoxy.

We must now turn to the question of benefits of aggregate consumption through time. Here the *Guidelines* are all at sea, for the orthodox model is timeless. It deals with the characteristics of equilibrium in a stationary state. (Recent efforts have been made to extend it to a situation in which the future, from 'today', is correctly foreseen by everybody concerned, although in the past, the position 'today' was not currently foreseen.)

The discussion of the choice of investment projects for a profit-seeking business is confused even in its own terms. Two criteria of choice are offered, the present value of a project when future profits are discounted at the ruling market rate of interest, and the internal rate of return, that is, the discount on expected returns that reduces them to equality with the cost of investment; the latter is the criterion for maximising net profit from an investment. After some discussion, they conclude that present value is the preferable criterion. The argument is posed in terms of a person who can lend and borrow at, say ten per cent per annum, as much as or as little finance as he pleases. Of course, there is no such person. If there were such a person, he would be planning to invest in all the possible projects in the world that are expected to yield a rate of return not less than ten per cent. But when will he carry them out? The analysis explodes, as the mathematicians put it, in the dimension of time. Its only purpose is to show that, in an ideal stationary neoclassical equilibrium, the total value of capital must be such as to make the rate of profit equal to the rate of interest.

An individual running a business has command, at any moment, of a limited quantity of finance of his own and a limited capacity to borrow, depending on his credit. He makes his plans in the light of the expected rate of return on the sum of finance which he has to invest. Moreover, he cannot borrow at *the* rate of interest. His credit standing dictates how much he must promise to pay for the amount of finance that he can raise. The rate of return on a project must exceed the rate of interest that he has to pay, with a margin to cover the risk, otherwise it would not be undertaken. The rate of interest may affect the amount that he will borrow, but on any sum to be invested, he aims at the maximum possible profit, irrespective of what rate of interest he will have to pay.

For a would-be developing country, the amount of investment to be planned, over any period, is limited by the availability of its own resources and the surplus of imports that it can borrow. It should plan to get the greatest possible return in terms of social benefit (however evaluated) on this amount of investment. The market rate of interest (if there is one) has nothing to do with the case.

This argument applies, however, to only one round in a process of accumulation. An important social benefit to be got from one set of projects is the capacity that they create for further investment. This is the most important and at the same time the most difficult of all the choices that have to be made. It involves the question of whether to follow the Soviet line of investment in basic industry at all costs, or to heed Mao Tse-tung's advice: 'if you really want heavy industry, you should invest in light industry and agriculture'. It involves the pattern of foreign trade, foreign borrowing and the aim of self-reliance; above all, it involves the distribution of income, which determines what type of productive capacity it is most profitable to create. (Presumably, the criterion of aggregate consumption measured by willingness to pay has been very useful to those, in many Third World countries, who have been pushing investment into the production of luxury goods.) On all this mainline teaching is a complete blank.

Another lacuna in the orthodox theory is the absence of a comprehensible analysis of the distribution of the proceeds of industry between wages and net profit.

'In textbook models of perfect competition, the market wage rate is the appropriate shadow price for labour, just as any market price is the

appropriate shadow price for a good or service.' This appears to mean that
the market wage rate measures the loss to society of removing a man from a
private employer and adding him to the labour force engaged on
investment in the public sector. But this, it is admitted, is in 'the dream
world of neoclassical theory'. How is it to be applied when there is massive
unemployment? Here the argument leaves the dream world only to fall into
a logical nightmare.

It seems that when a formerly unemployed man is put to work, the wage
that is paid to him is subtracted from the profits formerly accruing to
capitalists. This is taken for granted, not explained. Normally, when there is
an addition to employment, there is an addition to output, which is valued,
actually or notionally, at a price that exceeds the additional wage bill and
cost of other inputs, so that there is an increase in the actual or notional flow
of profit. Perhaps the point is that an addition to employment involves an
addition to working capital, before any additional product comes out, and
this must come from somewhere. But surely it comes out of the general fund
which is financing investment in the project concerned? It is impossible to
increase investment unless there are means to feed more workers while it is
going on.

The next step in the argument is even more mysterious. When
employment increases, the newly employed workers increase their
consumption. The proportion of saving in profit income is higher than in
wage income. Therefore this increase in consumption involves a reduction
in investment. Savings somehow create new equipment by an immaculate
conception without having to be paid out in wages to the men who will do
the job.

When the planners decide that saving is more valuable to society than
consumption, they must refrain from arranging to increase employment.

Now, it can well be argued that it would have been better for society if
the men now unemployed had never been born, but seeing that they have
already grown up, and are being kept alive somehow for the time being,
would it not be socially beneficial to put them to work on something or
other?

Perhaps the argument is that the most patriotic thing that the
unemployed workers can do is to cease consuming altogether and lie down
and die, taking their families with them.

All over the parish of UNIDO, calculations of cost-benefit are being
made according to the recommendation of the *Guidelines*. Apart from the
support that it gives to the prejudices of those who judge social benefit by
'willingness to pay', it is so vague that any adviser can always weight the B's

or fix the rate of interest to get out the result that he privately feels to be right. But one point is quite clear; it certainly confirms the opinion of those subtle exponents of orthodox theory who maintain that it has no application to real life.

22

EMPLOYMENT AND THE CHOICE OF TECHNIQUE

1

THE problems of the relation of the choice of technique to employment in the Third World have been discussed mainly in terms of the orthodox economic theory which has evolved in Western capitalist countries. Unfortunately, this theory is not appropriate even to the problems of capitalist industry.

The pre-Keynesian orthodoxy mainly concentrated upon what is now called micro questions, in particular, the formation of prices in a competitive market, but the treatment of micro problems necessarily implies a macro theory of the operation of an economy considered as a whole. In the macro theory there were two distinct streams, one derived from Walras and one from Marshall, nowadays often blended, or rather mixed up, in the mainstream text-books.

The Walrasian analysis begins with a market for the exchange of ready-made commodities. This found its application in the famous story of the prisoners of war swapping the contents of their Red Cross parcels.[1] It goes on to discuss production in terms of a market for inputs − workers of various capacities, areas of land of various types, and ready-made machines of various specifications. Technology, that is the feasible combinations of inputs to produce commodities, and the pattern of demand, determine an equilibrium position, in the perfectly competitive market, which establishes the prices of commodities, the rentals for the services of inputs and the incomes of their owners.

The stocks of inputs with which the story begins are quite arbitrary. To guarantee that a position of equilibrium exists, it is necessary to postulate that, for an input of which supply exceeds demand at any positive price, the rental falls to zero and part of the supply is not utilized. The Walrasian

[1] See R. A. Radford, 'The Economic Organisation of a P.O.W. Camp', *Economica*, November 1945.

From *Society and Change*. Essays in honour of Sachim Chaudhuri, Oxford University Press, 1977.

approach, applied to the question of employment in the Third World, leads to the conclusion that the *equilibrium* wage rate for unskilled labour is much below the level of subsistence. The only conclusion to be drawn is that wages would be higher if the supply of other inputs was greater, or the supply of labour smaller.

The Marshallian argument is not so completely vapid; it allows for production as a process going on through time; it draws a distinction between income from work, wages, and income from property, rent and interest; and it was designed to lead up to a discussion of accumulation and technical change. As it has been developed in mainstream teaching, however, it leads to the same conclusion: in the Third World the level of subsistence wages is too high to permit full employment.

The main difference between the Marshallian tradition and General Equilibrium lies in the treatment of 'capital'. The 'machines' which form part of the endowment of inputs in the Walrasian model are often referred to as 'capital goods' but they are more like the meteoric stones of Marshall's story, which fell from heaven long ago and can now be used as industrial equipment. These 'machines' were not produced by profit-seeking capitalists investing finance in equipment with a view to employing labour and selling output for a stream of receipts in excess of costs.

In Walrasian equilibrium there are no profits; the sales value of a batch of commodities just absorbs the rentals for the inputs required to produce it. (Production somehow results automatically from the process of exchange, or it is managed by special kinds of ghostly entrepreneurs who pay for inputs out of proceeds and themselves live on air.) In the Marshallian tradition, transmitted to the USA by J. B. Clark, 'capital' is a factor of production. It is derived from household savings which are embodied by businessmen in 'capital goods'. Each factor of production receives an income which corresponds to its contribution to the general productivity of industry. The income accruing to 'capital' is the interest received by rentiers (owners of wealth) while profits, in excess of the firm's interest bill, are the reward of the 'co-ordinating function' of the entrepreneur.

Keynes pointed out that in real life a market economy does not in fact normally establish and preserve equilibrium with full employment; that the wage bargain is made in terms of money and that a cut in wage rates is more likely to reduce prices than to increase employment; that accumulation comes about as the result of decisions by businesses and governments concerning investment, not by the desire of households to save, and that interest is the payment that has to be made for a loan, while profit is the return that a business hopes to make on an investment. All this is acknowledged by the mainstream economists and used in discussions of national policy, but when they turn to the question of the choice of technique, they relapse into the pre-Keynesian style of argument. The concept of a stock of means of production is fused with the value of the stock of capital and the rate of interest is identified with the rate of profit.

The argument is conducted in terms of a 'production function' (leaving land aside), in terms of labour and 'capital'.

The stock of means of production – equipment and other physical inputs – that is in existence at a moment of time is endowed with the qualities of a supply of finance in terms of money. It is 'malleable' and can be adapted to whatever line of production or whatever technique, in a given situation in the general market for commodities, promises the most profit. The 'production function' is based upon the concept of substitutability between 'capital' and labour. Any given output can be produced by a continuous series of combinations of the 'factors of production', a higher ratio of 'capital' to labour yielding a higher output per unit of work, with 'diminishing returns' from the application of 'capital' to labour, so that output increases is a smaller proportion than 'capital' per man. Or, with a given 'quantity of capital' it is possible to employ any number of workers, the output yielded being greater the greater the amount of employment per unit of 'capital' with 'diminishing returns' from labour applied to capital. Thus the marginal product of labour (the addition to total product due to employing an additional unit of labour with a given amount of 'capital') falls as employment per unit of 'capital' rises.

The combination of factors is dictated by the principle of 'marginal productivity'. With a given amount of 'capital' such an amount of labour will be employed as to make the marginal product of labour equal to the real-wage rate. In this model there can never be any long-run unemployment, for if some workers were unemployed, competition for jobs would lower real wages and the existing stock of capital would be spread more thinly and bring about employment of a larger number of workers. Thus, in this model, as in the Walrasian model, the existence of unemployment is to be accounted for by real wages being held above the equilibrium level.

The confusion between the rate of interest and the rate of profit brings a further absurdity into this theory. The marginal productivity principle is derived from the micro-economic argument, that an employer may be presumed to offer such an amount of employment with a given stock of equipment as will maximize the rate of return that he gets from it. With a lower cost of labour in terms of his own product, he offers more employment and gets a higher rate of profit on his investment. This is translated in the production-function model into the principle that a higher rate of interest will lead to the use of more labour-using techniques.

However far-fetched these models may seem, it is necessary to understand them, for they still underlie mainstream teaching, which is even more prevalent in the ex-imperial regions than in its homeland and provides the orthodox basis for discussions even of actual and urgent problems such as the employment of labour in the Third World.

2

The production function model is expressed in terms of a diagram of the form shown below.

There is a given stock of 'capital' which can be embodied in a continuous series of techniques. This is shown in the productivity curve, which is drawn so as to represent diminishing returns from labour applied to capital. The wage rate per unit of labour is shown by the angle φ and the wage bill for each amount of employment by the corresponding wage line. The rate of profit per unit of 'capital' is maximized when the excess of output over the wage bill is greatest, that is, where the tangent to the productivity curve is parallel to the wage line. (Here the marginal product of labour is equal to the wage per man.) It can be seen that with the higher wage rate φ_1, the more capital-using technique, a, is used; output per unit of 'capital' (OA) is less, and so is employment (OL$_1$), than with the lower wage rate.

This illustrates the underlying conceptions of the production-function approach in a simplified form.

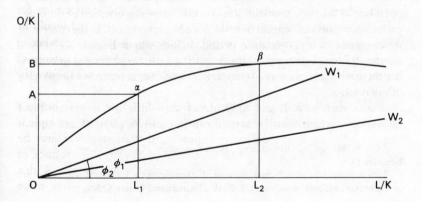

When applied to a given stock of 'capital' this is evidently absurd. Each technique has to be embodied in a set of physical means of production, and, once created, it cannot be changed instantaneously because the wage rate rises or falls. When challenged to say what a 'quantity of capital' consists of, the mainstream economists could only reply that they did not understand the question.[2]

The same approach, however, has been adapted to the discussion of the choice of technique in investment planning. Instead of a stock of capital, there is conceived to be a given amount of available investible resources, and a given objective of increasing productive capacity for a particular flow of future output. The production function is then conceived as an *ex ante* relationship, showing the known methods of production amongst which a choice is to be made. Now O/K means output per unit of investible resources and L/K the increment of employment that will be offered when the new investment is completed.

The famous problem of 'measuring capital' does not arise in this context as we are concerned with the choice of investment plans not with the stock of means of production already in existence. Here the labour to capital ratio, L/K, is used for comparing the cost of investment per man to be employed with various techniques. Such a measure, of course, is extremely crude. Investible funds may be reckoned at current prices, but investible resources really consist of particular workers and physical inputs available at particular places. The labour to be employed also has its own characteristics.

The concept of the capital to output ratio (K/O) is also extremely complex. To find out the inputs required, by different techniques, at only one stage in the production of a simple product, involves elaborate research.[3] Even then, the comparison can be made only for techniques in operation at the same moment. It leaves out the whole question of the time-pattern of inputs and outputs over the life of an investment. In the context of development, a long gestation period, before output begins, is clearly a greater drawback than a short life, requiring earlier replacement or repairs, but there is no sensible way of comparing these costs in terms of a simple rate of discount.

Ratios such as K/L and K/O are of very little use in the study of technology, which must be carried out in concrete physical and human

[2] Cf. R. M. Solow, 'Reswitching: Brief Comments', *Quarterly Journal of Economics*, February 1975.
[3] See for instance the study by F. Stewart of 'Manufacture of Cement Blocks in Kenya', in *Technology and Employment*, ed. A. S. Bhalla, International Labour Office.

terms; here, however, we are only trying to explore the basic conceptions underlying mainstream doctrines.

It is also necessary to clear up the confusion between interest and profits. For individuals or businesses to carry out investment, they must have control over some property which can be turned into a liquid form, to provide for the outlay to start a process of production that is expected to yield a return over a longer or shorter period of future time.

Where there are well organized institutions for bringing together lenders and borrowers – the banking system and the capital market – investors are not confined to disposing only of finance that they own. Rentiers – that is, passive owners of wealth – can get an income from lending, that is, putting finance at the disposal of active business, and there are flows of lending and borrowing between businesses which facilitate activity. The level of interest rates measures the cost of finance. It is *low* interest and *high* prospects of profit which encourage private investment.

The choice between more or less capital-using techniques depends upon the prospects of profit that they offer; it is only indirectly affected by the rate of interest. When finance has been raised by a loan, it will be embodied in the most profitable investment available, quite independently of the interest that has to be paid for it. Low interest and easy credit influences the *amount* of investment that profit-seeking businesses will plan to carry out but there is no reason why it should necessarily affect the amount of investment *per man* to be employed.

However, interest represents the cost of waiting for the return on an investment; a high rate of interest, therefore, biases investment plans towards those with the quickest yields, and quicker yields may be associated with smaller investment per man employed.

Moreover, the choice of technique for a particular project is very strongly influenced by the command of finance that the authority undertaking it can command. There are some highly mechanised, capital-using installations that require a large minimum size of investment to be able to work at all. They can be set up only when a large block of finance can be invested by a single authority (whether public or private). Those who command only modest resources can undertake only small investments and are confined to adopting simple techniques.

The miserable inhabitants of the shanty towns of Latin America and the street-dwellers in Indian cities are usually described as living in 'disguised unemployment' but rather they should be regarded as self-employed. Like any business, they have to seek a market, which they do by offering their services to their prosperous neighbours, operating at the lowest possible technical level of trading in tiny quantities of goods obtained on credit. Their productivity is low because of their inadequate command of finance. To make sense of the problem of choice of technique, we ought to draw a different productivity curve for each scale of investment.

In spite of all these complications, the production-function diagram has been adapted to the analysis of a programme of investment. For a given amount of finance, the productivity curve shows the technical possibilities that are assumed to be known and fully blue-printed. The ruling wage-rate, say φ_1, in the diagram, is expected to remain constant over the relevant future.

From the diagram it can be argued that a given amount of investible resources devoted to the Beta technique will add more to national income in the immediate future than if it is devoted to Alpha (assuming a choice between only these two techniques is available). It would have the further advantage of making a larger reduction in the mass of unemployment which is a burdensome problem in all the Third World.

Against this was advanced the so-called Dobb-Sen thesis that the technique should be chosen which maximizes the addition to surplus so as to help in speeding up the rate of accumulation. This thesis has had a considerable influence on the development of theory, though probably neither of the authors to whom it is attributed would want to defend it today.

The argument is that, supposing the wage rate φ_1 to represent some politically acceptable minimum real wage, then the Alpha technique should be chosen, because when the new productive capacity is in operation it will yeld a greater surplus over the wage bill than would the Beta technique.

This means that the profit-maximising technique, which would be chosen by a capitalist business faced with the same alternatives, is the most eligible also for a developing economy because it provides the largest surplus for further investment. The most obvious objection to this view is that, under private enterprise, a large part of the profit is consumed in relative luxury, and that, when it is invested, it is directed to increasing the profits of the businesses concerned, which is not necessarily the best contribution to national development.

But does it make sense in a fully planned economy? Even on the assumption that the whole investible surplus of the economy is controlled and wisely used, the case for choosing the surplus maximizing technique, before full employment has been established, is by no means convincing. Compare the profit-maximizing technique, Alpha, shown in the diagram by employment OL_1 and output OA with Beta, which offers OL_2 and

OB. A round of investment in Alpha, which has a larger surplus than Beta, adds more to investible resources, but the same amount of investment in Beta adds more to national income over the immediate future, more to employment and more to the total of wages. Choosing Alpha does not increase growth, it increases the acceleration of growth. Continuous reinvestment of the surplus from each, on the assumptions required by the argument, would produce two paths of development; at some date in the future the Alpha path would show a higher national income and more employment than the Beta path.[4] But meanwhile the workers who are not employed on the Alpha path are living in misery or even dying for lack of any wages to consume.

For a profit-seeking enterprise, the wage bill is the *cost of labour*. This concept is sometimes transferred to a national economy, so that the cost to the nation of employing a man consists of the consumption goods that he (and his family) buy with his wage. On this view, the most patriotic thing that a man could do would be to lie down and die (taking his family with him) so as to save the nation the cost of what he consumes. Of course, that is a point of view.

The way to generate the maximum possible surplus is to organise employment of all available workers, provide them with an acceptable minimum standard of life and to direct all who are not required to provide the ingredients of the minimum into investment industries. The surplus does not have to be first saved and then invested. Devoting resources to building up the stock of means of production is saving and investing at once.

The acceleration of accumulation depends, as was shown in the famous Fel'dman model, on the extent to which the output of machine-building industries is ploughed back into enlarging their own productive capacity. The criterion for the choice of technique, so long as investible resources are scarce relatively to availability of labour to be drawn into industry, ought surely to be to maximize product per unit of investment, not to maximize surplus. Where there is a choice such as that shown in the diagram, the Beta technique should be preferred to Alpha.

The problem of maximizing surplus is a political problem – that is, at what level the acceptable minimum should be set and at what pace it should be allowed to rise.

3

The conception of capital as a 'factor of production' has led the argument astray. It is not the means of production ('capital goods') that provide

[4] Cf. A. K. Sen, *The Choice of Techniques*, 1960, p. 22.

employment but finance, whether public or private, that organizes employment and is used to provide equipment to assist workers to produce output. The first question to be asked about a process of development should be: Who commands finance, how is it accumulated and for what purpose is it used?

The control of finance governs the quantity and form of investment. When finance is controlled by a central authority, investment can proceed on a conscious plan. Employment is organised and stocks of means of production built up with a view to the pattern of output that it is desired to produce. Idle labour is a waste of resources. Where finance is at the disposal of individuals and businesses, investment is guided by prospects of profit. Employment is organised and stocks built up, not in order to develop the resources of the nation but in order to supply the markets which offer the prospects of the highest returns.

For a planned economy, the choice of technique is bound up with the purpose of development. In the Soviet Union development was dominated by the motive of defence in a hostile world and therefore concentrated at all costs upon the development of heavy industry. This was effected through the pace of investment and its allocation between various objectives. The production-function analysis of the choice of techniques in any one line had nothing to do with the case.

The production-function approach is misleading also, in suggesting that there is one overall 'capital' to labour ratio that can be translated into the appropriate ratio of investment in productive capacity to labour to be employed. The ratio must depend upon the technical possibilities of each line of production.

The first step in the discussion of development strategy should be to examine the composition of the additional flow of output for which investment is intended to provide new capacity. The proper criterion for planning is then to secure the maximum possible output of the desired production per unit of investment. This requires a distinction between those products, such as iron and steel, which cannot be produced at all except in large-scale organisations with a high ratio of investment to labour employed and those for which there is a choice between more and less mechanised techniques.

The policy of maximizing output per unit of investment would, incidentally, provide the largest possible increment of industrial employment with each round of investment, for where there is a choice between feasable techniques (as illustrated in the diagram), the highest output per unit of investment involves the greatest employment per unit of investment.

Where an investment programme is planned for a whole economy, development on these lines can be carried out systematically. The Chinese policy of 'walking on both legs' aims at the most rapid possible modernisation of industry with the least possible sacrifice of consumption meanwhile.

A private-enterprise economy cannot proceed in this rational manner, for the choice of investment projects depends upon prospects of profit on the one hand and command of finance on the other. Generally, in the situation of a developing economy, the most immediately profitable investments are those in producing consumer goods for households who already have a margin of income to spend over mere necessities. The most important investments for growth, in basic industries, are the most slow yielding and the least attractive to private investment.

In India, for this reason, investment in basic industries was undertaken in the public sector, with foreign help. This led the Indian authorities to dream of following the Soviet example of planned development, but they lacked the essential precondition – control over the total supply of finance.

The growth model used by Mahalanobis, which had a great influence on Indian planning, was based upon the same conception as that of Fel'dman – that the fastest way to develop was to make the largest possible investment in basic industry and to plough back the product into enlarging the investment sector, leaving consumption to be provided for mainly by cottage industries with a very low level of mechanization.[5]

However, a private sector was already established and could grow by investing its own finance and inviting investment from abroad. Private enterprise must direct its investment towards an existing market and a market existed in the cities for manufactured consumer goods. The cottage industries failed to expand while profits and high salaries in the private sector enlarged the market for their own products. The output of the public sector, instead of being ploughed back into investment, was sucked into the profitable market. 'Thus hot- and cold-rolled sheets required for the manufacture of consumer durables have received considerable attention in some of the steel plants in the public sector despite the high capital intensity of the investment required for this purpose.'[6]

In India there has been a considerable effort to encourage cottage industries based upon traditional crafts. There has been some success in developing hand-woven textiles as a luxury product, dependent on the sophisticated taste of a middle-class market. The attempt to promote

[5] Cf. K. N. Raj, 'Linkages in Industrial Development Strategy', *UN Journal of Development Planning*, No. 8.
[6] Ibid.

spinning as a cottage industry, with the *ambar charkha*, was influenced by piety rather than common sense. It violates the first principle of the choice of the objects of investment, for yarn (as opposed to cloth) is a commodity for which the advantage of mechanization is very great.

Apart from the luxury market for goods with an artistic appeal, traditional handicrafts have largely been wiped out by the competition of factory products, but there has been some development of small-scale production of modern consumer goods, such as bicycles and sewing machines, working with a low level of mechanization.

For small businesses, where a large proportion of the labour force is provided by family members, the rate of profit required to attract investment is much lower than in capitalist enterprises, for the family lives off the profit, which is thus a substitute for a part of the wage bill, instead of something that has to be added on to it. Even when the business prospers, the ratio of employees to family members is kept low, because it is easy for a worker who has learned the job as an employee to set up in business on his own. Investment per man employed is by no means negligible in organisations of this type, but in the first instance it consists mainly of working capital – materials and the wages of employees – which offers better security for loans than fixed investments. The family have a strong motive for saving to invest in improving their equipment, so that mechanization can be gradually increased, as the market expands, without making any call upon national investible resources.

In India, the growth of the small scale industries is impeded by the extreme inequality of income, particularly in the agricultural sector. Landless labourers and small tenants have scarcely any margin over bare subsistence to spend on the kind of consumer goods that the small industries are able to provide, while purchasing power is concentrated in wealthy households who prefer the type of commodities that can be produced only in large-scale capitalist industry.

There is a notable exception to prove the rule. In Punjab, flourishing agriculture is conducted by medium and small proprietors, with very little wage labour. This provides a market which has permitted a considerable growth of small-scale manufactures. These have begun to expand into the urban market by producing components for factory industries.

4

It seems that the doctrine derived from the production function – that low wages and high profits (though called interest) promote the growth of employment – is the reverse of the truth, for it leaves out of account the reaction of the distribution of income on the pattern of demand.

It is true that there is some competition in cheap labour between different countries of the Third World, and even between regions in India, to entice capitalist business to come and set up factories in one rather than another, but that is quite a different story.

It is certainly absurd to suppose, as the production function suggests, that a higher value of investment per man employed is associated with a lower rate of profit. In the advanced industrial countries, technical progress was always pushed into a labour-saving direction, but this does not mean that it was continuously more capital-using. Superior techniques were always being evolved, that offered a higher output per unit of investment as well as a higher output per man.

When these techniques are imported into the Third World, for a business that can operate at the required scale, they yield enormously higher profits than small-scale, labour-using, techniques. Such businesses would not be induced to adopt a less mechanized technique by lower wages. Indeed, they often find it convenient to pay somewhat higher wages than the local level in order to enlist the loyalty of their work force.

Capitalists (both local and foreign) and the economists who support them, object that the small-scale industry is inefficient. They are willing enough to allow government investment in heavy industry (particularly if its products are handed over to them at cost-price) but they claim that any investment that is profitable to private enterprise is necessarily contributing to national development. It cannot be right, they maintain, to help the small-scale businesses with, for instance, cheap credit, because the very fact that they need help shows that they are 'uneconomic'. Certainly, it is often profitable for a business to use investible resources to displace labour by mechanizing production and competing small-scale businesses out of existence, but for the nation, in purely economic terms, this is substituting a scarce resource for one that is plentiful, and in human terms, increasing misery for many families and benefiting only a few.

Against this, the capitalists' spokesmen claim that they are benefiting the consumers of their products, for the fact that they buy them shows that they prefer them (preferences being helped by advertisement and salesmanship). Granting for the sake of argument that we could compare the *utility* contained in factory-made goods with that of the small-scale products, and that theirs is superior, we should credit the excess of investment per man in factory industry with a return represented by this difference in *utility*, not by the whole profit. A small benefit to consumers involves a large cost to the nation.

Moreover, if the benefit goes to richer households, for whom orthodox economics teaches us that marginal utility of consumption is lower than for those who are poorer, we cannot rightly claim any advantage even in *utility* for the factory products.

What is the moral of all this? The economists have too long allowed themselves to be bamboozled by mainstream teaching, which is no more than the pre-Keynesian doctrine of the defence of laisser-faire, and leads to no practical conclusion except: What is profitable is right. With the scene before their eyes, surely Indian economists ought to be able to think for themselves.

23

FORMALISTIC MARXISM AND ECOLOGY
WITHOUT CLASSES

BEFORE 1945, underdevelopment had not been heard of. Unemployment and poverty were problems in the capitalist world, but extreme misery in colonial territories was not seen as a problem in the imperial countries. In the colonies, nationalist movements concentrated on the aim of getting rid of foreign rulers. Little thought was given to the problems of development that would follow independence. Indeed, landlords and businessmen supported such movements because they wanted to be free to exploit their own people for themselves. Only in China was a war of liberation conceived in terms of a radical reconstruction of society.

When the old empires had disintegrated (all except the Portuguese) and successor states had come into existence, there was a great deal of talk about development, take off, and stages of growth, but the main object (conscious or unconscious) of the advice and 'aid' given to the new nations was to induce them to continue to make themselves a convenience to their ex-masters and, in particular, to the United States, providing supplies of materials and a sphere for profitable trade and investment.

In twenty-five years, certainly, some development has taken place but it has been accompanied by a growth of numbers that increases the reserve army of labour faster than organized industry can offer jobs; in a large part of the world, the mass of human misery is growing at the same time as statistics record a rise in national incomes. In this situation the advisers on development can do nothing but wring their hands and offer some pills.

The orthodox economic theory on which the advisers rely was developed out of Ricardo's argument against protection. The doctrine of comparative advantage is that a country can gain by allowing imports of commodities of which output per man employed at home is relatively low and paying for them by exports of which output per man is higher. The

Review of *Unequal Exchange, A Study of the Imperialism of Trade*, by Arghiri Emmanuel, N.I.B., 1973, and *Poverty and Progress*, by Richard G. Wilkinson, Methuen, 1973, reprinted from *The Journal of Contemporary Asia*, 1973.

argument is stated in terms of costs at a moment of time; it does not take account of the relative potential future growth of various commodities.

Ricardo took the case of trade between England and Portugal in cloth and wine. He argued as though it would be just as advantageous to Portugal to give up her textile industry and rely on exporting wine, as to England to do the opposite. He was not being consciously sophistical but his intuition was working entirely in terms of British interests and in terms of the interests of the rising capitalist class against the old landed aristocracy.

The case for free trade became the dogma of English economics and the ideology of imperialist expansion. It was not believed in America, Germany or Japan, where industry, at first developed under the shelter of protection from the British, was soon beating them at their own game.

In the industrial countries, accumulation overtook the growth of population, the reserve army of labour was absorbed into employment, scarcity of workers speeded up technical development and trade unions were able to take advantage of rising productivity to raise real wages. In the colonies there was no scarcity of labour; even when the slave trade was abolished there were plenty of landless labourers (for instance, in South India and China) to be moved to wherever it was required to develop exotic natural resources. Wage rates remained at rock bottom and cheap imports of food stuffs and raw materials contributed to the rising standard of life of the labour force in the industrial metropolis.

From the tangled skein of international economic relations, Arghiri Emmanuel picks out this thread – the terms of trade between primary products from the Third World and industrial manufactures from the West – and uses it as the main explanation of the contrast between the poverty and wealth of the two groups of nations. (He points out that a share in the benefit goes just as much to innocent countries like Sweden as to the old or new imperialists.)

He offers to explain the terms of trade by means of the labour theory of *value* and the Marxian transformation of *value* into prices. Wage rates (whether reckoned in dollars or in a basket of goods) are much lower in the Third World than in the West, while the overall rate of profit on capital tends to be equalized among trading countries, so that relative prices of commodities are such that the money-value of product per man hour is much less in the Third World than in the West, both for primary products and for manufactures.

What does this explanation explain? The labour theory of *value* is a way of exhibiting exploitation in an industrial capitalist economy. In any period, say a year, a flow of output is produced by labour applied to pre-existing equipment and stocks of materials. Deducting stocks used up and wear and tear of plant from gross output, we are left with the physical net output of the period. This can be represented as a list of specified commodities, as a sum of money at ruling prices or as a sum of *value*, that is, the number of man hours of work performed during the year.

To avoid a complication to be discussed below, let us assume that conditions in the various industries are such that the money prices of commodities are proportional to their labour *values*. Take the measure of net output in terms of money and subtract from it the total of wages paid over the year. We find that the money-wage bill is, say, half the money value of net output. Now go back to the calculation in terms of man hours of work. Half the time the workers were producing wages and half net profits. Marx puts it that an individual working, say, a ten hour day, is spending five hours producing what he consumes, but this is metaphorical; production is interlocked; no part of net output is produced by anyone by himself. The point of the argument is to show that a worker gets for himself only a fraction (in this example, half) of *value* that he produces. This is a very striking and picturesque way of expressing the fact of exploitation but it cannot be said to explain anything.

In particular, this way of looking at an industrial economy does not explain the level of real wages. In Volume I of *Capital*, Marx appears to expect that real wages will fluctuate around a more or less constant level so that, as capital accumulation and technical development go on, the rate of exploitation (the ratio of net profit to wages) will be rising as time goes by. In Volume III, there is a tendency for the rate of exploitation to remain more or less constant, so that real wages will rise more or less in step with total output per man employed.

The problem of the transformation of *values* into prices has attracted an enormous amount of confused controversy but it is only an analytical puzzle of no deep significance. When organic composition (the capital to labour ratio) is the same for all industries, the prices corresponding to a uniform rate of profit are proportional to labour *values*. This is a very useful assumption to make for what is nowadays called a macro theory of distribution, in which relative prices of commodities are a secondary consideration. (We made it above to simplify the calculation of the rate of exploitation.)

When technical or marketing conditions make the money value of investment per man employed different for different commodities, then, with a uniform rate of profit, prices are not exactly proportional to labour *values*. (In the above calculation, when the industries producing goods that wage-earners buy have a different organic composition from the average, there may be a discrepancy between measuring exploitation in terms of flows of money payments and in terms of labour time.) But even when prices are not exactly proportional to *values*, the two are related to each other in a systematic way. Marx's powerful intuition showed him where the analysis must lead but he left it only partially worked out. Piero Sraffa has shown how to find the only one uniform overall rate of profit and the one pattern of prices that is compatible with any given rate of exploitation.

No doubt the labour theory of *value* was a necessary step in the argument, but once the point has been made clear, there is no more need to go on making a fuss about it, as Emmanuel and Bettleheim do in the appendices to this volume.

There are a number of serious difficulties in applying the Marxian apparatus to problems of international trade. (Emmanuel spends a good deal of space on criticising Ricardo and modern theory but he does not quite understand it. It would be better to knock it out for total irrelevance.)

First, labour *values* in a single economy are reckoned in terms of 'abstract labour'. A skilled worker is held to generate more *value* than a labourer, to an extent roughly proportional to his higher wages. How is the unit of abstract labour to be reckoned for international comparisons?

Secondly, it is not to be expected that there is normally a uniform rate of profit as between colonial and metropolitan investment. When an imperialist government acquires territory, by force or fraud, suitable for, say, tea gardens or copper mines, and lets its own capitalists invest in them, employing local or imported low-wage labour, the rate of profit (while markets are good) may be very high, but, since the natural resources are limited, investment cannot expand to bring it down to the average level. Moreover, the profitability of such ventures depends enormously upon the state of markets. In this kind of business prices are strongly influenced by conditions of supply and demand. They do not fit well into the theoretical scheme of labour *value* or 'prices of production', which applies to industry using man-made equipment. The long-run fall in terms of trade for primary products (just now violently reversed) has been largely due to the fall in demand for them brought about by the use of synthetics in modern industry.

There is one important point, however, that Emmanuel draws from the labour theory of *value* – the effect of relatively high real wages upon the working-class movement in the industrial countries.

It is not the conservatism of the leaders that has held back the revolutionary elan of the masses, as has been believed in the Marxist–Leninist camp; it is the slow but steady growth in awareness by the masses that they belong to privileged exploiting nations that has obliged the leaders of their parties to revise their ideologies so as not to lose their clientele.

The diagnosis and the illustrations in this whole section of the book are very telling.

Even here, however, the argument is set up on too narrow a base. There is a great deal more than cheap tea or copper in the benefits that the industrial workers draw from imperialism; the greatest injury that they are now doing to the Third World is in supporting measures to prevent low-wage countries from developing exports of manufactures and so climbing into the capitalist world by the Japanese route.

The narrowness of Emmanuel's diagnosis of the problem of imperialism in trade is shown by the policy that he proposes for the low-wage countries: that they should try to restrict production of primary products and so improve their terms of trade. Such a scheme might gain them a temporary advantage, but it would only speed up substitution of synthetics for natural materials and reduce their export earnings in the future. Besides, even if this policy was successful, the benefit would go mainly to landlords, dealers and capitalists (including the foreign capitalists to whom the ex-colonies are still paying tribute). It would strengthen the position of the reactionary governments which are keeping the successsor states in thrall to the capitalist world.

Richard Wilkinson treats of poverty and progress in terms of economic history in general rather than of the modern problem of underdevelopment.

The present disintegration of orthodox economics leaves the field open to anyone with a bright idea. Wilkinson's bright idea is 'ecological equilibrium'. Each animal species that survives today remains in balance with its food supply.

Ester Boserup, in her brilliant little book *The Conditions of Agricultural Growth*, made two very striking points. The first is that the principle of 'diminishing returns' from a rising labour-to-land ratio applies to man hours of work, not to bodies. Output per man hour is at its highest and output per family at its lowest in primitive slash and burn cultivation. As population grows in a given area, fallow time is reduced and the forest soon disappears. Then technology develops so that a family can get a living from a smaller area by working harder. A community which failed to develop the appropriate technology would die out.

The second point is that when a peasant population has been absorbed into a 'civilized' state, the cultivator is made to part with half or more of his gross produce. Rising numbers in a given space reduce the cultivators' income per unit of work, partly by reducing average output (because of 'diminishing returns') and partly by weakening his bargaining position and reducing the share that he can keep for himself.

Wilkinson makes a great deal of the first point, which fits in with his ecological conceptions but he overlooks the second, for his whole argument is set out in terms of the ecology of a 'community' without regard to its internal structure.

When he treats the English Industrial Revolution as an example of technological response to growing numbers, the concept of 'the community' leads to a lot of special pleading.

He traces the story of how shortage of wood led to coal mining and coal mining led to steam pumps and so to all the rest. But how much was the despoiling of woodlands due to growing numbers in the countryside (as happened in India) and how much to rising middle-class consumption in the towns? He quotes a seventeenth century writer:

> . . . Such hath been the great expense of timber for navigation, with infinite increase of building houses, with great expence of wood to make household furniture, casks, and other vessels not to be numbered, and of carts, wagons and coaches, besides the extreme waste of wood in making iron, burning of bricks and tiles, that at this present, through the great consuming of wood as aforesaid, and the neglect of planting of woods, there is so great a scarcity of wood throughout the whole kingdom that not only the City of London, all haven-towns and in very many parts within the land, the inhabitants in general are constrained to make their fires of sea-coal.

Wilkinson treats the factory system, also, as an ecological response and remarks that it was 'soon' to reverse the fall in real wages which growing numbers had caused. He refers incidentally to the import of raw cotton and export of piece goods. Were the conquest of India and the export of slaves to the cotton states in America all part of the ecological response to growing numbers in England? (Of course, in Ireland and Scotland population was declining – what was that an ecological response to?)

With growing apprehension, the reader looks forward to a last chapter in which it will be argued that the multiplication of numbers in India will 'soon' lead to a take off. But at the end the discussion of underdevelopment is mainly a critique of the hollow orthodox theory, which is only too easy to expose.

Wilkinson sums up his case by saying that new technology is introduced when it is profitable. Yes, certainly, but profitable to whom? Merely formalistic Marxism does not get us very far, but ecology without classes gets us nowhere at all.

24

WHO IS A MARXIST?

DURING the dark years of McCarthyism and the Cold War, a small group of American Marxists, of whom Paul Sweezy was the leading spokesman, held the fort with courage and integrity. In those days, no doubt, it was natural to distinguish friend from foe by shibboleths rather than reasoned arguments, but it is sad that they should feel obliged to continue to do so now, when the scope for argument, at least with the young generation, is beginning to open out.

The leading case in point is the attitude of certain professed Marxists to Piero Sraffa's 'Prelude to a Critique of Economic Theory'.

The orthodox theory (which was produced in the first place as an answer to Marx) is that it is not true that only labour produces value, because 'capital' also produces value. The 'factors of production' are 'labour and capital' (we can leave 'land' out of the argument here). There is substitution between them; technology involves 'diminishing returns' – falling marginal productivity – as the ratio of one to the other increases; their 'rewards' are regulated by their marginal productivities, so that as 'capital' per man employed increases, with accumulation, the real wage rate rises and the rate of profit falls. This was essentially Marshall's theory (mixed, however, with elements of classical theory derived from Ricardo) though it was disguised in subtleties and contradictions. It was enunciated blatantly by J. B. Clark: 'What a social class gets is, under natural law, what it contributes to the general output of industry'. Underneath mountains of algebra, this is still the basis of modern teaching. (In trying to answer Sraffa, in 1962, Professor Samuelson appealed to J. B. Clark, and when he was caught out on a technical point, although he admitted that he was wrong, he did not in any way change his view.)

Bukharin[1] and Thorstein Veblen[2] produced penetrating criticisms of this set of ideas but the general run of latter-day Marxists did not press the argument home. They merely reiterated the slogan that only labour

[1] *The Economic Theory of the Leisure Class.*

[2] 'Mr. Clark's Economics', reprinted in *The Place of Science in Modern Civilizations.*

produces value. They could not explain how it is that men operating machines produce more output, though not more labour value, than men with simple tools. This left the theory of the productivity of 'capital' in possession of the field.

The orthodox theory contained another element – that the relative prices of commodities are determined by the interaction of supply and demand. Marx took it for granted that there is a tendency for the rate of profit to be at a uniform level throughout a competitive capitalist economy, so that the normal prices of commodities are proportional to their labour values only when organic composition (which governs the capital to labour ratio) is the same in all lines of production. The Marxists allowed themselves to be drawn into an intricate and inconclusive controversy about the relation of labour values to normal prices ('prices of production') losing sight of the main point – the distinction between the Marxian theory of prices and the orthodox theory of supply and demand.

Sraffa confronted the orthodox theory with a simple example (though it must be admitted that his book is not very simple to read). Let us suppose that we can observe a process of industrial production going on. The labour force, operating particular techniques of production, is using a particular flow of inputs (materials) to produce a flow of output which reproduces the inputs used up and adds to them a flow of net output. The net output of any period is a list of products expressed in physical terms – tons, pints or yards. The stocks of inputs available at the beginning of a cycle of production are added to and subtracted from the gross output of the period. Thus we can say that the whole labour force, working so and so many hours over the period, produces the whole net output. The existence of available stocks of inputs was a necessary condition for workers to produce, but there is no way of attributing a particular part of the product to the stocks, and another part to labour. The marginal productivity theory has nothing to bite on. Moreover, there is no way of distinguishing the influences of supply and demand. The requirement for inputs is geared to the composition of output by the technique of production. Because the economy which the model represents is a going concern, inputs, outputs, and employment are in line with each other, and there is no sense in asking which causes which to be what it is. The analysis can be extended to deal with fixed equipment, with differences in technique, and other complications, but the simple model is sufficient to exhibit the essential point.

The technical specifications of the model make it possible to distinguish the amount of labour time required, directly and indirectly, to produce a unit of each commodity, subject to the condition that inputs used up in the process are replaced. These quantities of labour time express the Marxian values of the commodities. Prices would be proportional to labour values with zero profits. When a certain part of net output accrues to capitalists (that is, when there is a particular rate of exploitation) there is a particular pattern of prices which insures that the production of every commodity yields the same rate of profits on the value, at these prices, of the inputs required for its production. These are Marxian 'prices of production'. They are proportional to labour values (as Marx showed) only in the fluke case where organic composition is uniform in all lines of production.

Sraffa does not attempt to offer a theory of the rate of profit or the rate of exploitation. He is only concerned to show that when we know technical conditions and the ratio of net profit to wages in the economy as a whole, we can find the rate of profit on capital, the prices of commodities and the wage rate in terms of any bundle of commodities. Alternatively, if we know technical conditions and the wage rate as a bundle of commodities, then we can find prices, the rate of exploitation and the rate of profit.

Incidentally, the analysis shows that there is no meaning to be attached to the productivity of physical inputs separable from the productivity of labour and that the 'quantity of capital' represented by a stock of inputs has no meaning independent of the rate of profit.

Sraffa offered this argument as a battering ram to knock down orthodox theory and clear a space in which the Marxian theory of distribution and of prices could be elaborated. A certain group of professed Marxists have refused to accept it.

The reason perhaps is the sentiment towards Marx which Schumpeter detected:

> It is easy to see why both friends and foes should have misunderstood the nature of his performance in the purely economic field. For the friends, he was so much more than a mere professional theorist that it would have seemed almost blasphemy to them to give too much prominence to this aspect of his work.[3]

However, the group of professed Marxists who reject Sraffa do not admit that they object to precise analysis as such; they maintain that there is a clear theory in Marx which is incompatible with Sraffa's analysis. They claim that he derived his treatment of profits from Ricardo rather than Marx but they have not offered any alternative formulation. Objection is made to the very name of Sraffa's book *Production of Commodities by Means of Commodities* as though it meant: as opposed to production by labour, rather

---

[3] *Capitalism, Socialism and Democracy*, p. 21.

than as opposed to production by 'capital'. An elaborate attack[4] was based on confusing two meanings of the word 'surplus' as net output – the excess of product over the replacement of constant capital $(v + s)$ and as profits – the excess of net output over the wage bill(s). They complain that Sraffa does not use Marxian terminology – *value*, *exploitation* and *constant capital*. These are all merely verbal points, without any analytical substance.

It is true, however, that there is a difference between Sraffa's set of categories and that used by Marx. Marx treats the rate of exploitation as s/v, which represents the division of the working time of the labour force between producing the commodities that are acquired by capitalists (investment and luxury consumption) and commodities consumed by workers, while Sraffa's system leads up to P/W, the division of the value (at prices corresponding to the ruling rate of profit) of net output between profits and wages.

In fact, it is Sraffa who has shown how it would be possible to distinguish the ratio s/v (in his highly simplified model) but there is no advantage in doing so, for P/W is much more useful concept than s/v if we are interested in trying to understand how a capitalist economy operates. The decisions of capitalists are influenced by the search for profit – they could not care less how much labour-value they are getting, except in so far as labour-value means profit. For the observing economist, P/W is an operational concept; it can be roughly observed in terms of statistics and compared between countries or over time, while s/v can be distinguished only 'in the abstract', as Marx himself asserted.

In translating Marx's system into operational terms, we come upon a puzzle. When we write the flow of gross output per annum in terms of Marxian value as $c + v + s$, v evidently corresponds to the year's wage bill, but Marx refers to it as variable *capital* and in some contexts it corresponds to the wage fund. When the rate of exploitation is written s/v, clearly v corresponds to the wage bill, while when the rate of profit is written, $s/(c + v)$, v corresponds to that part of the stock of capital which is embodied in the wage fund. (It could be argued that Marx's analysis was sometimes thrown out of gear by this confusion; but even if his was not, that of his followers often is.)

The wage bill for employing a man continuously for a year is the weekly wage multiplied by 52. The purchasing power of this sum constitutes his real income (the value of labour power). The wage fund required to employ a man depends on the length of the period of through-

[4] Mike Lebowitz, 'The Current Crisis of Economic Theory', *Science & Society*, Winter 1973–1974.

put of the process of production (the turnover of working capital). This is the length of time over which wages have to be advanced before they are recovered from the product. (For Ricardo, with an annual harvest, the turnover period was one year.) The wage fund required to employ a man is the weekly wage multiplied by the number of weeks in the turnover period, minus one. (The worker who is paid at the end of a week is continually lending one week's wage to his employer.)

Marx wrestled with the problem of varieties of turnover period in the notes that were published as Volume II of *Capital* but these are not very easy to follow.

In Sraffa's system, the wage fund is deliberately eliminated by the assumption that wages are paid out of the net product. There is no point of principle involved in this. Anyone who wants to, can postulate a particular turnover period and take variations in the wage fund into account in showing the relationship between the level of real wages and the rate of profit on capital. This is only a minor complication in Sraffa's argument; however, it is a challenge to the verbal Marxists to make clear the meaning of 'variable capital' as they understand it.

There is another important subject on which the verbal Marxists eschew analysis, that is, effective demand.

Marx took it for granted that the realization of surplus value depends on expenditure of profits – a view summed up in Michal Kalecki's epigram – the workers spend what they get and the capitalists get what they spend. The most important and the most variable object of capitalists' expenditure is investment.

In the orthodox theory which was intended to answer Marx, accumulation depends upon decisions of households to save. That 'saving is a form of spending' was the basis of the equilibrium theory that came to a crash in the great slump. Keynes rediscovered the obvious fact that accumulation depends upon investment and that the motive for investment is to increase the capacity to acquire profits in the future. (The orthodox school have adopted a bastard version of Keynes' theory and wrapped it up again in equilibrium.)

Considering the political use that has been made of his ideas, it is natural enough for Marxists to be suspicious of Keynes, but what is the objection to Michal Kalecki, who set out almost exactly the same analytical system as the *General Theory* on the basis of the schema of expanded reproduction in Volume II of *Capital*?

Marx's theory of effective demand is mainly in long-run terms. 'Accumulate? Accumulate! That is Moses and the prophets.' So long as businesses reinvest profits, as they are made, in expanding productive capacity, there is no problem of instability – the economy enjoys a continuous boom. The problem, as Rosa Luxemburg saw, would be how to find outlets, over a long future, for the ever growing flow of profits to be invested. The saying: 'The last cause of all real crises always remains the poverty and restricted consumption of the masses,' again, seems to envisage long-run stagnation rather than instability. Marx also offered a number of suggestions to account for a ten-year trade cycle, which contain most of the elements that have been elaborated in modern theories.

All this needs to be sorted out and brought to bear on the experience of the last hundred years. To this task, indispensable contributions have been made by Kalecki, but the verbal Marxists refuse to accept anything that is not expressed entirely in Marx's own terminology.

With the light that Sraffa has thrown on the theory of value and Kalecki on the process of realization of the surplus, we can develop a complete system, not of *neo* Marxism but of *intelligible* Marxism, and, what is more important, adapt it to the analysis of contemporary problems of capitalism, socialism and so-called 'development'. Who wants to build a verbal wall to shut themselves off from this prospect?

It would be better to heed Chairman Mao's advice to look first for the principal contradiction. In teaching economics and in trying to understand economic history (including the present as history) the principal contradiction is between an adaptation of the tradition of classical political economy, developed by Marx, to modern problems, on the one side, and orthodox mumbo jumbo on the other. At the present time, orthodoxy is still entrenched, particularly in American universities, but its supporters are quite unable to answer the criticisms that are being made of their system. They have to fall back on authority over appointments and publications to keep their pupils in line. The verbal Marxists, however, are not much of a menace. In an argument with them, neither party pretends to understand the other's analysis and the debate is purely on ideological grounds, where the orthodox professors feel quite secure. Indeed, the verbal Marxists are doing them a good turn, by helping to shield them from Sraffa's logic.

25

IDEOLOGY AND ANALYSIS

IT is natural that a student of the social sciences should choose the school to which he attaches himself according to his ideological sympathies. But when he judges all points of logical and factual analysis by ideological standards and refuses to learn anything from the work of any school whose ideology he does not accept, he cuts himself off from making any useful contribution to the development of his subject and ends by substituting slogans for the insight that led him to form his ideological beliefs in the first place.

Some writers purport to deny that analysis and interpretation of evidence can have any validity apart from ideology. (I say purport to deny, for the fact that they deploy arguments in favour of the ideology that they support shows that they do not accept in practice that argument cannot have any validity.) This point is discussed by Dr. Barrington Moore in a book entitled *Reflections on the causes of Human Misery and upon Certain Proposals to Eliminate Them*:

> There are many people today who apparently believe that once moral judgments enter a discussion, science necessarily flies out the window. Since, they agree, moral considerations are unavoidable, there can be no such thing as a scientific approach to human affairs. Moral judgments are inevitably arbitrary, this line of argument continues, and therefore no two people with different moral positions can possibly agree in their interpretation of social facts.
>
> That aspect of the issue may have stirred up more dust than is really necessary. If the factual evidence and the logic in a political treatise are sound, the moral starting point plays a very minor role towards the intellectual contribution that the treatise can make. One can reverse the moral premise without affecting the rest of the argument. In the case of this little book, if the general arguments are correct, presumably

---

A contribution to the Festschrift for Eduard März, Europaverlags AG Wien, 1973.

anyone who wished to increase human suffering would find the discussion pertinent.[1]

In what follows I offer a few examples of how confusing logic with ideology has impoverished the development of economics.

It is obvious enough that the academic schoolmen, from Böhm Bawerk to Samuelson, cut themselves off from studying the classical problems of accumulation and distribution for fear of being contaminated by Marxism. This has reduced latter-day orthodoxy to mere triviality. There is no need to dwell upon that point. I want rather to discuss some aspects of academic economics of which Marxists might have made good use if they, also, had not been nervous about ideological contamination.

1

VALUE AND PRICES

The flow of production taking place in an industrial economy is an extremely complex entity that cannot be represented in any simple measure. It is something which exists. It is *there* in reality. It is not affected by the way we chose to represent it, but various ways of representing it are connected with various alternative ways of diagnosing its behaviour through time, its distribution between classes and so forth.

In a drastically simplified schematism, it may be represented as a flow of money values corresponding to the market prices at which goods change hands or are entered in the books of business and government organizations. Or it may be represented in money values deflated by a chosen index of prices. It may be represented as a list of quantities of commodities, in tons, pints and yards. Or it may be represented in labour *value*, that is as a number of man hours of work.

When 'gross national product' is represented by labour *value*, it consists of two parts – c, the pre-existing 'constant capital' used up during, say, a year and net labour *value* $(v + s)$ – the labour time worked during the year. The constant capital was produced in the past by labour time working with then pre-existing constant capital and so on, *ad infinitum* backwards. It therefore cannot be reduced simply to a number of labour hours that can be added to the net *value* of the current year. And there is no advantage in trying to do so. The constant capital used up and replaced can be subtracted in physical units from the gross physical product of the year's work. The

[1] Op. cit., pp. 4–5.

physical net product is then represented by the man hours of work performed during that year.

What is the relation between a calculation in money values and in labour *values*? Total net national product in terms of money and in terms of labour hours are two different ways of presenting the same physical facts, but when we want to discuss the division of the total between wages and surplus we cannot treat them as identical.

As a first approximation, let us suppose that money prices are such that there is a uniform rate of profit on capital throughout the economy and that workers are all alike, so that a man hour is a simple unit in which values can be measured.

Now, in the special case where 'organic composition of capital' is the same in all lines of production, money value and labour *values* coincide, not only for total output, but for each segment of output. In that case the rate of exploitation, s/v, is identical with the ratio of profits to wages in money terms, P/W. Moreover, the real wage regarded as what the workers get is identical with the real cost of labour that the capitalists have to pay.

When prices do not correspond to labour values, we have to work out the 'prices of production' in the particular economy that we are examining. This involves valuing the stock of capital, for the value of his capital determines the profit that each capitalist receives.

Marx made this calculation in a very rough and ready way. He identified c, the means of production used up in a year, with C, the stock in existence, and v, the annual wage bill, with V, the wage fund. And he valued both elements in capital in terms of labour *values* instead of at prices corresponding to the ruling rate of profit. With the assistance of Piero Sraffa, we can work out the 'transformation problem' correctly, at least in principle. When the physical conditions of production and the over all share of wages in net output are given there is one pattern of prices of commodities, including the elements making up the stock of means of production, and one rate of profit on capital. Or, the other way round, there is one share of wages and profits in total net income corresponding to each rate of profit on capital. Thus, when either the rate of profit or the rate of exploitation is given, the relation of labour *values* to prices of production is determined.

Now consider the meaning of s/v and P/W. We may consider the real wage – the value of labour power – as a specific bundle of commodities (as in von Neumann's system, or like Ricardo's 'corn'). The commodities the capitalists receive as net profit are a different bundle, containing inputs for investment and luxury consumption goods. When money prices of the two bundles of commodities are not proportional to their labour values, P/W does not necessarily coincide with s/v.

This is a significant difference when the real wage is, in real life, a specific bundle of goods that remains more or less constant through time. But in modern conditions, with the composition of output continuously changing and the level of consumption of industrial workers rising, there does not seem to be much point in calculating labour values. For practical purposes, P/W is both more accessible in terms of statistics and more significant in terms of the diagnosis of the behaviour of the economy. However, it is still necessary to distinguish between W deflated by the prices of commodities that workers consume (that is the real wage) and W deflated by prices in general (that is, the cost of labour to the capitalists as a whole).

There has been a great deal of unnecessary controversy and fuss over all this because the ideological aura attached to the labour theory of *value* has dazzled Marxists and blinded academics so that neither could find their way through the analysis.

2

EFFECTIVE DEMAND

In the three volumes of *Capital* there are a number of theories of the instability of production under capitalism – the mechanism of the absorption and recreation of a reserve army of unemployed labour; the problem of realization of the surplus; an echo cycle, due to bunching of replacements of equipment at ten-year intervals; under-consumption ('the last cause of all real crises') due to unequal distribution of income – but in the main line of the argument, capitalists continuously invest the surplus that they extract. ('Accumulate! Accumulate! That is Moses and the prophets.') There may be in some far future an absolute overproduction of capital, or there may be a falling rate of profit because organic composition rises, as time goes by, relatively to the rate of exploitation, but before the Keynesian revolution, no one found in Marx a systematic treatment of chronic or cyclical deficiency of effective demand in a market economy.

Marxists, of course, have no sympathy with Keynes' ideology. His meliorist philosophy, his 'moderately conservative' politics and his ludicrous comments on Marx naturally raise prejudice. But this is not a valid reason for refusing to understand his analysis.

In this connection we have a striking illustration of the independence of analysis from ideology (when logic is not deliberately fudged or evidence cooked). Michal Kalecki found out independently all the main points in Keynes' analysis. He, in spite of much disillusionment, was all his life devoted to the cause of socialism and he found the basis for his theory in the Marxian schema of expanded reproduction. His version of the general theory of employment is in some respects more coherently argued than Keynes', but Keynes is more useful in shooting down academic orthodoxy, because he understood it from within.

With the aid of Kalecki's analysis, it is possible to sort out all the various elements in Marx's theories of crises, get them into perspective and apply them, with necessary adaptations, to the problems of capitalist, socialist and so-called developing economies in the world today.

3

THE RATE OF PROFIT

In reality, of course, there is no such entity as *the* rate of profit. Investment by capitalist firms is guided by estimates of future profits while the distribution of income is governed by realized profits. The two are never exactly in line with each other, for expectations never turn out to have been exactly correct. Moreover, the level of profits (either ex ante or ex post) is not uniform throughout an economy. There are systematic variations due to differences in monopolistic power and there are chance variations in the fortunes of particular industries or particular firms.

All the same, it is useful to set up a model of an economy developing in sufficiently tranquil conditions to make outcomes fairly consonant with expectations, with sufficiently pervasive competition to make the rate of profit uniform. Moreover it is convenient to assume that organic composition is the same in all sectors, so that we do not have to bother about whether s/v has the same meaning as P/W.

Before discussing Marx's treatment of the rate of profit, we must clear up some points in his notation.

When $v + s$ and c, or $W + P$ and A, represent the flow per annum of net income (wages and net profits) plus replacement (amortization) of wear and tear of equipment and stocks consumed, then we cannot write $s/(c + v)$ as the rate of profit on capital. The stock of capital as a quantity of labour time embodied in physical means of production should be written as C and the wage fund (which is related to v, the wage bill, by the average of the periods of through-put in different industries), should be written as V.[2] Then (assuming that labour value prices have always ruled) $s/(c + v) = P/K$

[2] See p. 262 for a slightly different interpretation.

where K is the value of the stock of capital in wage units, at the ruling rate of profit.

Marx habitually assumed that $v = V$, because he had taken over the Ricardian system based on an annual harvest. Given the wage rate, V per man employed is a stock of corn in the barn after harvest, to be used to pay out v, a week at a time, over the year until the next harvest. In industry, the period of through-put varies with technology and is neither uniform between industries nor constant through time. It is important in relation to finance – bank loans are used for working capital rather than for investment in equipment – but on the level of generality of Marx's argument it is not of any importance at all.

Clearly, the rate of exploitation must be written s/v. The extent to which an employer exploits labour does not depend upon the amount of V that he owns or borrows but on the amount of v that he pays out, relatively to the net output $(v + s)$ that he makes the workers produce.

Organic composition cannot be written as c/v or C/V. Neither of these ratios is of any interest, either technologically or economically. Technically C and c consist of two parts, fixed equipment, and materials, power, etc. used up in the process of production. The latter element together with V, constitutes working capital. The distinction between working and fixed capital is of importance in some connections but it has only a remote connection with the power of capital to exploit labour or with the determination of the rate of profit. The important relationship is $(C + V)/v$ which, on our assumptions, is the same ratio as K/W.

Now, what is the theory of the determination of the rate of profit in *Capital*?

In Volume I, the mechanism of the reserve army will keep commodity wages more or less constant, while accumulation and technical change are raising output per head. Therefore the rate of profit on capital is rising over the long run.

Rosa Luxemberg pointed out that it is impossible to predict a falling rate of profit if commodity wages are to remain constant, and that the danger for capitalism lies in the sphere of realization.

In Volume III, it seems that the rate of exploitation (s/v) is expected to be more or less constant. This implies that commodity wages will be rising. The tendency to a falling rate of profit will be due to technological changes raising K/W faster than P/W. In the counteracting causes, Marx points out that the labour *value* of the physical ingredients in C may fall but he did not emphasize the point that the labour *value* of a constant commodity wage falls towards zero as output per man rises so that there is no necessary limit to s/v.

What technology tends to raise K/W through capital-using innovations is a matter of fact, not of logic. No doubt in the phase of industrialization that Marx was observing, C/v was rising. Nowadays the 'stylized facts' seem to correspond to more or less neutral innovations that raise the money value of capital per man in more or less the same proportion as the money value of output per man. Then an overall rate of profit on capital, constant through time, is compatible with a constant rate of exploitation (s/v or P/W) which entails commodity wages rising in proportion to output per head.

Once he has left the anchorage of constant commodity wages, Marx does not give any systematic account of what determines the rate of exploitation, but from his general argument we can see that there are two interconnected forces at work.

The first is the relation of accumulation to the growth of the labour force. When capital is accumulating rapidly, the reserve army is absorbed into employment and the share of wages in net income rises. Marx refused to admit that growth of population is deleterious to the interests of the workers, but his argument clearly shows that it is, and modern experience certainly confirms this.

The second element, which is not unconnected with the first, is the growth of political power of organized labour. This also is clearly seen in modern times. We find that the share of wages in value added in industry is highest in countries like Australia, Sweden and Finland; in the capitalist countries in general it is twice or three times that in the Third World. It has been rising in Japan since the reserve army from agriculture was absorbed into industry.

It is easy to understand why the academic economists have not devoted much attention to this subject. The Marxists, absorbed in theological arguments about the relation of surplus *value* to profits, have also neglected to study it.

To return to formal theory, Sraffa has shown that, when we know the technical conditions of production and the overall rate of exploitation, we can find the unique set of prices that is compatible with a uniform rate of profit. This determines the wage in terms of commodities and the cost of labour to each group of capitalists. There is then no need to continue to confine the argument to the case of labour-*value* prices. When organic composition varies between industries, prices are not simply proportional to labour *values* but are related to them in a systematic way.

Sraffa does not offer any theory of what determines the rate of profit. His argument begins and ends with the relation of the rate of profit to the rate of exploitation in one system of technical relationships. His purpose was to vindicate Marx by showing that the orthodox theory is quite empty, rather than to discuss how to fill the void.

A Marxian analysis of the historical evolution of the rate of exploitation provides the setting, in broad terms, for a theory of profits; some detail can be fitted into it with the aid of Kalecki.

In an industrial economy, there is, at any moment, a particular amount of productive capacity in existence. Prices of commodities are formed, not by supply and demand, but by the decisions of firms, who fix the gross margin or mark-up on prime cost, at levels calculated to cover total cost of production at some standard rate of utilization of plant, plus an allowance for net profit which depends mainly on the weakness or strength of competition in the various markets in which the goods are to be sold.

The amounts that will be sold, at these prices, of the total flow of output, depends on the level of effective demand. When the economy can be divided exhaustively into two classes – workers and capitalists – and when the workers are spending their wages week by week as they receive them, it follows that total gross profits going to the capitalists as a whole are equal to their expenditure on investment and on their own consumption. 'The workers spend what they get and the capitalists get what they spend.'

There are many complications that have to be introduced into Kalecki's simple model to analyse a modern economy, but the basis is there.

It is possible also to work out a long-period version of the theory, in which accumulation is going on at a steady rate. This, however, is only a first step which should not be given much weight. In reality, all the interesting and important questions lie in the gap between pure short-period and pure long-period analysis.

Analysis that is put at the service of ideology is not interesting, because we know in advance what the answer is going to be. When we consider the world evolving around us, we see a great number of questions that need to be explored because the answers are not obvious at all.

26

THE ORGANIC COMPOSITION OF CAPITAL

THE concept of 'the organic composition of capital' is an important element in Marxian analysis; because of its connection with a theory of a falling rate of profit, it has been taken to resemble the neoclassical concept of 'the ratio of capital to labour' and since the latter has been pulverized by Sraffa's critique[1] it is necessary to re-examine the former in the same light.

1

The notation in which Marx set out his formal analysis is very confusing. A flow of production, say per week or per year, in terms of *value* is expressed as $c + v + s$, that is, the *values* of the depletion in the pre-existing stock of means of production, of wages and of surplus. Net output, $v + s$, represents all the man-hours of work performed over the period. (The labour-force is partly engaged on replacing means of production, but this is compensated for by c, the *value* released from the means of production used up.)

At the same time, Marx writes $c + v$ for the stock of capital and c/v for organic composition. Clearly the stock of constant capital is a multiple of c, the depletion of the stock, say *per annum*, that has to be made good over the period. Let us write C for the stock of physical means of production in existence at a moment of time. But then what is v, regarded as part of the stock of capital? At one time I believed that 'variable capital' should be treated as a wage fund, represented by V, so that the stock of capital should be written as $C + V$. But now I think that this was a mistake. A wage fund is essentially a financial concept – the sums required to pay out wages over the period of turnover of working capital.

In Ricardo's corn model, the turnover period was given by nature – the period from harvest to harvest, which is a year in high latitudes, and the wage fund had a physical existence as a stock of grain, available after the harvest to be paid out week by week until the next harvest. In tropical

---

[1] *Production of Commodities by Means of Commodities*, Cambridge University Press, 1960.

agriculture and in manufacturing industry, the turnover period of working capital may be much shorter than a year or sometimes longer, and it varies for various lines of production and for various techniques; there is no standard turnover period to define the wage fund required for output as a whole. Furthermore, the equipment and stocks required for producing a flow of output of wage goods cannot be distinguished (like corn in a barn) from the rest of the stock of means of production. Thus it seems best to write C for all existing physical capital, including stocks of grain, and to use v only in one sense – the flow of *value* of wage goods being produced.

It is clear that Marx thought of the stock of capital as consisting of two parts; one part was the physical means of production and the other part somehow represented labour employed, organic composition being the ratio between them, but there does not seem to be any way of representing this in his notation as c/v.

An alternative definition of organic composition is 'the ratio of dead to living labour', that is the quantity of labour embodied in the stock of means of production, required for a particular technique, per man employed on current production. Here, as we shall see, we can find a clue to guide us through the mazes of 'capital theory', but it has to be handled with care.

2

A change in methods of production brought about accumulation and technical improvements is an extremely complex process. It is best to begin by comparing 'islands' each using a different technique, each equipped with the stock of means of production that its technique requires. Since the comparison is a pure intellectual experiment with no pretension to realism we can simplify it as much as we like provided that we introduce no inconsistencies into the picture.

The concept of the *technique* for producing the whole output on an island is basically the same as Sraffa's 'system' of equations depicting all the physical relations between the ingredients in a flow of production and the labour force that operates them. However, we modify the details of Sraffa's picture to suit the requirements of our problem.

Sraffa's system was designed to emphasize the effects of differences in the rate of profit in a single economy, while we are interested in differences between economies that are independent of differences in their rates of profit.

Instead of Sraffa's distinction between basics and non-basics, we depict a physical difference between net (consumable) output and means of production. Net output is measured in 'baskets' made up of commodities in fixed proportions, the same on each island. The labour force on each island consists of the same number of men, working the same hours per day, per week and per year. Each labour force produces a flow of output of baskets while keeping intact the stock of means of production required for the technique that it is operating.

We can compare flows of production growing through time provided that the growth rate is the same on each island, but the most convenient growth rate to take is zero. On each island the whole net output is consumed and the stock of means of production is continually being replaced, item by item. We need not bother about the distinction between equipment, say 'machines', and stocks of materials being used up in the process of production, for the whole stock on each island has existed in its present form from time immemorial; a photograph of it taken on a given day in any year would always look exactly the same. Consumption of workers and of rentiers is of baskets of uniform content so that the distribution of income does not influence the composition of net output.

Now we come to the difficult question. How are we to compare the stocks on different islands, each being composed of the entirely different physical items required for different techniques?

Marx was content to treat the stocks as 'dead labour', that is, he measured a stock by the number of man-hours of work performed in the past to produce it, but this is very rough, for a stock of means of production was not produced by labour alone. The flow of net output *per annum* can be represented by its *value*, $v + s$, a number of man-hours of work, but to produce a physical output workers require a pre-existing stock, appropriate to the technique in use, of which a part, c, is used up and replaced during the year. Marx treats c as a quantity of *value*, formerly created and now released, but this year's c could not have been produced without the aid of some earlier pre-existing c.

This conception plays an important part in Sraffa's argument. It means that the cost of investment cannot be reckoned in terms of labour alone. It depends also on the time-pattern in which the work was done and this entails that the value, in any *numéraire*, of a specific physical stock of available inputs varies with the rate of profit.

We cannot get out of this difficulty merely by postulating that the same rate of profit is actually ruling on each island. We do not have any theory of what determines the ruling rate of profit on any island, only, following Sraffa, an account of the relationship, for any specified technique, between the rate of profit and the share of wages in net output. But we can escape the difficulty, for the purpose of an intellectual experiment, by postulating that the time pattern is the same for all techniques.

Divide the labour force into two sectors. In one sector, workers are operating 'machines' to produce a flow of 'baskets'. Here the period of through-put is very short, so that work in progress as part of the stock can be neglected. In the other sector, workers (with the aid of machines) are replacing machines as they wear out. Now suppose that, on each island, the stock, whatever it may be is completely replaced every ten years. Then C, the stock measured in labour-time, is ten times c, the annual depletion of stock. An island where C is larger has to have a greater proportion of the labour force in the machine-making sector and requires, in a clear sense, a higher capital to labour ratio to operate its technique. By this, or some equivalent set of assumptions, we can justify treating differences in stocks as differences in 'labour embodied' and we can write organic composition as C/L where L is the number of men employed.

In this part of Marx's argument the problem of effective demand (realization of the surplus) does not arise, so that we assume given employment (not necessarily full employment) on each island.

We can now present a technique in a modified version of Sraffa's wage-profit diagram. Sraffa's curves, though with a consistent negative slope, are full of wiggles. This was very important in the capital controversy but in the present context we are not interested in re-switching and all that. We will suppose that on any island, labour-value prices rule, that is to say that the relative prices of items in the basket and in the stock of that island are the same (at any rate of profit) as they would be at a zero rate of profit. Then on each island the wage-profit curve is a straight line. (This is in no way necessary to the logic of the argument; it is introduced merely to simplify exposition.)

A given labour force, L, is providing a flow of work ($v + s$ per man) which produces a flow of net output, O/L, while keeping intact the physical stock of means of production represented by C. Net output, in 'baskets', is shown on the vertical axis and the rate of profit on the horizontal axis. The maximum rate of profit, corresponding to the imaginary position of zero wages, is shown by R. K, the value of capital, in terms of a unit of output is O/R. (With labour *value* prices for all items of current output, the value of capital is independent of the actual rate of profit.) The capital to labour ratio, K/L, is shown by the slope of the wage-profit curve, OR, and the output to capital ratio, O/K, is shown by R, the maximum rate of profit. Thus, a higher capital to labour ratio is shown by a steeper slope and a lower capital to output ratio by a higher maximum rate of profit. In the diagram,

Figure I

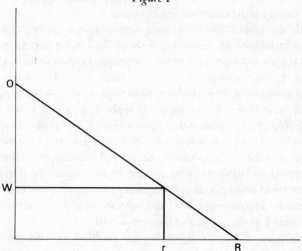

the actual rate of profit is shown as *r* and the wage as *W*. The rate of exploitation (s/v) is shown as $O-W/W$.

We are interested in comparing five typical islands. *Beta* is the basis for comparison; on three superior *Alpha* islands, output, O/L, is greater than on *Beta* without requiring a higher capital to output ratio, K/O. There is also

Figure II

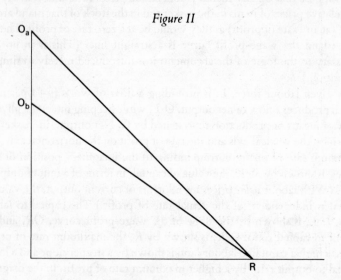

The intermediate case, quasi-*Alpha*, is shown in *Figure V*. Here higher net output per man, O/L, requires a cost in terms of labour embodied in the stock of capital per man employed higher in a greater proportion. Thus the capital to output ratio in this case is greater than for *Beta*. $K_a/O_a > K_b/O_b$. The maximum rate of profit, R_a, is lower than R_b.

Here there are two ranges of cases. On an island where the wage rate was below the level corresponding to the intersection of the curves (W' in the diagram) if the *Beta* technique was known, the quasi-*Alpha* technique would not have been installed, but at any higher level of wages, quasi-*Alpha* offers the greater rate of profit.

Over that range, $O_a - W'$ is greater than $O_b - W'$ in a greater proportion than K_a/L is greater than K_b/L. Similarly, if the rate of profit is less than r, quasi-*Alpha* provides the higher wages.

Marx wanted to argue that rising organic composition would cause the rate of profit to fall (though when he was working on Volume III of *Capital* he was evidently very uneasy about this proposition).[2] The above analysis indicates a missing link in his argument which he evidently overlooked.

3

In a recent contribution to the debate,[3] Professor Okishio purports to provide the assumptions which would justify Marx's proposition, but he falls into a trap of Marxian terminology. He treats $v + s$ (labour time) as the measure of product and so identifies the capital to output ratio with the capital to labour ratio. A rise in organic composition, by definition, is a rise in the capital to labour ratio. It lowers or raises the capital to output ratio according to the technique which it embodies. Furthermore, a rise in the capital to output ratio does not cause the rate of profit to fall, for a capital-using technique would not be adopted unless it raised profit per man employed at least as much as the cost of investment per man.

Okishio goes on to construct a diagram of the same type as those used above, with output in terms of wage goods on one axis and the rate of profit on the other. He emphasizes the character of a superior technique (*Alpha* compared to *Beta*) but he maintains that Marx's theorem would be correct if technical progress was confined to the type, quasi-*Alpha*, which requires an increase in the capital to output ratio. He noticed, in the diagram, that the quasi-*Alpha* technique has a lower maximum rate of profit than *Beta* but he

[2] *Capital*, Vol. III, Ch. 14.

[3] N. Okishio, 'Notes on technical progress and capitalist society', *Cambridge Economic Journal* March, 1977.

failed to notice that at any wage above W' (at the level of the intersection of the curves) the rate of profit is higher for quasi-*Alpha* than for *Beta*.

The ratio of the quasi-*Alpha* to the *Beta* wage, at a common rate of profit, is less than the ratio of the outputs. To yield the same profit with a greater K/O the share of profit in the *value* of output (s/v) must be greater. Thus Marx was correct in saying that, if the rate of exploitation (in terms of *value*) was unchanged, a rise in organic composition would lower the rate of profit. But here we are not concerned with *value* but with physical output. In a comparison of quasi-*Alpha* with *Beta*, when the rate of profit is the same, the real-wage rate in terms of output is higher.

There is another inconsistency in Professor Okishio's analysis, besides identifying organic composition with the capital to output ratio. He writes L for the flow of *value* being produced without distinguishing between the number of men and the hours of work that each performs. In order to keep in touch with this argument, we assumed above that hours of work were the same on all islands, so that both L, the number of men employed, and $v + s$ were the same everywhere but it would be much more natural to suppose that hours of work are less on the islands where output per man is greater.

Marx argued that normally a capitalist employer must maintain a rate of real wages sufficient to support life (the *value* of labour power) while the more effort per day he can squeeze out of the workers and their families, the greater the surplus *value* that he extracts. This applies to a one-technique, one-shift system. It is painfully true of situations where unorganized, under-employed workers are being absorbed into a capitalist labour force. But where a strong trade-union movement has been able to claim a share in the fruits of advanced technology, the advantage has been taken partly in reducing the working day and increasing holidays.

Where the technique in use requires heavy investment, multiple shifts make the working day of equipment twice or three times that of the average wage-earner. This has to be taken into account in measuring the capital to labour ratio. It cannot well be represented by lumping L and $v + s$ together.

4

The discussion of the Marxian theory of a falling rate of profit has been heavily impregnated with ideas drawn from neoclassical doctrines, but meanwhile those ideas themselves have been discredited.

In pre-Keynesian theory, 'saving', that is accumulation of financial capital, forces down the rate of interest (identified with the rate of profit) and so induces the use of more capital-using techniques. This concept has not survived the abrogation of Say's Law by Keynes and Kalecki; the concept of 'the marginal productivity of capital' which falls as the 'capital' to labour ratio rises has not survived the 'Cambridge criticism' which draws a clear distinction between financial capital and a stock of man-made means of production.

The neo-neoclassics have shifted their ground and adopted the concept of a pseudo-production function.[4] This can be represented by a series of islands in which each requires a higher capital to output ratio than the last (as in the comparison of quasi-*Alpha* with *Beta*).

A technique with a higher capital to output ratio, K/O, has a lower maximum rate of profit and a smaller share of wages in net output, but since net output is higher, it is not necessary that the rate of profit should be lower.

We can run over the series of techniques assuming the same rate of profit to be ruling on each island (shown as r in the diagram).

With a common rate of profit, the ratio of the wage to output falls as we ascend the series. In the limit, the increment to output is only just sufficient to yield the constant rate of profit on the increment to the cost of investment, so that the wage rate remains unchanged. Beyond this point, no further 'deepening' of the stock of capital takes place.

This is a version of the neo-neoclassical theorem, that the maximum output obtainable by deepening the stock of capital (raising K/L) is that which requires zero consumption by capitalists.

The explanation is that, on an island where the stock of means of production is greater, the proportion of the labour force required to maintain it is higher. The limit is reached at the point where the increase in net output due to a more capital-using technique is no greater than the output lost by transferring the requisite amount of labour into the investment sector.

We may observe that the lower the rate of profit at which the comparison is made, the higher the maximum value of K/L. This would not necessarily be true if we had not eliminated reversals and reswitches from the psuedo-production function by assuming labour-value prices to rule on each island. In fact this construction is exactly the same as Professor Samuelson's 'surrogate production function' which was devised to answer the Cambridge critics. Yet Samuelson seemed to believe that his construction was supporting the neoclassical doctrine of a falling marginal productivity of increments of capital applied to labour.

[4] See P. Samuelson (1962), 'Parable and Realism in Capital Theory: The Surrogate Production Function', *Review of Economic Studies*, Vol. 29, pp. 193–206.

Figure VI

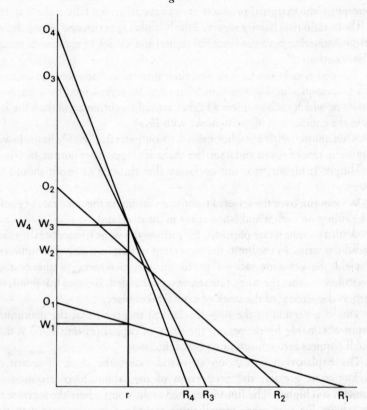

It seems to me to be a great insult to Marx to foist this conception upon him. It is far more honourable to him to admit that his *value* system is not all-inclusive than to try to make out that he was really a neoclassic at heart.

This limitation on the *value* system is precisely that it does *not* provide a unit of physical output. Marx listed among the counter-acting causes that check the tendency for the rate of profit to fall, the fact that technical progress may reduce the cost in terms of labour-time of the physical ingredients in the stock of means of production, thus reducing C while leaving $s + v$ unchanged. (This is our case of *Alpha II*, but without taking account of the increase in O/L.)

He failed to notice the main counteracting cause. A superior technique does not necessarily require a rise in the capital to labour ratio (as Marx admitted) but when it does, it raises the output to capital ratio. Even a quasi-superior technique leaves room for a constant rate of profit with a rise in real wages, or a rise in the rate of profit with constant real wages.

There are many influences that may cause the overall rate of profit to fall as capitalism develops, but rising organic composition has not been shown to be one of them.

5

The foregoing argument is conducted in terms of comparisons of economies each adjusted to its own technique. Marx was actually interested in a historical process of accumulation and technical change going on through time.

This involves the whole of economic theory and most of economic history as well. Our model is too limited to contribute much to it. We have not discussed changes in the labour force and in the types of work required, nor the availability of natural resources, nor problems of the uneven development of national economies. The assumption of rising consumption per head of identical 'baskets' of goods is unnatural, for technical change is largely devoted to changing the nature of commodities. We have not touched upon the manner in which innovations are made by profit-seeking firms or the process by which competition diffuses them. We have not discussed the finance of investment or the conception of technological obsolescence.

All the same, there are three very important generalisations towards which our argument can be seen to point.

First: if real wages do not rise when productivity is increasing, the rate of profit, in general, will not be maintained, for there will be insufficient expenditure to make a market for the greater flow of output (unless investment happens to increase or thriftiness to fall sufficiently to make up the deficit in effective demand). This is the paradox of capitalism. Every individual employer gains by reducing the cost of labour in terms of his own product but, taken together, they cannot prosper unless real-wage rates are rising.

Second: when accumulation has been going on for some time with more or less neutral progress on balance and then the latest eligible techniques take a capital-using form, there will be a gradual decline in employment offered at full-capacity operation of the stock of means of production, unless the flow of gross investment rises sufficiently to equip the labour force at the same rate as before with the new, more capital-using plant. This was Ricardo's argument about the introduction of machinery.[5] It is seen today

[5] David Ricardo, *Principles*, 3rd edition, Ch. 23.

in dramatic form in Third World countries which are being invaded by modern capitalism.

Third: when accumulation has been going on for some time with increasing employment and a moment comes when the reserve army of long-run unemployment is exhausted, a scarcity of labour develops in the sense that capitalists want to continue to increase output but cannot get any more hands. This situation is a strong stimulus to technical change, but there is no reason to expect the capital to labour ratio to be raised. On the contrary, in this situation, the motive is all in the direction of saving labour, that is, raising output per man, and this applies just as much, if not more, in the production of means of production as in the output of consumable commodities.

These reflections show that when Marxian analysis is disentangled from its false association with the neoclassical production function, it is seen to be all the more cogent.

27

FORMALISM VERSUS DOGMA

WHEN Piero Sraffa came to England in 1928, to keep out of trouble with Mussolini, he had already worked out the main concepts of the book, *Production of Commodities by Means of Commodities*, which he was finally persuaded to publish only in 1960. Meanwhile he was editing the *Works and Correspondence of David Ricardo*. As he had already understood the point for himself, he was able to find that Ricardo had seen that the rate of profit on capital is determined by the technical conditions of production and the share of wages in net output, that his so-called labour theory of value arose out of his search for a unit in which the product of industry could be measured, and (though this was not specifically mentioned) that his system of prices was a more consistent version of what was intended by Marx's 'prices of production'.

Prices of production correspond to Marshallian normal long-run prices, with a uniform normal rate of profit, but not to the Walrasian supply and demand prices which appear in modern textbooks.

Sraffa's *Introduction* to Ricardo's *Principles* was published in 1951 (*Works*, Volume I). This started off the great 'capital' controversy though it did not hot up till after 1960. Sraffa's aim was to expose the logical incoherence of the prevalent doctrine that the rate of profit corresponds to the 'marginal productivity of capital'. In this he was perfectly successful though to this day the neo-neoclassicals cannot bring themselves to recognise the ruin of their system of thought. Incidentally, he provided, as Ian Steedman shows, 'the simple, definitive solution of certain issues which had long been debated by Marxists'. A number of dogmatists, who prefer political rhetoric to logical analysis, were hostile to Sraffa. They declared that he was not a Marxist and invented a new category – neo-Ricardian – to put him into. Steedman indignantly exposes their many confusions of thought and counter-attacks with what he calls a Sraffa-based critique of Marxism.

The critique concentrates almost exclusively on the concept of *value* – the labour time embodied in commodities. Marx did not succeed in getting the Ricardian theory of the rate of profit into final form, but he took up the suggestion, which Ricardo had tried and rejected, that labour time provides the requisite unit of measurement of total output. This saved him from getting lost, as Ricardo had been, in the mazes of what is now known as the problem of aggregation. In terms of *value*, Marx expressed his conception of capitalism as a system of exploitation and many large ideas of historical analysis and political prognosis. To the dogmatists, these large ideas depend upon *value* and cannot be explained in any other language. Because Sraffa never used the word *value*, they supposed that he was rejecting all that Marx had expressed in terms of it.

Like any other word, *value* cannot yield any more meaning than is put into it by its definition. Whatever ideological overtones it carries, on the plane of formal analysis a quantity of *value* is a quantity of labour time. Steedman points out that when we have a description of capitalist production and distribution in terms of physical processes and flows of payments, a description in terms of *value* adds nothing at all. (The present reviewer pointed this out in 1942 and has been treated as an enemy by the professed Marxists ever since. It will be interesting to see if Steedman meets with the same fate.)

One of Marx's strong points is that he had learned from Ricardo to draw a clear distinction between gross and net output (a point on which both Adam Smith and the neo-neoclassicals are rather hazy). Only current labour time produces *value* but to produce physical output, workers require a pre-existing stock of means of production to operate upon. In Marx's formula for the flow of output in terms of *value*, $c + v + s$? $(v + s)$ is the total man-hours of labour being performed in a particular period, while c is interpreted as *value* embodied in means of production in the past, now being released as they pass into use. In Sraffa's simple input-output model, all material inputs are replaced in kind over the period in which they are used up. Physical net output of the period is the excess of production over replacements. Now, Steedman's main point is that when net output is divided between wages and profits, it must be reckoned at normal prices. When the prices of commodities are not proportional to *values*, s/v is not the rate of exploitation and $s/(c + v)$ is not the rate of profit. (He does not try to clear up the further confusion involved in treating v, the flow of wages, as part of the stock of capital.)

To reinforce his point, Steedman elaborates his famous proposition that *surplus value* may be negative in a situation where the rate of profit is positive. Of course, this is just a tease; when the flow of net profits is positive, capitalists are acquiring a flow of investment goods and luxuries, and the labour time that they are employing is more than is necessary to replace the depletion of stock and produce wage goods. In physical terms and in command of labour there is a positive surplus all right. The only issue is that in the case of joint products, the *value* of individual commodities is ambiguous. Suppose that there are two types of wheat, one with heavier ears and shorter straw than the other. When the requirements for bread and thatching in the flow of output are such that both types are grown, then a particular amount of labour is producing wheat and straw in the appropriate proportions, while replacing the stocks of seed, but the *value* of the net output of each commodity separately is indeterminate. Steedman adopts a particular method of attributing *value* to each commodity separately and constructs an example in which *surplus value* on this definition is negative. He conscientiously explains afterwards how he put this rabbit into the hat in order to perplex dogmatic readers by pulling it out.

Joint production gives a neat illustration of his point, but the point is quite general. In any period, the whole employed labour force, working certain hours per day, per week and per year, operating on an appropriate pre-existing stock of inputs, is producing a specified flow of gross output. The flow of hours of work cannot be separated into those needed to replace stock and those needed to produce wage goods and the other elements in net output. Marx's statement, that a man works every day some hours to produce his own wages and the rest for his employer, is not to be taken literally for no one by himself produces anything at all.

However, the pattern of prices appropriate to given input-output relationships and a uniform rate of profit entails the corresponding distribution of net output between wages and surplus. Using a unit of money-wages as numeraire (which is more convenient than Sraffa's standard commodity), we find the money value of gross output and subtract from it the costs (at normal prices) of replacements and wage goods to find net profits. Then the rate of exploitation (s/v) can be interpreted as the ratio of net profit to the wage bill.

It seems that Sraffa provides an illumination of Marx, rather than a critique.

The sarcasm that Steedman heaps upon the dogmatists is well deserved but he over-estimates the importance of his own formalistic argument. In an actual capitalist economy, there is never a moment when a perfectly uniform rate of profit is ruling and all products are exchanging at long-run normal prices; but there always is a share of wages in value added. This is something that actually happens and can be exhibited (more or less) in actual statistics. On this basis, all the propositions that Marx expressed in terms of *value* in Volume I of *Capital* can be perfectly well understood. His intuition was correct in starting from the share of profit, which exists here and now, and leaving the *rate* of profit until he could get round to working it out. Perhaps it was a lurking doubt about *value* that finally prevented him from doing so.

Reckoning in *value* did create confusion in Volume III, for the supposed tendency of capital-using technical change to reduce profits arises from identifying the capital to output ratio with the capital to labour ratio. Steedman falls slap into the same error.

The illusion that *value* can explain something that cannot be explained in any other way is illustrated by the doctrine of unequal exchange in trade between the industrial centre and the underdeveloped periphery of the capitalist world, for short, between North and South.

Wages for a representative worker (and income for independent peasants) are very much lower in the South than in the North. From a human point of view, what matters is real income, say in terms of calories, but to discuss trade we must compare wage rates in dollars, as the international unit of account.

Profit margins for primary products vary enormously both in time and space but for the sake of argument suppose that on average (excluding oil) they bear the same relation to wages in the South as in the North. Then the dollar value of output per worker is lower in the South in the same proportion as wages, and the comparison of value per man-hour is still more unfavourable. A further disadvantage to the South is that the difference between the value of its exports FOB and its imports CIF accrues mainly to Northern shippers and dealers.

What does it add to calculate the terms of trade in *value*, showing that the South exchanges goods which require a particular amount of labour to produce for goods which require a particular amount less?

The interesting questions is what determines the difference in wage rates; the answer must be found, not in terms of *value*, but in terms of history. In the North, a slow growth of the labour force with rapid accumulation of capital led to the installation of techniques yielding ever higher outputs, for, as Marx observed, capitalism ripens the productive power of labour as though in a hot-house. With liberal politics and a strong labour movement, it was possible for workers to catch a share of rising productivity in the form of higher wages and shorter hours. In the South, growth of numbers, limited investment and oppressive regimes keep wages low.

Low wages in the South have contributed something to the standard of life of Northern workers in so far as they kept down the prices of, say, tea and bananas, or copper and jute; but now cheap exports of manufactures from the South are a serious threat to employment in the North.

The ideological tendency of the doctrine of unequal exchange is not progressive, for it teaches Southern intellectuals (who do not themselves live on wages) to moan about injustice instead of showing workers and peasants the causes of their misery.

This kind of argument is outside the scope of Sraffa's analysis and Steedman does not venture into dynamics beyond von Neumann's path of maximum growth without technical change.

There are other areas of Marxian theory which need to be illuminated by *value*-free inquiry. Michal Kalecki, also reviled by dogmatists, has analysed the process of realization of the surplus (which Steedman expressly excludes) and linked it to the principle of effective demand and the instability of capitalism, to class war in the North and to quasi-feudalism in the South, as well as developing the analysis of expanded reproduction in capitalist and planned economics.

By refusing to understand Sraffa and Kalecki, the dogmatists are disrupting an intellectual alliance of the left which aims to bring Marx's insights to bear on the problems of our own day.

28

THE LABOUR THEORY OF VALUE

BEFORE 1956, Ron Meek was a rigid dogmatist. It was his leg that I was pulling in 'An Open Letter from a Keynesian to a Marxist'.[1] He took it very much amiss, and it was still rankling when he was writing the original version of this book, *Studies in the Labour Theory of Value*. His extremely high standard of doctrinal purity was shown by the fact that he treated Oskar Lange and Rudolf Schlesinger (both life-long students of Marx) as hostile critics, along with me. Lange was suggesting that some problems that arise within a market economy can best be treated by orthodox methods, and Schlesinger was pleading to relax the strict quantitative calculation of the 'transformation of *values* into prices' in order to deal with monopoly. These suggestions were dismissed as heretical. I did not intend my *Essay on Marxian Economics* (1942) as a criticism of Marx. I wrote it to alert my bourgeois colleagues to the existence of penetrating and important ideas in *Capital* that they ought not to continue to neglect. In this the book had some success, which it certainly would not have done if it had been written in Marxist terminology, but since I was a bourgeois myself I must have been trying to reconstruct orthodox equilibrium theory. (In fact, that book was the first round in the 'Cambridge criticism' which, with the aid of Piero Sraffa, finally pulverized equilibrium theory twenty years later.)

The year 1956 was one of political shocks (including the riots at Posnan, when both Ron and I happened to be there on a visit with some colleagues). It broke through the crust of dogmatism. Ron became a professor and drifted back towards equilibrium theory, though he continued to work on the pre-Marxian classics (the best part in this book). When he was finally persuaded to prepare a second edition, he found that he regretted the 'defensiveness and didacticism' of his manner of writing, but he did not see much need to change the matter. The present volume is a reprint of the original with a new introduction and postscript by Professor Meek.

[1] Reprinted in *Collected Economic Papers*, Vol. 4 (Oxford: Blackwell's 1971).

A Review of *Studies in the Labour Theory of Value*, by Ronald L. Meek, 2nd edition, 1976. from *Monthly Review*, December 1977.

VALUE

The labour theory of *value* provides the particular language and set of concepts in which Marxist doctrines are expounded. It is also a shibboleth; to 'be a Marxist', it is necessary to 'believe in' labour *value*. But regarded as a *theory*, what does it assert? For the classics, a theory of value was required to account for the relative prices of commodities; so long as the real wage rate is constant, their theory of 'natural prices' is quite straightforward, but Marxian *value* is independent of wages. Marxists frequently suggest that it provides a theory of prices, but we all know that the prices of commodities cannot be proportional to their *values* when there are different capital-to-labour ratios in different lines of production. When there is a uniform rate of profit, in a competitive capitalist economy, 'prices of production' rule. Yet somehow *values* 'ultimately', 'basically', or 'in the long run' do determine prices.

We are told that the law of *value* governs the distribution of resources between different lines of production; but surely that could be better discussed in terms of the process of accumulation and the evolution of technology? Sometimes we are told that it is impossible to account for exploitation except in terms of *value*, but why do we need *value* to show that profits can be made in industry by selling commodities for more than they cost to produce, or to explain the power of those who command finance to push around those who do not? For some, *value* theory includes the whole grand sweep of the materialist interpretation of history. But something that means everything means nothing.

We must go back to the first chapter of *Capital* to see what *value* meant to Marx.

'Let us take two commodities, e.g., corn and iron. The proportions in which they are exchangeable, whatever these proportions may be, can always be represented by an equation in which a given quantity of corn is equated to some quantity of iron: e.g. 1 quarter corn $=x$ cwt iron. What does this equation tell us? It tells us that in two different things – in 1 quarter of corn and x cwt of iron, there exists equal quantities of something common to both.' This common something is the property of being products of labour. Here we have it. *Value* is an otherwise indefinable quantity which is put into commodities by the man-hours of labour time required to produce them.

This is not something that one can 'believe in' or 'not believe in'. It is a mental construction that may or may not be useful in analysing reality.

The great advantage of this concept is that it enabled Marx to think quantitatively without being hung up, as Ricardo had been, over the problem of measurement. Along with broad historical and political argument, there are a number of economic 'models' in *Capital*, set out in terms of *values*. The central model, the schema of expanded reproduction, has been absorbed, via Kalecki, into post-Keynesian theory and translated into operational terms.

Some Marxists object to translations. They maintain that a flow of output is a quantity of *value* and cannot be represented in any other way. This is mere dogmatism. Last year's national income is something that actually occurred. It is now part of history, an extremely complex set of events. There are many ways of representing it, none of which is perfectly satisfactory. If we had full information, we could present a flow of industrial production as an input-output table of physical goods, making allowance for the wear and tear (but not financial depreciation) of the stock of means of production. We could represent it in terms of flows of money payments and depreciation allowances, or as *value*, that is, the total number of man-hours of work performed over the year $(v + s)$ plus c, the depletion of the pre-existing stock of means of production, valued by the labour-time embodied in it. When prices in terms of money are not exactly proportional to *values*, the share of net profit in proceeds is not exactly equivalent to *surplus value*. In that case, it is the calculation in terms of money that is operational, for the decisions of businessmen who control investment and the distribution of income are influenced by profits, not by *values*.

The concept of *value* enabled Marx to dispense with an exact treatment of relative prices. There are no prices in Volume I of *Capital* and the discussion in Volume III (the transformation problem) is very sketchy. I have always felt that it was a mistake for Marxists to allow themselves to be lured onto the terrain of price theory, where the orthodox economists could score some hits (though their own analysis of prices is far from satisfactory). The Marxists should have said: Do not worry about prices. We will get around to that later. Meanwhile we are interested in the mode of production, the rate of accumulation, and the distribution of income. We have a theory of the share of profit – the rate of exploitation. The *share* of profit is far more important than the *rate* of profit. The *share* of profit is something that actually happens, and affects people's lives – the *rate* of profit is a mental calculation.

But Marxists, of course, would never admit that there was any problem that *value* does not solve, and they floundered about proving that prices are proportional to *values*, and that they are not.

The theories that Marx put forward in terms of *value* are the indispensable basis for a treatment of the economics of capitalism, which the orthodox school fails to provide. Many of the Marxian concepts are even more relevant in our own day than they were a hundred years ago. For instance, a *commodity* is something which is produced by employing labour in order to be sold. Marx said that a commodity must have *use value*, otherwise no one would buy it, but nowadays use value becomes less and less essential. Packaging, advertisement, and salesmanship are what generate demand.

The Marxian concept of the nature of an economic system, characterized by the manner in which production is controlled and a surplus extracted from it, is more important than ever, since there are now many systems coexisting in the world and reacting on each other – several types of socialism, and overlapping stages of the development of capitalism, as well as remnants of feudalism in the Third World. The central topic in teaching economics ought to be the nature of productive systems, but this is generally avoided for fear that capitalism would not necessarily always get the best marks.

To interpret history, the interplay of the forces of production and the relations of production is an invaluable clue, even though Marx's predictions of how it was going to work out have not yet been fulfilled.

Marx saw all this in terms of *value*, but the parts of the theory that are most closely bound up with that concept are the least satisfactory. There are some statements that seemed to Marx to contain important truths which now appear only as metaphor. Labour power is sold like a commodity, and, like all commodities, it exchanges for its *value*. The *value* of labour power means a wage rate sufficient to permit the workers to maintain their families at some customary standard of life. But calling it *value* does not explain anything. We know that, in rich countries, the minimum acceptable standard of life is always a little above the average actually obtained, so that the majority are living below it; in poor countries there is no bottom to the level of subsistence; undernourishment makes people grow up smaller (in height and weight) and reduces the length of life. *Value* does not help us here.

Again, Marx expresses the rate of exploitation as the division of the working day into the time that a man is producing for himself (creating wage goods) and the time he is working for the capitalist. But a man by himself cannot produce anything. The whole labour force is producing the whole output. We have to go round about to find out total net output and the ratio of net profit to wages, before we can apply the ratio to the division of the working day. The time that a man works for himself is a striking metaphor, not an analytical proposition.

The worst case is the confusion between stock and flow in the concept of *variable capital.* (It was this that I was teasing Ron Meek about in my 'Open Letter'.) Because labour alone produces *value*, Marx maintains that only the part of capital invested in employing labour generates surplus. Constant capital – the stock of physical means of production – passes on to the flow of *value* only the *value* embodied in it in the past. But what is meant by the part of capital that employs labour? Is it a wage fund? The wage *fund* is a financial concept, depending on the turnover periods of particular processes of production. Surely it is the flow of expenditure on the wage *bill* that employs labour and generates surplus (net profit)?

Marx writes the flow of output, say, per annum, in terms of *value* as $c + v + s$ (replacement of means of production used up, wages, and surplus). Here, obviously, v is a year's wage bill. But then Marx writes $(c + v)$ for the stock of capital and $s/(c + v)$ for the rate of profit.

These are all points of exposition that could be cleared up if Marxists would consent to amend the formulae, but there are some cases in which the *value* concept seems to be actually misleading.

Marx suggests that when simple commodity production prevailed, that is when peasants and artisans owned their own means of production, they exchanged the goods that they produced amongst themselves as *values*; this is inconsistent with his own analysis. How can the products of the blacksmith and the handloom weaver be treated as *values*? It is true that they are *commodities* designed for exchange, not for self-consumption, but how is the labour-time involved in each to be counted? For an artisan, there is no hard and fast distinction between work-time and leisure; there is no hard and fast distinction between investment and consumption – the working capital of an artisan, which he replenishes from time to time by sales, includes the consumption of his family. Moreover, each kind of work is qualitatively different and is inseparable from the appropriate means of production. Blacksmithing is work at a forge, weaving is work at a loom. Only employment for wages, as Marx said, is reduced to *abstract labour*, measured in numbers of undifferentiated man-hours.

There is another point at which an argument in terms of *value* is treacherous. The *organic composition of capital* is written as c/v, but it means the 'ratio of dead to living labour', that is the *value* of the stock means of production per unit of labour currently employed. (It would be better to write it as C/L.) Marx believed, as was natural in the railway age, that accumulation is associated with continuously rising organic composition (a strong capital-using bias in technical progress). He argued: c/v will rise indefinitely, and s/v, the rate of exploitation, cannot rise indefinitely. Therefore, sooner or later, $s/(c + v)$, which corresponds to the rate of profit on capital, will tend to fall. But this is a *non sequitur*. Organic composition is the capital-to-labour ratio, not the capital-to-output ratio. The very purpose for which capitalists raise organic composition is to raise output per man, not in terms of *value* (which cannot alter) but in terms of physical saleable commodities. As output per head rises, there is room for a rise in either or both the real-wage rate in terms of commodities and the rate of profit on capital – how the rise is distributed between the two depends on the market power of the parties, that is, on the fortunes of the class war. This mistake must be attributed to the habit of thinking in terms of *value*. A rise in organic composition means a fall in the *value* of output $(s + v)$ per unit of capital. So what?

Many devoted Marxists have tried to rescue the argument by mixing it up with a neoclassical production function, which only makes it worse.

The concept of *value* certainly helped Marx to arrive at his interpretation of history, politics, and economics; but we can learn from his ideas without remaining stuck in the groove that led him to them.

PRICES

In his new introduction, Meek reformulates what he believes to be the essence of the labour theory of value in terms of Piero Sraffa's *Production of Commodities by Means of Commodities*, but he does not really throw much light on it. There are no helpful explanations in that book of what it is about. My own view is that it should be understood as follows:[2]

The equations of production represent a formalized picture of a supposed actual economy, in which actual production is going on – as it were, an x-ray showing its bones. There is a certain labour force being employed and there is a specified flow of materials being continually used up and recreated in the process of production. (Fixed capital is treated separately.) In each period, a certain surplus product emerges, over and above the replacement of materials used up. This is surplus in the sense of net output $(v + s)$ not *surplus value* (s).

Sraffa's equations describe the technique of production in use in terms of an input-output table. (This was a more original concept when it was

---

[2] I must insist that this is only my own view. Piero has always stuck close to pure unadulterated Marx and regards my amendments with suspicion. The dogmatists say he 'is not a Marxist', and they have invented a special category – neo-Ricardian – to put him into. It seems that a neo-Ricardian is someone who thinks it worthwhile to take a lot of trouble to express his ideas precisely, while to 'be a Marxist' it is necessary to repeat undigested phrases out of the book.

conceived than it appeared thirty years later when it was published in 1960.)
The question is often raised: What about economies of scale? What about
demand? In the economy whose picture is being drawn, there is some
particular composition of output being produced in some particular
proportions; there is no scope for variations in scale. Since there are no
unsold goods, there must be just sufficient demand to absorb net output,
with the prices and incomes ruling. There is no scope for variations in
'tastes'. The output is being absorbed because it is being produced and it is
being produced because it is being absorbed.

Nor is there any variation in technique. The stocks of inputs in the
pipelines today were produced in the past by the same processes that are in
use today, and the stocks are being restored so as to be available for use in the
same processes tomorrow.

Now, by manipulating the equations, we can calculate the labour time
directly and indirectly required to produce a unit of each commodity (by
the method of subsystems). Here, for the first time, we have an exact
statement (within the specifications of the model) of the meaning of *value*.
The *value* of any commodity is a number of man-hours only, but labour
could not have produced that commodity without a pre-existing stock of
appropriate inputs; part of the labour indirectly required to produce the
commodity is that which replaces the inputs. However far we go back, in
imagination, we should never come to the first man who produced the first
output with his bare hands.

To go back is a movement in logical time. In history, of course, if we
traced production back, we should soon come to an earlier technique, out of
which this one grew, and if we go right back to the hunters catching
beavers and deer, the inputs were provided by nature. (Logical time can be
traced from left to right on the surface of a blackboard. Historical time
moves from the dark past behind it into the unknown future in front.)

Now we come to the point. The technical equations alone cannot
explain prices. In the actual economy, some prices are ruling. We may
postulate a uniform rate of profit, and when it is given – a rate per cent per
period of turnover – we can work out what the prices must be. But this is
what they happen to be. They are not determined by the technical
conditions.

This is demonstrated by another conceptual calculation. Run the rate of
profit through every value from zero to the maximum, with the
corresponding share of wages in net output falling from unity to zero, and
observe how the pattern of prices behaves. In historical time, of course, it
would not be possible to have the same physical composition of output with

widely different shares of wages and profits – the capitalists would want to take their share in steel and caviar and the workers in cheese and boots. The calculation is a movement only in logical time.

Now what was the object of this meticulous construction (and of the many elaborations of the simple case which the book contains)? The object was a *Prelude to a critique of economic theory*. It knocks out once and for all the marginal productivity theory of distribution. That theory purported to show how the physical conditions of production determine the 'rewards' of the 'factors of production' in accordance with the contribution that each makes to the output of industry.

Of course, you and I always knew that that theory was nonsense, but however long the Marxists battered at it from the outside they could never knock it down. Now it has been exploded from within.

Piero Sraffa's aim was focused on orthodoxy, but incidentally he has shown the Marxists how to solve the 'transformation problem' and he has answered the old conundrum – does the labour theory of *value* provide a theory of prices? The answer is that normal prices are not, in general, proportional to *values* but, through the rate of profit, they are related to each other in a precise and systematic way. (If the rate of profit is not uniform, prices may be all over the place, as indeed they usually are.)

The next question is: What determines the rate of profit? For all the model tells us, it could be anything.

Some readers have interpreted the calculation of the movement up and down of the rate of profit and the share of wages as a story about the class war. But that is a complete misunderstanding. With a single technique and a given net output, there is little scope for fighting over wages and, anyway, the movement is only the movement of the eye running up and down a curve on the blackboard.

In the actual economy, at the moment when its picture was being taken, the share of wages had already been brought into existence by past history, and in the actual future, in front of the blackboard, it will be influenced by the interplay of technical change, the accumulation of capital, the growth of monopoly, the bargaining power of trade unions, and the benevolent or hostile intervention of the state.

Sraffa's model says very exactly what it can say and nothing more.

On this point, Meek is mistaken. He tries to squeeze out of amendments to the equations an historical process of moving from a precapitalist world where *value* prices ruled into capitalism with a uniform rate of profit. To project the transformation problem into history seems very far fetched. Nothing like that can possibly have happened. Moreover, to present it in terms of Sraffa's model is quite illegitimate. Simple commodity production was not an input-output technology but a set of independent groups of producers each with their own lore and their own equipment. Professor Meek ought to have remembered enough of Ron's Marxism to recognize the difference between different modes of production.

Sraffa's contribution to Marxism is mainly negative, to dispose of the rubbish of orthodox theory. Now it is up to the Marxists to break out of the husk of dogmatism and set about building the political economy of today in the space that he has cleared.

29

THE LABOUR THEORY OF VALUE AS AN ANALYTICAL SYSTEM

1

INTRODUCTION

JOSEPH SCHUMPETER, in *Capitalism, Socialism and Democracy*, described Marx as a learned and painstaking analytical economist.[1]

> It may seem strange that I should think it necessary to give such prominence to this element in the case of an author whom I have called a genius and a prophet. Yet it is important to appreciate it. . . . This incessant endeavor to school himself and to master whatever there was to master went some way toward freeing him from prejudices and extra-scientific aims, though he certainly worked in order to verify a definite vision. To his powerful intellect, the interest in the problem as a problem was paramount in spite of himself; and however much he may have bent the import of his final results, while at work he was primarily concerned with sharpening the tools of analysis proffered by the science of his day, with straightening out logical difficulties and with building on the foundation thus acquired a theory that in nature and intent was truly scientific whatever its shortcomings may have been.
>
> It is easy to see why both friends and foes should have misunderstood the nature of his performance in the purely economic field. For the friends, he was so much more than a mere professional theorist that it would have seemed almost blasphemy to them to give too much prominence to this aspect of his work. The foes, who resented his attitudes and the setting of his theoretic argument, found it almost impossible to admit that in some parts of his work he did precisely the kind of thing which they valued so highly when presented by other hands.

[1] Op. cit., Ch. III.

A contribution to the Conference of the Economic Section of the Academy of Sciences of Montenegro, October 1977.

It is clear that orthodox academic economics has been very much impoverished by refusal to take Marx seriously. The shallow theory of the Austrians, which Bukharin mocked as the *Economic Theory of the Leisure Class*, Marshall's conceptions of the rate of interest as the 'reward of waiting', which was reduced by J. B. Clark to the 'marginal productivity of capital,' and the elaboration of the Walrasian model of the general equilibrium of exchange in a market where production itself is treated as a kind of exchange, were all built up as a defence against Marxism. They are all now palpably disintegrating both through internal criticism, which the academics attempt to repress because they cannot answer it, and through its obvious inability to offer any means to deal with the problems of the present crisis in the world market economy. This pitiable state of academic teaching is largely the result of refusal to take account of the questions raised by Marx.

At the same time Marxism has been impoverished by refusal to refine and develop the analytical apparatus that Marx bequeathed. Schumpeter observed that Marx was both a prophet and a scientist. The difference between the pronouncements of a prophet and of a scientist does not lie in what is said but in how it is received. The duty of the pupils of a scientist is to check his results and refine his hypotheses as knowledge advances; the duty of the disciples of a prophet is to believe what he says. Beliefs easily slip into dogmatism, for a disciple can never be sure that he has understood the doctrine correctly; the safest thing is to repeat the lessons of the master in his own words.

Marxists in the West have been so battered and trampled upon by the academics that they adopt Marx's terminology as a defence mechanism and refuse to translate it into language that would deprive academics of the excuse that it is incomprehensible. Now that the orthodox academics are in evident disarray, this way of arguing is impeding rather than promoting the renaissance of political economy that Western Marxists are intending to promote.

2

The Nature of Capitalism

Marx founded his economic analysis upon the English classics, particularly Ricardo, but he imported into it an element that they lacked – the view of capitalism as a particular economic system that had grown up in particular historical circumstances and would evolve according to its own inherent characteristics.

The emergence of industrial capitalism required the existence, on the one side, of a proletariat – that is many families who had no rights in land or possession of means of production so that a great number of individuals were available to be employed for wages – and, on the other side, a few families with large accumulations of wealth which could be used to employ them in such a way as to yield profits. I do not think that any academic economist could deny this obvious fact, but they have elaborated their theories in such a way as to conceal it.

A proletariat was created in England by the introduction of capitalism into agriculture at the same time as a population explosion was going on. Instead of growing numbers of cultivators being absorbed into agriculture by fragmentation of peasant holdings, the ratio of labour to land was limited by the numbers that it was profitable to employ at the going wage rate.

There is a sharp break between the economic theory of the Physiocrats and that of Adam Smith. The Physiocrats took it for granted that producers, that is tenant farmers and artisans, own and manage their own working capital, which they continuously reproduce, and their working capital includes the subsidence of their families. (The peasants have to pay rent; their reproduction yields a surplus, while the artisans earn gross receipts from sales of their products which permits them just to live and to maintain their stock of inputs.) Adam Smith takes it for granted that workers are employed at wages and that a surplus is extracted in the form of profits to their masters.

The expulsion of a potential labour force from agriculture in no way guarantees employment in industry. In England in the 18th century, some large fortunes had been accumulated from commerce in the hands of families who did not have the aristocratic traditions of gentlemanly extravagance so that capital was available to be invested in industry.

There was a third ingredient in the historical development of capitalism – the scientific revolution from which developed the growth of technology. The factory system was a means of getting more work out of a given labour force than they would have been willing to perform as self-employed artisans, and as Steve Marglin has pointed out,[2] Adam Smith's division of labour was rather a means of enforcing discipline than a source of technical economies. All the same, industry would not have got very far by such means.

The essence of the application of science to technology was harnessing energy (at first only the flow of streams) as an adjunct to human muscle. This required the employment of large groups of workers under a single

[2] 'What do the bosses do?'. Harvard Research Institute, Nov. 1971.

control and it required an investment of finance that no individual artisan could command. From this, industrial capitalism took off. (There was a fourth requirement for the development of industry which Marxists have not sufficiently emphasized – the emergence of a sufficient surplus of the products of agriculture over its own requirements to supply the needs of an urban population and of national administration and warfare.)

Marx described the development of capitalism in terms of the labour theory of *value*. Profit is *surplus value* extracted from the toil of the producers, or unpaid labour; investment and technical progress result from the greed for ever more *surplus value* that actuates the capitalists. A class war arises from the struggles of the workers over the share of wages and conditions of work. The apparatus of the state is erected to help the capitalists to keep labour repressed.

This way of describing the system carries a powerful charge of ideology, intended to help the workers in their struggle, but freezing it into dogmatism has impaired its usefulness as a method of analysis.

There are two serious weaknesses in the theory of *exploitation*. First, while it gives a convincing description of the origin of the industrial revolution, and of its penetration today into many ex-colonial territories, it cannot easily be reconciled with the great rise that has taken place in the level of consumption of goods and services by the working class in the successful capitalist nations.

On a straight-forward reading, Volume I of *Capital* seems to predict that the level of real wages will remain more or less constant as capitalism develops. When accumulation overtakes the growth of population, so that the reserve army of labour is absorbed into employment, real wages rise; for that very reason, accumulation slows down, while the growth of numbers continues; at the same time, labour-saving inventions reduce the number of jobs per unit of investment; thus a reserve army is recruited again and the temporary rise in real wages is reversed. In Volume III (which Marx never completed to his own satisfaction) it is clear that real wages are expected to rise, because it is assumed that the rate of exploitation will remain roughly constant while technical progress goes on. A constant rate of exploitation means a constant share of wages in net product; when net product is a rising flow of output of commodities, real wage rates are rising. There are many passages in the writings of Marx and Engels where rising wages are mentioned but they evidently did not foresee to what an extent modern capitalism could buy off the revolutionary indignation of its own labour force. To tell these workers that their standard of life is kept up by super-exploitation of the Third World contains a grain of truth though it is politically unfortunate to exaggerate it since it feeds racism and undermines class loyalty.

The second drawback of using the language of labour *value* and exploitation in discussing the modern world is connected with the concept of socialism. Marx expected the revolution that would supersede capitalism to break out in the most advanced industrial centres, where the great historic task of accumulation and technical development would have been fulfilled. The class war could then come to an end and society could thenceforth make use of its resources in a rational manner to meet its social needs.

Socialism is no longer a day-dream. There are now in existence a number of what the United Nations documents delicately refer to as 'fully planned economies'. Contrary to Marx's prediction, revolutions have so far taken place in industrially backward countries. Their prime need, therefore, was rapid accumulation and planning has proved to be an effective means of carrying it out.

Accumulation means working to produce means of production (and means of defence) which are not available to be consumed. The extraction of an investible surplus, in the Soviet sphere, is naturally not described as exploitation. Under capitalism, it is said, *surplus value* is extracted by the capitalists for their private benefit; under socialism, workers are carrying out investment for their own future. But the future is a long way off and meanwhile industrial technology imposes much the same conditions of life wherever it is set up.

The 'law of value', in the Soviet sphere, has completely changed its meaning. There it means the need to maintain a balance between supply and demand in the market for consumer goods — a concept which is closer to academic economics that to anything in Marx.

The great vision of an international labour movement was shattered in August 1914, yet it was that war which created the setting for the first revolution made in the name of Marxism. Instead of trying to fit everything that has happened since into the lines of Marx's predictions, it is better to try to use Marx's own method of historical analysis to understand why those predictions have not been fulfilled.

3

A MEASURE OF OUTPUT

One aspect of the labour theory of *value* is the method which Marx used to describe a process of production. The *value* of a commodity consists of the hours of labour time required to produce it. The flow of output, say per annum, resulting from the employment of a given labour force, is represented by a flow of labour-time performed. Ricardo had been tormented by the search for a unit of absolute value in which to measure national income. Marx jumped over the problem by taking labour-time as the unit. This had the great advantage that he was able to think in quantitative terms without getting entangled in the old puzzle about the relation of value in use to value in exchange.

He had a clear grasp of the distinction between gross and net output. In the formula $c + v + s$, c means the depletion of a pre-existing stock of means of production, while $v + s$, wages plus surplus, is the *value* of the excess of output over replacement of the stock, that is, net product.

Marx treats c as *value* which was put into the stock when it was produced in the past, released as it is currently used up. This is not quite satisfactory. As we are all now well aware, part of the materials and energy used in current production result from mining irreplaceable resources; their contribution cannot be evaluated as only the labour that went into extracting them. However, Marxian notation enables us to see this point clearly, while in the academic treatment of 'capital' everything is muddled up.

The *value* of the flow of net output, $v + s$, consists of all the man-hours of work performed over the year; v is the *value* of the wage-goods consumed by workers and s is the *value* of rentier consumption and investment, that is, the expenditure of profits.

This method of aggregation suited Marx's way of thinking, but it is not the only possible one. Last year's national income for a particular country is something that actually happened. It is part of objective reality. It consisted of actual flows of goods produced and actual flows of money payments. No simple way of representing it can be quite satisfactory, for it is an extremely complex entity. Any measure has to be used self-consciously with due regard to its limitations. Since nowadays statistics are available in terms of flows of money payments they provide the best measure to use. We are not betraying the labour theory of *value* and surrendering to the view that profits measure the 'productivity of capital' by making use of information that is presented in terms of 'bourgeois' categories.

The rate of exploitation, s/v, can be interpreted as the ratio of net profit to the wage bill for industry as a whole. The share of wages in value added is a useful and important piece of information and we should not reject it because it does not fit exactly into the Marxian categories of *value*.

If we know the average money wage per man year and the amount of employment, we know the wage bill, corresponding to v. If we know the rate of exploitation we know the money value of the flow of net profits corresponding to s. Adding replacement cost of c, we know the flow of gross profits. The calculation in terms of money is more convenient than in *value* for two reasons: statistics, though never perfect, are easier to get, and gross and net profits in terms of money influence the decisions of businessmen, who know nothing about *value*.

4

PRICES

Marx took over the theory of the determination of the prices of commodities from the classical economists. For them, a theory of value was an essential and puzzling problem and Marx acquired from them the sense of its great importance as a key to understanding the essence of capitalism.

He took over from Adam Smith the doctrine that in a precapitalist economy exchanges of commodities (beavers and deer) must have taken place at prices proportionate to labour cost. Thus he believed that in an economy of simple commodity production – independent artisans – products would be exchanged at *values*. This seems to me to be quite unconvincing. Exchange entails specialization. If every family could catch the type of game or produce the type of goods that it needed for its own use, there would be no exchanges and no prices (though there might be differences in subjective costs for goods easier or harder to get). Artisans are specialized by the skill and lore of their trades, so that every type of labour is different and cannot be compared only in terms of hours. The artisans own each the appropriate equipment and manage their own working capital, which as we have seen, includes the subsistence of their families. Maintenance of stock as well as work is comprised in their costs of production. Their earnings may be set by some concept of a just price or they must be influenced by supply and demand. In fact, the orthodox theory of market price applies to this sort of economy, not to capitalism.

Ricardo's theory of prices under capitalism, as it has been reconstructed by Piero Sraffa, is perfectly coherent. The rate of profit on capital is determined by the technical conditions of production – including the length of the turn-over period for each commodity – and the cost of production of wage goods. To eliminate the influence of rent, production is considered on marginal, no-rent land. The real wage is not fixed at subsistence but is something like Marx's *value* of labour power. The cost of each type of commodity is then determined by the labour-time required to produce it plus an allowance for profit at the ruling rate on the value of the capital invested over the period of production and of bringing goods to market. The divergence of prices of commodities from their labour *values* depends upon the capital to labour ratios involved in the various techniques of production.

Marx starts the other way round. He begins with a uniform rate of exploitation so that the share of profits in proceeds is given. In one sense the *share* of profits is much more important than the *rate* of profit. It represents actual flows of payments and of incomes while the rate of profit is a mental calculation. In Volume I of *Capital*, the argument is all conducted in terms of *values* and there is no discussion of the relations of the *values* of commodities to their prices. In Volume III, a uniform rate of profit is introduced and 'prices of production', which correspond to Ricardo's prices, are worked out (though Marx did not complete the calculation exactly). There has been an enormous amount of confused controversy about the relation of prices to *values* but it is all a fuss about nothing. Sraffa provides a clearly specified one-technique model which shows the meaning of *value*, the labour-time directly and indirectly required to produce a commodity, and he shows how *values* are systematically related to prices by the level of the rate of profit. This gives a simplified picture of how exploitation works in a capitalist economy which is producing output at a steady rate, without crises.

Incidentally, it has the great advantage of having knocked out the academic theory of profit as the measure of the 'productivity of capital.'

'5

ACCUMULATION AND EFFECTIVE DEMAND

One of the most valuable parts of Marx's analysis is the schema of expanded reproduction. It was on this basis that Michal Kalecki produced his version of what became known as Keynes' theory of employment and his treatment of accumulation in capitalist, socialist and underdeveloped economies.

The argument as Marx left it has to be adapted to deal with modern problems. Marx described the exchanges between departments being made in terms of *value* but it is more convenient to deal with prices; and second, Marx treated the process of creating *value* by employing labour as separate from the process of realizing *surplus value* by selling commodities.

In Kalecki's model the two aspects of profits are integrated. Expenditure on Department I, that is, gross investment, and expenditure out of rentier income on Department III, luxury goods, accounts for the total flow of profits, while the wage bill of all three sectors purchases the flow of output of necessaries, produced in Department II.

When there is a reserve of unemployed labour, an increase in investment increases profits and increases employment in all three sectors. When prospects of profit fall off, for any reason, investment slackens and there is a decline in actual profits and in employment. These are the short-period aspects of realization.

There are also long-period relations to be considered. When accumulation has been going on for some time faster than population has been growing, the reserve army of labour is absorbed into employment. The bargaining power of the workers is then strong and real wage rates may be pushed up, so that the share of profit falls. This may discourage investment, but it does not necessarily do so. If the competitive urge to accumulate is strong, the shortage of labour is a stimulus to technical innovations designed to raise output per man employed; this may cause an increase in investment that offsets the tendency for the rate of profit to fall.

The broad sweep of Marx's analysis of accumulation and the development of crises provides the basis for understanding the history of capitalism and the problems of planned economies, but his treatment of technical change is blemished by some confusion in the concept of organic composition of capital and by the view that innovations which require a rise in the capital to labour ratio cause the rate of profit to fall.

This trouble arises because Marx measures output only in *value* and does not have any unit for physical product. The essence of technical progress is to raise output per unit of *value*. Technical innovations, even if they are capital using, permit the rate of profit to rise when real wages remain constant, or wages to rise at a constant rate of profit. There is nothing to compel capitalists to install equipment for techniques that increase investment per man employed unless they increase profit per man employed correspondingly. It would always be open to them to go on using the old technique if nothing better offered.

The rising capital to labour ratio in modern technology is creating extremely serious problems, not because it reduces the rate of profit but because it reduces the requirement for labour and threatens the highly developed economies with permanent unemployment, even during a short-period boom. This is a problem which planned economies, in principle, should be able to avoid, but it is severe where capitalist investment is being made in the so-called developing economies of the Third World.